SUETONIUS

HAVERING SIXTH FORM
COLLEGE LIBRARY

WITHDRAWN FROM HAVERING COLLEGES
SIXTH FORM LIBRARY

D1340885

SUETONIUS

Andrew Wallace-Hadrill

PAPERBACKS

This impression 2004
This edition published in 1995 by
Bristol Classical Press
an imprint of
Gerald Duckworth & Co. Ltd.
90-93 Cowcross Street, London EC1M 6BF
Tel: 020 7490 7300
Fax: 020 7490 0080
inquiries@duckworth-publishers.co.uk
www.ducknet.co.uk

© 1983, 1995 A. Wallace-Hadrill

All rights reserved. No part of this publication
may be reproduced, stored in a retrieval system, or
transmitted, in any form or by any means, electronic,
mechanical, photocopying, recording or otherwise,
without the prior permission of the publisher.

A catalogue record for this book is available
from the British Library

ISBN 1 85399 451 0

Printed and bound in Great Britain by
Antony Rowe Ltd, Eastbourne

Contents

To
J.M. W-H.
and
J.C. W-H.

Note to the Second Edition

I have taken the opportunity of this reissue to correct a handful of slips and misprints. Since this book was written, much has been published on Suetonius, including two long studies by Barry Baldwin[1] and Jacques Gascou.[2] It would be misleading to update the bibliography without rewriting the text, and I have not attempted to do so. My original aim was to get away from debates about the author, his career, and his literary quality, that I felt had become sterile, and to ask new questions about how we can use his imperial biographies as a window on the society, culture and ideology of the early empire. Since then, interest in Roman social and cultural history has grown markedly, and the dominance of Tacitean narrative history has been further eroded. I hope that the questions I asked about Suetonius remain relevant.

A. Wallace-Hadrill

Reading 1995

1   Barry Baldwin (1983), *Suetonius* (Hakkert; Amsterdam).
2   J. Gascou (1984), *Suétone historien* (École Française de Rome).

Preface

Suetonius has never lacked readers. Many biographers of late antiquity and the early middle ages took him as their model. For us he remains one of the most informative and vivid sources for the history and society of the early empire. He has been made popular in non-scholarly circles by numerous translators and adaptors, from Philemon Holland to Robert Graves. Yet he has enjoyed less than his due of serious study. There has been no full-length study of the author to supersede that of Alcide Macé at the turn of the century, and to date no book on him of any sort in English.

There are reasons why scholars have hesitated to take Suetonius seriously. Most important, he did not handle his Caesars in the fashion traditionally thought appropriate to a historical subject, through a narrative of great events. Matters of high state are neglected for intimate, even trivial, biographical details; and the material is presented not chronologically but 'gathered into titles and bundles', as Francis Bacon put it, whereby it seemed to him, as it has to others, 'more monstrous and incredible'.[1] The distinction between biography and historiography has not always proved a sufficient defence. But now fashions in the writing of history have changed and invite a reassessment of Suetonius. 'L'histoire événementielle' has lost its position of dominance and topics like sex and superstition are no longer ones for which the serious historian need apologise.

It would be rash to try to build Suetonius up into a sort of precursor of the modern *Annales* school. Only by placing the author in the context of the intellectual and cultural currents of his own day can we begin to make sense of him. It is this which has been my main aim in this book. I have by no means touched on every aspect of the author which could be discussed. In particular I have abstained from the sort of literary analysis which has become common in recent Suetonian scholarship. Instead I have concentrated on reconstructing the social and cultural world of this scholar and

1. *The Advancement of Learning* book 2, ch.8.

imperial servant and so on explaining the unusual angle from which he views his Caesars. My hope is that the resulting picture may be of use not only to professional Suetonians, but also to anyone interested in the society and culture of the early empire.

Over the years since I first embarked on my researches, I have incurred more debts than I can now catalogue. Numerous friends and scholars have given up time to help me: I name only the most long-suffering. Peter Brunt has read successive drafts with untiring vigilance. John Crook's enthusiasm for Suetonius revived my own at a time when it was flagging. Gavin Townend has given me expert advice and encouragement to write a book he would have done better himself. None of these can share responsibility for the book's shortcomings. Magdalene College, most recent in a line of benefactors, allowed me the brief but precious leisure in which to write. Colin Haycraft made valiant efforts to lick my text into something resembling English. Iris Hunter typed the final draft with painstaking care and the resources of modern technology at her fingertips. Jamie Masters, by his aid and good humour, took the drudgery out of indexing. My final and greatest debt is to the support of a medievalist and a classical schoolteacher: I tried to write a book which they too could understand, and to them this is gratefully dedicated.

Magdalene College
Cambridge, March 1983   A.F. W-H.

Note on style of references

References to the works of Suetonius are given where possible in the body of the text. Where the context leaves no doubt as to which life is under discussion, the title of the life is omitted and only chapter numbers are given. Other references and bibliography are given in the notes, usually at the end of a paragraph. Books and articles that bear directly on Suetonius are listed in the Bibliography at the end, and are referred to in the notes by author's name and date of publication. For editions of Suetonius see also Bibliography. Suetonian lives are abbreviated as follows:

Jul.	-	*Divus Iulius*
Aug.	-	*Divus Augustus*
Tib.	-	*Tiberius*
Cal.	-	*Caligula*
Cl.	-	*Divus Claudius*
Ner.	-	*Nero*
Galb.	-	*Galba*
Oth.	-	*Otho*
Vit.	-	*Vitellius*
Vesp.	-	*Divus Vespasianus*
Tit.	-	*Divus Titus*
Dom.	-	*Domitianus*
Gramm.	-	*de Grammaticis et Rhetoribus* (the numeration is continuous as in Brugnoli's Teubner text. The Loeb text numbers the rhetors separately. Thus *Gramm.* 26 = Loeb *On Rhetoricians* 1 etc.)

No chapter or paragraph numbers are given for the lives of the poets since there is no agreed system of reference.

Fragments of other works are cited from both the edition of Roth (Teubner 1858) and that of Reifferscheid (1860) as appropriate.

PART ONE

THE AUTHOR

Chapter One

THE MAN AND THE STYLE

Suetonius' *de vita Caesarum* appeared within a decade or so of the accession of the emperor Hadrian in AD 117. No exact publication date can be fixed. The preface bore a dedication to one of Hadrian's current praetorian prefects, Septicius Clarus, and the author must still at the time have held office in the imperial secretariat as *ab epistulis*. Both officials were to lose their posts in an incident dated (though not on unimpeachable authority) to 122. But the eight volumes that contained the collection may well have appeared serially over the decade. Nor can we tell when composition commenced; and it should be remembered that the prevalent fashion of literary recitations may have allowed the Roman public a foretaste of the *Caesars* before publication.[1]

Given the time of writing, there was a certain temerity in the enterprise. The work embraced the lives of twelve Caesars; from Julius, as precursor and eponym of the first imperial dynasty, to the last of the Flavii, Domitian. There decency required a halt; for though two further Caesars had reigned and died in the mean time, the formal ties of continuity between Nerva, Trajan and the reigning emperor were so strong that convention would have insisted on panegyrical treatment; and these lives were to be no panegyric. The temerity lay in touching again so soon on a topic recently covered by a classic of historiography. Tacitus' *Histories*, spanning the

1. The date of publication of the *Caesars* has been much debated. It is tied by the dedication to Septicius' prefecture, but there is no agreement when that ended. The traditional dating of Septicius' fall to 122 has recently been defended by Alföldy (1979) and Syme (1980a) against the arguments of Crook (1957) and Gascou (1978) for 128 or later. Syme, *Tacitus* (1958) 780 (cf. 1980b, 120) pointed out that *Tit.* 10.2 refers to Domitia Longina, the widow of Domitian, still alive in 126, in terms that suggest that she was by then dead. If Septicius fell in 122, it may well be that later volumes were published after the fall, as suggested by Townend (1959). The case put up by Bowersock (1969) that the last six lives were published first is refuted by Bradley (1973).

period of the last six lives, from Galba to Domitian, had appeared in the first decade of the century. His *Annals* of the reigns from Tiberius to Nero were even fresher: perhaps completed before Trajan's death in AD 117, possibly not even then. Publication of the *Annals* and *Caesars* may even have overlapped. Suetonius was undoubtedly looking over his shoulder at Tacitus. Tacitus, whose status as the leading literary star of the age was long since established, hardly paid him the same compliment. Suetonius, the younger man, knew that he stood in the shadow of a giant. He has tended to remain there since.[2]

The first two lives, however, of Julius and Augustus, stood well clear of the shadow, since Tacitus had provocatively opened the *Annals* with Augustus' death. It may have been the success of these two lives that encouraged Suetonius to follow up with the remaining ten. More important, lives were not the same as history. Suetonius was able to minimise the overlap. Even if Tacitus towers above, he stands on foundations of his own. So much would hardly have been possible had he not brought with him a very different intellectual background from that of the historian, former consul and orator. Before looking at the character of the *Caesars*, it is helpful to consider briefly this background.

The biographer's life

There are few ancient authors of whom it is possible to construct more than the sketchiest of biographies. Suetonius is relatively well served. A number of sources cast light on different aspects of his life, while new discoveries have thrown up new controversies over the details of his career. But rather than attempt a premature synthesis or extend the controversy, it may be useful to look at the different sources separately like pieces of a jigsaw, reflecting on why they provide the different information they do. It will be easier then

2. The dates of publication of the *Annals* remain in dispute. The arguments of Syme, *Tacitus* 465ff. in favour of publication extending into Hadrian's reign are not universally accepted: see F.R.D. Goodyear, *The Annals of Tacitus* 2 (1981) 387-93. Syme (782) thinks that the Neronian books may be later than Suetonius: *contra*, J. Beaujeu, *Rev. Et. Lat.* 38 (1960), 234-5. All attempts at precise relative chronology are dangerous: the habit of recitation made it possible for authors to know each other's views before publication.

to fit the pieces together, and to relate the man to what he wrote.[3]

Suetonius lays the basis with autobiographical notes scattered through his writings. Since the period he writes about comes to an end with the death of Domitian, it is only his family background and his early days of which he tells us anything. The family's contacts with the Caesars stretched back three generations. The grandfather had an indirect contact with the court of Caligula: he could report on the authority of sources in the palace an explanation of one of the emperor's follies, the bridge over the bay of Baiae (19.3). That does not mean that the grandfather was himself a courtier; but it suggests that as a young man he was in Rome, on the periphery at least of court circles. Perhaps he was able to make other use of his contacts: for his son, the biographer's father, was relatively well placed. Suetonius Laetus served in AD 69 as an equestrian military tribune in the camp of the unfortunate Otho and witnessed his emperor's courageous end after the defeat of Bedriacum (10.1). His legion (XIII Gemina) transferred its loyalties to the victorious Flavian cause; he may have gone with them. It would be no surprise to discover that Laetus served the Flavians as procurator. Whether his son was born before or after the battle of Bedriacum is unclear. His name, Tranquillus, might point to an era of peace after war, but it may have been family tradition (Peaceful son of Joyful). Tranquillus could describe himself as adolescent by AD 88 when rumours of a false Nero in Parthia reached Rome (*Ner.* 57.2). Rome is clearly where he was; for in the reign of Domitian he witnessed there an anti-semitic incident at court (12.2). There too he attended lectures on grammar and rhetoric; he recalls a certain Princeps teaching both in the same day (*Gramm.* 4.9). No doubt he also sat at the feet of more famous men than Princeps: Valerius Probus was the foremost grammarian of the day, and Quintilian held the new chair of rhetoric.[4]

---

3. S's career has been much discussed since the first collection of the evidence by the humanist Politian, on whom see Brugnoli (1968) 187ff. Macé's thorough study (1900) superseded all previous accounts, and even correctly predicted that an inscription might one day be discovered which would show him to have been a *bibliothecis* (228). Since the discovery debate has been rife.

4. S's date of birth was placed in 69 by Macé (35ff.), rejecting Mommsen's date of 77; in 67-72 by C.P. Jones, *Phoenix* 22 (1968) 129. Baldwin (1975a) thinks a date as early as 62 possible, implausibly. Syme, *JRS* 67 (1977) 44 suggested that the name Tranquillus pointed to the year 70. On S as a follower of Quintilian, see Dalmasso (1905/6) and D'Anna (1954) 87ff. On Probus, see below, ch.2.

Suetonius never refers to himself as an adult, for the period he writes of ends with the death of Domitian and his approaching manhood. But the picture is filled out by the correspondence of a friend, the younger Pliny. These letters present an invaluable picture of Roman society at the turn of the second century: of the studiously polished cultural veneer of the intelligentsia, of the self-proclaimed reawakening of letters under Trajan after the repressive atmosphere under Domitian, and of the web of patronage and recommendation by which men rose in public life. They show Suetonius rising with Pliny's aid and encouragement both in literary circles and in public life.

His literary début is hesitant. Like most of Pliny's young protégés, he will have thought initially of a career at the bar, and Pliny refers to him as his 'tent-mate', *contubernalis*, a military metaphor commonly applied to the relationship between a master and his pupil.[5] We meet him first in the late 90s, begging postponement of a court case after a bad dream (his surviving works give the impression that he would never have made a good orator). Not long after, Pliny helped to buy a small estate, where this scholarly character (*scholasticus*) could reflect in peace among the vines in the garden. At last in AD 105 he was on the brink of his first major publication, and Pliny prodded him gently to take the plunge. The start of his public career was also uncertain. Pliny secured him the favour of a military tribunate; but Suetonius changed his mind and passed it to a relation. It is unlikely that he took any commission subsequently; for his purposes the mere offer of a tribunate may have been honour enough. It looks as if he joined Pliny's staff when the latter was governor of Bithynia at the end of the decade. There Pliny secured for him a final favour from Trajan, the legal advantages of fatherhood to compensate for his sterile marriage. Pliny speaks of growing admiration on closer acquaintance; we

---

5. Pliny refers to S as in his *contubernium* at 1.24.1 and 10.94.1 (*in contubernium adsumpsi*). Sherwin-White (*The Letters of Pliny* 690) rightly refers this to a literary relationship, comparing the literary *contubernales* at 1.2.5. We may also compare the *contubernium* between the orator Fronto and his pupils, discussed by E. Champlin, *Fronto and Antonine Rome* (1980) 45-6. The same metaphor is found in S of the relationship between master and pupil (*Gramm.* 7, Gnipho and Dionysius, ib. 30, Albucius and the orator Plancus) and between emperors and men of learning (*Aug.* 89.1, the philosopher Areius; *Tib.* 14.4, Thrasyllus; 56, Seleucus). It appears from these passages that *contubernium* involved staying under the same roof.

sense that he had had his doubts at first about a young man so diffident and unsure of himself in spite of all his scholarship.[6]

Pliny's letters show how literary studies and a public career intertwined for Suetonius, as for many others in Trajanic Rome.[7] But now the evidence falls into two artificially separated spheres. His public career received unexpected documentation from an honorific public inscription discovered in Algeria, in the ancient town of Hippo Regius where later Augustine became bishop. It is often local men risen to fame who are so honoured by provincial town councils. If Suetonius did come from Hippo, he was the first of a long line of men of literary distinction who came from North Africa in the second century: Fronto the orator, Sulpicius Apollinaris the grammarian, Apuleius the philosopher and novelist, and Tertullian the Christian apologist. But even if Suetonius was African, no trace of his origins remains in his writings. He passed a good part at least of his formative years in Rome, and Rome remained the centre of his universe. From the inscription we hear of some of his public distinctions: membership of the jury panels under Trajan, some honorific priesthoods, and then (after a substantial gap in the text), the crown of his career, three prestigious posts in the imperial service, *a studiis, a bibliothecis, ab epistulis*. He held the last and most important under Hadrian, the others probably under Trajan.[8]

6. Pliny *Ep.* 1.18 (the court case), 1.24 (the estate), 5.10 (brink of publication), 3.8 (military tribunate), 10.94 (favour from Trajan). There are two main uncertainties. Did S ever hold a military tribunate? Della Corte (1967) 143 assumes so; Syme (1981) 106 rightly doubts that he ever took any military post. Possibly the mere fact that he was offered the tribunate was an honour that conveyed prestige: for parallel cases, see Champlin, *Fronto and Antonine Rome*, 99. The second uncertainty is whether S accompanied Pliny to Bithynia: Syme (1981) 107 argues that he did. In both these contexts Pliny's use of *contubernium* has been misunderstood as implying a military relationship (see Macé 77-80 against Roth, and recently Baurain (1976) 124f.).

7. The importance of the part played by literary culture in public life in the second century is brought out by Fergus Millar, *The Emperor in the Roman World* (1977) esp. 83ff. For a comparable picture of Rome a generation later than Suetonius, see Champlin's *Fronto* 29ff.

8. The Hippo inscription was first published by E. Marec and H.G. Pflaum (1952). Townend supported the inference that S was a native of Hippo. Crook (1957), however, followed by Gascou (1978), argued that S only visited the town with Hadrian. Syme, *Tacitus* 780f. pointed to Pisaurum as the ultimate origin of the family; but accepts Hippo as the *patria*, cf. (1980a) 80. F. Grosso, *Rend. Acc. naz. dei Lincei* 14 (1959) 263-96 put up a case for Ostia, but new epigraphical discoveries made this impossible: see R. Meiggs, *Roman Ostia*[2] (1973) 584. For argument over the details of S's public career, see also H.G. Pflaum, *Les Carrières procuratoriennes équestres* (1960) 219ff., Townend (1961a), van't Dack (1963), Baurain (1976), Syme (1981).

Inscriptions only divulge formalities, not the background of patronage and intrigue that in practice made a career. But the life of Hadrian, probably drawing on the earlier biographer Marius Maximus who admired Suetonius and took his *Caesars* as a model, reveals tantalising information: both the *ab epistulis* Suetonius and the praetorian prefect Septicius Clarus fell from Hadrian's favour together and were dismissed. The charge was greater familiarity with the empress Sabina than court etiquette allowed.

It is hard to assess this somewhat lurid information. Was there a serious rift between emperor and biographer? What bearing does the incident have on our interpretation of the *Caesars*? The source appears to date it to Hadrian's British tour of AD 122; and if, as seems plausible, the publication of the *Caesars* stretches through the decade, disgrace will have come mid-flow. Should we look for traces of fundamental disagreements? Perhaps, but this sensationalist source should not tempt us into overestimating the significance of the episode. Marius Maximus made much of Hadrian's petty jealousies, and catalogued former literary favourites whose careers were blighted by the emperor's rancour. They include Favorinus the sophist, Apollodorus the architect and a certain Valerius Eudaemon. There is a strong suspicion that Marius blew up such incidents out of proportion. Emperors were constantly replacing officials, who had no fixed term.[9]

The secure point is that Suetonius fell with Septicius, and therefore is likely to have risen with him. Septicius belonged to Pliny's circle of mandarin *literati*. He was the dedicatee of the first book of Pliny's letters as well as of Suetonius' *Caesars* and supplies a missing link between Pliny's death and Suetonius' court appointment. The network of Pliny's patronage of literary men extended into the new reign. Even the disgrace did not destroy it: Septicius' nephew Erucius Clarus, whose learning impressed Pliny, was to be City Prefect under Hadrian's successor.[10]

9. *SHA Hadrian* 11.3. For speculations as to the cause of S's disgrace, see Crook (1957), Baldwin (1975a&b). Carney (1968) examines at length the relationship of S with Hadrian, arguing that in some points they saw eye to eye and in others disagreed profoundly. But Syme (1980b) 128 and (1981) 112f. rightly plays down the episode.
10. On S and Septicius see Macé 87ff. Della Corte (1967) 22 sees Septicius as replacing Pliny as S's patron; he goes too far in supposing that this involved a major reorientation of the ideas and loyalties for S. Cizek (1977) 181ff. goes to further extremes. For Pliny's support of the nephew, Erucius Clarus, *Ep.* 2.9.

There survives one biographical sketch of Suetonius, and it shows him in a very different light from the Hippo inscription and the life of Hadrian. The Byzantine encyclopedia, the *Suda*, includes him among its potted biographies of important authors. Suetonius is known to the encyclopedia (as to most ancient scholars) as Tranquillus. He is seen not as a public figure, but as a *philologos*, a scholar, author of a long list of erudite works among which the *Caesars* is almost lost from sight. The length of the list suggests a lifetime in libraries, stretching from well before Pliny's chiding letter in the first decade of the century to his fall from grace in the third, and possibly well after.[11]

The sources, fragmentary by accident of survival, give a disjointed picture of Suetonius' life. The council of Hippo regards him as a public figure with a string of titles, the *Suda* shows him as an author, with a string of titles of a different sort, while Marius Maximus sees in him a specimen of Hadrian's vindictiveness. Of himself he reveals no more than the young man growing up in Rome. The danger is that we too may fragment his personality, forgetting the scholar in the official, and missing both in the *Caesars*. Only Pliny's letters begin to relate his public and literary life, and they stop short at the Palace door. It is the relationship between these aspects and the problem of locating the author and his work in the correct social and intellectual setting that will be one of the concerns of this book.

When Suetonius put his hand to imperial biography he must have been in his late forties or early fifties. He was established as a scholar and as a public figure. Already in about 110 when Trajan granted him the privileges of fatherhood he was presumably a well-known author: Martial had been granted the same distinction in recognition of poetic merit. His first post in the imperial secretariat may have come in the middle of the same decade shortly after Pliny's governorship in Bithynia: the appointment was at least in part recognition of literary worth. His reputation as biographer was already made before he started the *Caesars*. The *Illustrious men*,

---

11. The date of S's death is unknown: see Macé 220ff., showing that he is not the Tranquillus mentioned in Fronto's correspondence in the 160s (*ad Ver. Imp.* 1.5, Loeb ed. vol. 1, 306). Macé, in order to account for his prolific output, guesses that S lived until *c*.141; but the bulk of his scholarly works probably preceded the *Caesars* (below, ch.2).

sketches of notable Roman authors, proved a classic, much drawn on by succeeding generations, and his promotion to *ab epistulis* by Hadrian may have celebrated the recent appearance of this work.[12]

The author of the *Caesars* is far from the hesitant beginner revealed by Pliny's letters. His reputation is won. Moreover, his cast of mind, his habits of thought, his method and style are already formed and mature. They could not but affect the way he approached his new subject – the lives of great men who were no authors.

Between lives and history

History or not history? The problem faces every biographer in varying degree. Biography occupies an ambivalent position on the outskirts of proper historical writing. As the role played by the individual in his society varies, so does the historical component in his life. The spectrum ranges from men who are no more than unimportant specimens of social life to those who wield a formative influence. The problem is at its most acute when an individual plays a dominant role in the historical narrative of the period. Then history is most likely to take the form of biography and biography of history. It is therefore when Plutarch came up against the colossal figure of Alexander that he voiced his awareness of the dilemma. 'We are writing biographies, not histories ... A battle with ten thousand dead may tell us less of a man's character than a brief anecdote.' It is when history most threatens to swamp biography that the biographer feels most intensely the need to assert his independence. Plutarch's *Lives* are shot through with this ambivalence, which is not satisfied by any simple distinction between chronological and typological passages. Plutarch asserts the primacy of his interest in *ēthos*, the inner moral core of personality. Yet the Aristotelian doctrine which he followed held that character was only revealed in *praxeis*, actions. In consequence his *Lives* contain a high proportion of historical narrative. In the groups of lives especially that criss-cross a single period, such as the late republic, he both conjures up a historical picture of the time, yet is scrupulous in pursuing the theme of the individual concerned.[13]

---

12. Millar, *Emperor* 90-1 rightly sees S's official posts as recognition of literary distinction. The date of publication of the *Illustrious men* is unknown, but it is not the work announced by Pliny in 105, as many have supposed. For detailed discussion, see below, ch.3.

13. On the general problems of biography and history, see the discussion of A. Momigliano (1971) 1ff. The distinction between the two was a much

For Suetonius the dilemma was as acute as it could be. The nature of the early principate was such that even historians found it difficult to avoid writing a series of imperial biographies. Tacitus made a show of imposing the year-by-year annalistic format that derived from republican historiography: yet, as his book divisions reveal, the lives and deaths of Caesars articulated the structure. Cassius Dio was more open: he habitually prefaces a new reign with a discussion of the ruler's personality. For the period after Dio we have to rely largely on the series of imperial biographies that acted as a continuation of Suetonius; and although at some points these lives profess a contrast between lives and history, the ambivalence of their status is summed up in the technically incorrect name by which they are known – Augustan History.[14]

Suetonius' reaction to the dilemma was vigorous. Rather than let biography become history, he would write not-history. His *Caesars* can be defined as much by the options he avoids as by those he embraces. To view it as a sort of alternative history, let alone a misfired history, is a temptation that must be resisted at all costs. There is no reason to suppose that he thought imperial history *ought* to be more biographical: history for him was what Tacitus wrote. He had no reason not to admire it. Written by one who understood public life as it was traditionally defined, devastating in its exposé of the springs of human action and stylistically a self-conscious masterpiece, it could hardly be rivalled on its own terms. Suetonius was too modest or honest to challenge Tacitus. But there was still room for a supplement. As a man of learning and a servant

repeated commonplace: see Momigliano 99. Plutarch's handling of the problem is discussed by Alan Wardman, *Plutarch's Lives* (1974) 2ff. On Plutarch's biographical aims, see also D.A. Russell, *Plutarch* (1973) 100ff. and C.R. Pelling, 'Plutarch's adaptation of his source material', *JHS* 100 (1980) 127ff. J. Ginsburg, *Tradition and Theme in the Annals of Tacitus* (1981) perceptively argues that Tacitus exploits annalistic form, especially in the Tiberian books, to underline the contrast between form and content under the principate.

14. On this extraordinary agglomerate of biographies, inappropriately called *Scriptores Historiae Augustae* (SHA), there is ceaseless debate. Their imitation of S is acknowledged by all, but oddly there is no satisfactory study of their debt. On the tension between biography and history in these lives, see R. Syme, *Ammianus and the Historia Augusta* (1968) esp. 94ff. with the criticisms of Momigliano, *English Historical Review* 84 (1969) 568. See also H.W. Bird, 'Suetonian influence in the later lives of the *Historia Augusta*', *Hermes* 99 (1971) 129ff.

of Caesars, he had something to add. Historian and biographer complement each other; there is no need to make a choice.[15]

Negatively Suetonius wrote not-history; positively he wrote scholarship. We should not regard this as a sort of blunder. Friedrich Leo, whose classic study of the ancient biographical tradition first established the scholarly character of the *Caesars*, apparently felt that Suetonius had perpetrated a misclassification; he assumed that the biography of a historical figure ought to be historical, and that history ought to be narrative. This is a strange value-judgment, attributing an absolute value to the ancient conception of history and ignoring the claims of ancient biography to be independent of history. Suetonius' avoidance of what, by ancient standards, counted as historical techniques is not just a casual byproduct of his employment of scholarly techniques. It is of the essence. Suetonius establishes the independence of his genre by distancing himself from history the further, the more his subject-matter brought him up against historical material. His *Caesars* were to be in technique a mirror-image of history. Three criteria defined history for the ancients: structure, subject-matter and style. In each we find the scholar where the historian might have been.

Structure

In form Roman historiography was both chronological and narrative. The labels are not identical. The Pontifical Annals, the yearly calendar of the priests in which magistracies, triumphs, corn shortages, portents were listed day by day, were evidently chronological. These the earlier Roman historians imitated, appropriately enough since the annual cycle reflected the political structure of republican life. But Cicero, like others before him, found such listing jejune, stylistically and intellectually lacking nourishment. Historians therefore turned to the Greeks for a model of narrative history and learnt to tell a tale in a tradition which stretched back to the *Iliad*, and which satisfied stylistically by dramatic story-telling, and intellectually by setting events in an explanatory chain of cause-and-effect.[16]

15. S's relations with Tacitus are discussed by Macé, 80ff. and by Syme, *Tacitus* 781-2. But though the two were not competitors, S was not above scoring points off Tacitus: see Townend (1967) 88f.

16. The debt of Roman historiography to the pontifical annals is described by Cicero, *de Oratore* 2.52ff. On structure in Roman historians, see the convenient survey of A.H. McDonald, 'The Roman historians', in M. Platnauer (ed.), *Fifty Years (and Twelve) of Classical Scholarship* (1968) 465ff.

Biography had (and has) its own framework. It is chronological, though the chronology is not dictated by the calendar, but by the rhythm of human biology, reproduction, birth, growth and death. Few accounts of a life, ancient or modern, from a newspaper obituary notice to a full biography, fail to draw on this simple framework of parentage, birth, early years, career, death. Biological rhythm is refined by social rhythm. The life of a Roman aristocrat, whether described by a member of his *gens* in the customary funeral address, or by a Plutarch or Suetonius, passed through a necessary progression of stages, such as the assumption of the *toga virilis* at the turning-point to manhood, the first military campaign and the progression up the ladder of office or *cursus honorum*. Chronological like history, inasmuch as it involves a succession of events, the subject-matter distinguishes this pattern as 'biographical', and it can be recognised as such in the body of a history.[17]

Beyond that, rules are few and possibilities many. The chronological frame can be expanded in various ways, both descriptive and narrative. Description of character, habits and physical appearance is almost inevitable. So are some passages of narrative. The death narrative, for instance, is a familiar feature of biography and by Suetonius' day there had spawned the fashionable sub-genre of 'Deaths of Famous Men'. Moreover the more involved a man was in exciting incidents, the more susceptible his life to narrative treatment. Potentially both chronological and narrative, ancient biography could draw near to ancient historiography.[18]

Suetonius could not reject entirely either chronology or narrative. His *Caesars* are chronological in following the biological and social rhythms; and they contain fine passages of biographical narrative, notably the death narrative of Nero. But he could and did reject the

17. The still classic study of ancient biographical form is Leo's *Die griechisch-römische Biographie nach ihrer literarischen Form* (1901). For a more detailed discussion of the question of biographical form, see below, ch.3. There is a handy introduction to the problems of modern biography in the series 'The Critical Idiom' by Alan Shelston, *Biography* (1977). The importance of the social rhythm was first brought out by Stuart (1928) 189ff., further developed by Steidle (1951) 108ff. and by Lewis (forthcoming).

18. On the genre of 'Deaths of Famous Men' see H. Bardon, *La Littérature latine inconnue* 2 (1956), 207-9. No specimen survives, but several titles are known from the first century AD; by Fannius on the victims of Nero (Plin. *Ep.* 5.5.3), by Junius Rusticus on Thrasea Paetus and Herennius Senecio on Helvidius Priscus (Tac. *Agricola* 2.1) and by Titinius Capito (Plin. *Ep.* 1.17.3 and 8.12.4). All these were evidently martyrologies, mostly with a marked Stoic tinge: that element is missing from S.

narrative that lay in the province of the historian. The danger was at its greatest in the discussion of a Caesar's reign: and where there was no biographical element in the chronology, he decided to abandon chronology completely. Even here, however, he could preserve chronological elements. Tiberius' reign fell into different phases as his personal behaviour changed, and his life preserves these phases. So much was 'biographical'. The rule is best expressed as an avoidance of *historical* narrative, whether within the reign or outside it.

Take the campaigns of Julius Caesar. Caesar made his name as a general; his campaigns, especially the conquest in Gaul, should be central to any biography. Plutarch gives a very adequate section to the narrative (*Caesar* 18-27). But Suetonius dismisses the Gallic wars in one brief paragraph, reducing a decade of campaigning to a numerical summary of successes and reverses. The general's own *Commentaries* survived, already a school classic, and Suetonius knew that they rendered emulation superfluous (*Jul.* 56.3). Instead he offered something of his own, an analysis of Caesar's generalship. He looks at his personal energy (57), his mixture of caution and daring (58), his attitude to omens traditionally observed in warfare (59), his strategy in deciding when to engage in battle (60), his personal participation in battle, the figure he cut and the example he set (61-4); his handling of the troops, in training them for action (65), promoting confidence (66), exercising discipline (67.1) and winning their loyalty (67.2). The reader is now in a position to understand the devotion and effectiveness of the Caesarian army (68), and the general's position of (almost) unchallenged authority (69-70). The biographer of poets does not shy from the fact that Caesar was a general, though he emphasises that he was also considerable as an author (55-6). The analysis suggests not only careful reading of the *Commentaries*, but an impressive understanding of what the command of armies involved. The analytical technique is that of a hellenistic scholar and literary biographer: but it was not from hellenistic literary biography that he borrowed these categories of analysis.[19]

19. Note however the possibility that the ground was prepared by some earlier biographer. Plutarch has a much more restricted analytic section describing the valour Caesar inspired in his troops and the personal example he set (16-17). Oppius, the friend of Caesar who wrote a life of him, cited by Plutarch *Caes.* 17.4 and S.*Jul.* 53 may have had anecdotal material arranged in this fashion.

The rejection of narrative was a policy he made explicit: 'having summarised Augustus' life, I shall go through the individual details not chronologically, but by aspect, in order to demonstrate them and evaluate them more distinctly' (9). *Neque per tempora sed per species*: 'by rubric' as this is traditionally glossed. 'Rubric' is a suitable word to apply to Suetonius because so often the first few words of a chapter act as a heading. It would be well if modern editors picked such words out in bold type, if not actually in red. But 'rubric' describes the end-product, not the method. Suetonius' characteristic process is analysis; the dissolution of narrative into fragments, and their reconstitution under heads of analysis.

The processes of dissolution and reconstitution may be illustrated. First, dissolution. The conspiracy of Varro Murena and Fannius Caepio against Augustus was an important historical incident – some modern historians believe it to have been a turning point in the reign. Cassius Dio indicates its importance by a narrative of the episode. Suetonius suppresses all narrative, but he draws on the incident for four separate points: he records the conspirators' names in a list of other conspirators against Augustus (19.1); he notes as an illustration of Augustus' refusal to abuse prerogative that he only once intervened in court to save a guilty man – Castricius who betrayed the Murena conspiracy to him (56.4); he talks about the difficulties Augustus had with his friends – Maecenas let him down by telling his wife Terentia that the plot had been discovered (66.3); finally he records that among Tiberius' first public duties was the successful prosecution of Murena's accomplice Caepio (*Tib.* 8).[20]

If Suetonius had intended his method as a substitute for history, he should have explained a little more about the circumstances of the conspiracy. But he simply assumes knowledge of it in the reader. We are expected to take as read that Murena and Terentia were close relatives, that Maecenas' betrayal resulted in the flight of the conspirators, and that Augustus had to conduct their trial in absence. This process can be frustrating for us when the historical narrative which Suetonius assumed is lost. And in the process of compressing a tale to illustrate one particular point, he could distort, oversimplify, even fall into error by excluding what was irrelevant.[21]

20. The Murena conspiracy attracts endless controversy: for a neat summary of the debate, see R.G.M. Nisbet and M. Hubbard, *A Commentary on Horace Odes Book II* (1978) 151ff. Dio's narrative is 54.3.
21. The dangers of S's analytic approach are excellently brought out by Flach (1972), building on Townend (1959) 288ff. Bradley's Commentary on

There are compensating advantages, however, in the process of reconstitution. Narrative histories were Suetonius' basic, but not his only, source material. Throughout, his account is enlivened by anecdote and small detail, of a type hardly suitable to the grandeur of history. He uses this supplementary material to cast further light on problems raised by the historical accounts. Indeed, he is more valuable the further he gets from standard historical material, his treatment of which tends to be cavalier. The discussion of Vespasian's financial dealings will serve as an illustration (16-19). Suetonius moves from a phenomenon well attested in the historians, Vespasian's constant anxiety to raise funds, and he enumerates briefly some of his methods – increased taxàtion, commercial transactions, sale of office and connivance at maladministration – though he is frustratingly unspecific (16.1-2). This raises the problem whether the emperor was naturally stingy (as anecdotal evidence suggests) or in the grip of a fiscal crisis, as indicated by historical evidence (16.3). Suetonius resolves the problem thus. Natural stinginess is unlikely because of Vespasian's generosity in making grants, particularly in support of the arts – which is substantiated by a mass of specific detail (17-19.1) – although his popular reputation for stinginess persisted, and this is illustrated by two anecdotes (19.2).

The methodology of the ancient scholar is easily recognisable here. A problem (*quaestio, zētēma*) is set up, and an assortment of evidence is adduced on either side. The information is unlikely to derive from the standard histories (that Terpnus and Diodorus the lyre-players were given 200,000 sesterces each is an improbable item for a historian). The scholar's interests are also evident in the weight attached in Vespasian's favour to the support of the arts. But as a result of the attention to small, 'unhistorical' details we gain interesting information: an insight into the workings of imperial liberality, the scale and distribution of grants to professors, poets, craftsmen, inventors and musicians; and a vivid and surprising picture of an imperial funeral, at which a leading actor takes the dead emperor's part and raises laughter by mimicry of his failings.

Analysis is not Suetonius' only method. Inevitably there are also passages of narrative in the *Caesars*. But even here Suetonius does not narrate after the fashion of a historian, enlivening the tale with tension and drama. Take his account of Nero's murder of Britannicus (33.2-3). At first sight it is straightforward narrative; but set beside

the *Nero* (1978) brings out the distortions and false generalisations that mar this life; Bringman (1971) does the same for the *Tiberius*.

Tacitus it is little more than a catalogue of colourful items. Suetonius omits the scene-setting that gives Tacitus' narrative its atmosphere – the anxious circle of dinner-guests who witness the poisoning and by their reactions betray their own understanding of palace life. Suetonius homes in only on the detail that directly illuminates Nero's behaviour. The contrast is between a stage on which several characters play out a drama and a close-up focus on a single man.[22]

Extraction of the relevant detail is Suetonius' characteristic method. Sometimes we get the impression of a large card-index system at work, reducing the sources to an endless series of one sentence items that can be reshuffled and redeployed at will. It would be interesting to know more about the technology behind the writing of the *Caesars*. We should pause before assuming that Suetonius actually had at his disposal anything so useful as a card-index. There is no evidence that antiquity had developed such systems. Scroll-form was normal for books; even library catalogues and the official records of imperial transactions were, to our knowledge, kept in scrolls rather than files. The philologist had to rely on a prodigious memory and much verbatim learning of texts in order to recall the passages where a given word occurred; naturally it also helped to be able to lean on those who had already done the donkey-work. The chances are that Suetonius worked from sources in scroll-form without the prop of an index and had to rely on memory to an extent no modern research student could expect to have to do. If there are imprecisions, errors and omissions in his material, this is a factor to be borne in mind.[23]

Subject matter

The thematic content of ancient historiography, revolving round the two poles of war and politics, was well defined. History was about the state, the *polis*, and its conflicts, external and internal: its

22. Venini (1974) examines the parallel narratives of the civil war in the lives of Galba, Otho and Vitellius and shows that when S does turn to narration, he does not do so in a historian's fashion. The concentration on the individual and the 'linearity' of his account set him apart not only from Tacitus but from Plutarch.

23. The ancient library catalogue (*pinax, index*) took the form of a list of names of authors and their works: Seneca commented that it might take a lifetime to read a library *index* (*de Tranquillitate* 9.4). For the details, *RE* XX, 1408ff., s.v. Pinax. The official records (*hypomnēmatismoi*) of petty Egyptian officials and those of emperors (*commentarii*) are known to have been kept in diary form: von Premerstein, *RE* IV (1901), 735ff., s.v. Commentarii.

relations with external powers in peace and war and its internal power relations in the arena of public, political life. Biography had a different subject – the life, personality and achievements of an individual. Suetonius goes out of his way to avoid making his subject-matter historical. This can be shown both negatively and positively.[24]

Negatively, Suetonius reduces the element of war and politics to a minimum. His treatment of Julius' Gallic war is in fact typical of his treatment of foreign wars. The enormous military achievements of Augustus' reign are reduced to a list of peoples conquered, successes won, reversals sustained (21-3). There is of course no narrative; but there is an interesting analysis of Augustus' attitude to military discipline, recruitment, decorations, and his views on strategy (24-5). Augustus was more significant as a supreme commander than as a general in the field (20); but Suetonius affords the same treatment to Tiberius, an active campaigner. The circumstances of Tiberius' German assignments under Augustus are perfunctorily summarised (*Tib.* 16-17); detailed discussion focusses on his style of life in camp and his strict discipline (18-19). In fact it is not war and battles but military institutions that concern Suetonius. Behind his treatment is not only an avoidance of narrative but a strict conception of what is relevant to biography. The total omission of Corbulo from the *Nero* is clearly justified by the irrelevance of Armenian campaigns to Nero as an individual. So much is confirmed by the constant exception to the rule that there should be no military narrative: civil wars which are important for the rise or fall from power are narrated chronologically for Julius (34-6), for Augustus (9-18) and for all those involved in the strife of AD 68-69. But even here, it is not a historian's narrative. No battle is described (the forte of the historian) and the emphasis is on the anecdotal detail that reveals the individual.

Suetonius' attitude to politics is even more revealing. The settlements of 27 and 23 BC, so central to the constitutional history of

For a recently discovered excerpt from the imperial *commentarii* (the Tabula Banasitana), see *Comptes Rendues de l'Académie des Inscriptions* (1971) 468ff. On the senatorial archive, see now J.M. Reynolds, *Aphrodisias and Rome* (1982), 65f.

24. The fundamental character and limitations of the subject-matter of the ancient historian are identified by H. Strasburger, *Die Wesensbestimmung der Geschichte durch die antike Geschichtsschreibung* (1966). His insights are taken up by M.I. Finley, 'Myth, memory and history', in *The Use and Abuse of History* (1975) 11ff. and by A. Momigliano, 'Tradition and the classical historian', in *Essays in Ancient and Modern Historiography* (1977) 161ff.

Augustus, are also of great potential interest to the biographer. But Suetonius' paragraph on the topic is woefully inadequate, to the point of being misleading: Augustus twice thought of restoring the republic, but changed his mind (28.1). Indeed political life under autocracy, when so much goes on behind closed doors, is not easy to document; but at least there was the occasional eruption of resistance. Yet the Pisonian conspiracy against Nero is only cited in passing to provide anecdotal evidence of cruelty (36); and the conspiracy of Murena and Caepio against Augustus is, as has been seen, simply listed with others (19.1). At the end of this bare list, there is a sudden plunge into specific detail – about a forger called Lucius Audasius, a half-caste Parthian, Asinius Epicadus, a slave by name of Telephus who was *aide-memoire* to a certain woman, and finally a half-witted camp-follower in Illyria who made at Augustus one night with a cleaver (19.2). These details are of no historical consequence. Why else did Suetonius give them, and say nothing of Murena, except that, unlike Murena, they were absent from the standard history books?

Even if a biographer should choose to treat a public figure in a manner more or less 'historical', there is a range of subjects he would need to consider in addition to the public aspect. These may conveniently be summarised as 'private' life: family, friends, personal characteristics, habits and inclinations, education and beliefs are topics the modern biographer too would take for granted as his province. Suetonius makes the distinction himself. Thus after discussing Augustus as a public figure, he proposes 'to go on to his more intimate family life, to his ways and fortunes at home and in private' (61.1). The point is that both public and private aspects were the proper material of biography; in fact, as will be seen later, Suetonius does not always keep them distinct. But in private as well as public aspects, he sets the maximum distance between himself and historiography.

By separating out the private aspects and gathering them together, Suetonius underlines their non-historical nature. Plutarch is again a useful contrast. Suetonius' *Julius* has a section of some thirty chapters (45-75) on personal details; these have no counterpart in Plutarch. Some of Suetonius' 'private' topics have strong and obvious connections with public life, but in treating them as private he plays down the public component. The imperial family is a clear example. An emperor's relations with members of his family had potential political significance: thus the relations of Augustus with his descendants, or of Claudius with his wives, are central features of the historiographical accounts of their reigns. But we search in vain in Suetonius for the colourful stories of the disgrace of the Julias or the fall of Messalina: they are only alluded to. And though he describes Nero's murder of Agrippina in its full grotesque detail, he gives no hint that the causes were political: Nero appears simply to have found his mother's nagging irritating (34.1).

In treating private life as a separate section Suetonius was no doubt extending the method he had used in his literary lives. It does not follow that he is treating emperors 'as if' they were authors, under the wrong category so to speak. The abundance of the material he was able to assemble about the literary interests of Caesars, in addition to their eating and drinking, sexual behaviour and religious beliefs, shows that he was not asking inapposite questions. To dismiss this material as gossip unworthy of mention in a life of a major historical figure is to fall into the trap of swallowing the prejudices of ancient historiography. A biographer has a plain duty to depict his subject, especially when he is an autocrat, as an ordinary human, existing in the dimension of social as well as political life. Unless we allow the emperor to take off his state robes, we cannot see him as contemporaries did.[25]

Suetonius does not delve into the private side to the neglect of the public. Naturally he is well aware of the public dimension of his subjects' lives and its importance. The topics he chose to expand on were not those of traditional historiography; but neither were they those of literary biography, which had, and could have, no appropriate categories. In place of high politics and great events, which he shuns, he gives details of the everyday and business side of imperial administration: supervision of the senate, of the jury panels, of the citizen-roll; reforms and corrections of military and civil institutions; the administration of justice; maintenance of public order and care for the city, its corn-supply, its fire-brigades, its police force; public expenditure on distribution to plebs or troops, on buildings, on games. These are topics the modern historian so takes for granted as 'historical' that he forgets how disdainfully ancient historians pushed them aside. So far from being the residuum remaining after 'high politics' had been sifted out of annalistic writing, they formed a positive contribution, which was made

---

25. See further below, ch.3.

possible only because the author set his work apart from the historian's, both in structure and in content.[26]

Style

The stylistic gulf between the *Caesars* and history is no less marked. Ancient historiography had a grand subject, and convention demanded for it a style of suitable grandeur. It eschewed the vulgar and the trite; it set itself apart from everyday prose by the use of poeticisms, archaisms, and syntax either elliptically abrupt or polished with elaborate artistry. Homer was the precursor of the historians; historiography remained in debt to epic for elevation of tone and pathos of narration. Rhetoric too made fundamental contributions: not to tempt the historian to deceive (that pitfall was obvious, and was only too often pointed out) but to persuade and impress. The ancient historian sought to sweep his reader with him, and to dazzle him into admiration; not just (as he claimed) to tell a plain unvarnished story, but to enlist his sympathies, to impose (without arguing) his interpretation, and to excite emulation of his heroes and disgust for his villains.[27]

Suetonius is innocent of all these devices. He is mundane: has no poetry, no pathos, no persuasion, no epigram. Stylistically he has no pretensions. No writer who sees himself as an artist, one of the elect, could tolerate the pervasive rubric; the repetitiveness of the headings, the monotony of the items that follow, the predictable ending 'such he did; and such he did; and such he did'. Suetonius is not sloppy or casual; he is clear and concise, but unadorned. His sentences seek to inform, with a minimum of extraneous detail. Ablative absolutes, present participles, subordinate clauses fill in the essential background, while the main verb conveys what the emperor said or did. The style is neither conversational nor elevated. It is the businesslike style of the ancient scholar.[28]

26. On S's handling of these topics, see below, ch.6.
27. The stylistic pretensions of ancient historiography are well illustrated by Pliny *Ep.* 5.8, a letter to Titinius Capito in which the writer turns down the invitation to write history partly on the grounds of its exacting stylistic demands. The very different expectations of biography are betrayed in Pliny's characterisation of the works of Fannius: 'somewhere between conversation and history' (*Ep.* 5.5.3). On the contribution of rhetoric, see T.P. Wiseman, *Clio's Cosmetics* (1979), with important qualifications by P.A. Brunt, 'Cicero and historiography', in *Miscellanea . . . E. Manni* (1979) 311-40. The contrast between the style of S and historiography has been demonstrated in detail by Sage (1979), who shows S's avoidance of the historian's stock-in-trade.
28. The scholarly nature of S's style was understood by Leo (1901) and Funaioli (1932 and 1947). There are useful analyses of his style by Bagge

Three particular features point to the scholar rather than the historian: the inclusion of technical vocabulary, the admission of a foreign language (Greek) and the verbatim citation of documents. Technical vocabulary undermines an elevated style and is avoided by historians: Suetonius uses the vocabulary proper for his mundane subject. So Nero was an addict of the techniques of Greek lyre-playing; Suetonius uses the correct terms for a player (*citharoedus*), the method of clearing the voice (*clyster*), the types of applause (*bombi, imbrices, testae*) and the artist's dress (*sythesina*). He correctly employs legal, secretarial and bureaucratic technicalities. Often he is the first or only author who does so. Such words aim at precision, not at fine style.[29]

The intrusion of a Greek word into a Latin text was also felt to be offensive to fine style. Suetonius notes that Tiberius actually made the senate remove the Greek *emblema* from the wording of a decree (71). On another occasion the grammarian Pomponius Marcellus reminded Tiberius that he had no power to 'grant citizenship' to a foreign word (*Gramm.* 22). Suetonius himself felt no scruples: a high proportion of his technical terms are Greek words transliterated; he cites single words and phrases of Greek where they represent *ipsissima verba*; he cites letters of Augustus which, like those of Cicero, frequently seek the *mot juste* in Greek; and his text is peppered with citations of Greek verse, whether from Homer and tragedy or from popular pasquinades. Some of these Greek quotations may just derive from Latin historical sources. But the total indifference with which he includes Greek in his text is inconceivable in a historian: it is the mark of a scholar, who himself had written in Greek.[30]

(1875), Freund (1901) and (most conveniently) in Mooney's Commentary (1930) 611-39. The repetitiveness of the rubric style emerges from the investigations of Mouchova (1968). On the use of the perfect verb, see Dihle (1954) 50. For those who take a rather different view, see below, n.32.

29. On S's vocabulary, see the lists in Mooney 611ff.; Slusanski (1975) examines some of his technicalities, particularly literary ones, Tomulescu (1977) his use of legal terminology and Ramondetti (1977) his terminology relevant to senatorial procedure. Among bureaucratic terms, which S is the first or only surviving literary author to employ, I note: *officium* in the sense 'department' (*Vesp.* 14, cf. *ILS* 1921), *ducenarius* of procurators (*Cl.* 24), *rationarium* (*Aug.* 28.1), *formalis epistula* (*Dom.* 9.3), *ordinatio* of appointment to a post (*Dom.* 4.2), *fiscalis* (*Dom.* 9.3), *confisco, instrumentum* of a collection of documents (*Vesp.* 8.5), *angusticlavius* (*Oth.* 10: the only occurrence of a word much used by modern textbooks), *amanuensis* (*Ner.* 44, *Tit.* 3).

30. Townend (1960) emphasises the exceptional nature of S's use of Greek citations longer than a single word. He plausibly suggests the Greek savant Ti-

Suetonius' willingness to cite documents is perhaps the most exciting and valuable product of his non-historical approach. Ancient historians sometimes made use of documentary material. Tacitus (almost certainly) owes his accounts of senatorial debates, and particularly of imperial orations, partly to first-hand consultation of the senatorial minutes. But no more than any other historian was Tacitus prepared to cite his sources verbatim. We can still see how he remodelled an oration of Claudius rather than allow him speak in his own words. The fictional speech rather than the authentic document was the hallmark of the ancient historian. Those who cited documents were not historians but scholars: whether Aristotle in his series of *Constitutions*, Craterus who collected Athenian decrees or Varro illustrating the diction of old censorial or consular records. Suetonius had made verbatim citations as a matter of practice in his literary lives and other scholarly works. He continued to do so in the *Caesars*: imperial edicts, inscriptions, invectives, snatches of verse chanted in triumphs or the theatre, wills, and above all, the letters of Augustus, a priceless contribution. These, together with anecdotal sayings, took the place of the historian's set-piece speeches.[31]

Suetonius' lack of stylistic pretension enabled him to preserve these precious fragments. It has also led to the verdict that he was 'no true artist'. A school of critics has recently leapt to his defence, anxious to prove that he is more than an amasser of facts, 'tipping out for his readers', as Benedetto Croce put it, 'his cornucopia of information'. The new school has demonstrated the not inconsiderable degree of control and skill with which he can organise his material.[32] But we must not be swept away and miss the point. Suetonius belonged to a culture in which art-prose (the 'Kunstprosa'

Claudius Balbillus as the ultimate source for certain of them (115ff.). A minor Greek anecdotalist is precisely the sort of author S was likely to draw on. Greek technical terms in S are listed by Mooney 611f.

31. On Tacitus' use of the senatorial *acta*, see Syme, *Tacitus* 186ff. and 278ff.; *JRS* 72 (1982) 73ff. Claudius' oration preserved at Lyons (Smallwood, *Documents . . . of Gaius, Claudius and Nero* no. 367) has been frequently compared with Tacitus' recasting (*Ann.* 11.23-4): most recently see M.T. Griffin, 'The Lyons tablet and Tacitean hindsight', *CQ* 32 (1982) 404ff. For citation of documents in Varro, see e.g. *de Lingua Latina* 6.86-8. The value of S's contribution is appreciated by Flach (1972) 285. On the gulf between historiography and antiquarianism, see Momigliano, 'Ancient history and the antiquarian', in *Studies in Historiography* (1966) 1ff.

32. The verdict of Croce comes from 'Variazioni intorno a Svetonio', *Quadri della Critica* 14 (1949) 16. For the reasons for his distaste, see Piero Treves,

of Eduard Norden's classic study) was a category apart: canons of
propriety, figures of speech and rhythmic clausulae deliberately
sought to raise it above the banal, conversational or technical. On
all the tests, Suetonius does not seek to identify his writing with this
category. The usual tricks which historians employed to produce
variety and excitement – historic presents and infinitives, syntactical
variations, rapid parataxis and variety of tempo, inversion of word
order – are absent from his style.[33]

Suetonius' natural affinities are with the abundant technical
literature of the early empire – Vitruvius on architecture, Frontinus
on aqueducts, Celsus on medicine, the jurists, physiognomists,
agronomists, metricians and grammarians. His greatest predecessor
in the scholarly-antiquarian tradition, Varro, was known for his
neglect of style. It did not diminish his stature. The elder Pliny was
not a 'good' writer either, even if the *Natural histories* contain a
sprinkling of purple passages. Literary critics do not normally pay
attention to such technical literature. Considered against such a
background of 'artless' prose, the positive virtues of Suetonius'
writing might be more apparent: his clear organisation, his succinct
expression, and above all his eye for vivid detail. But whatever the
verdict, neither his virtues nor his vices are those of the historian.[34]

'Biografia e storia in Svetonio', preface to *Svetonio: Vita dei Cesari* (Milan
1962). The reaction to the critical view of S was started by the important book
of Wolf Steidle, *Sueton und die antike Biographie* (1951). In his wake, various
scholars have sought to demonstrate S's 'artistic' control: Hanslik (1954) in the
Augustus, Croisille (1969/70) in the *Claudius* and *Nero*, Brutscher (1958),
Gugel (1970) and Müller (1972) in the *Julius*. More recently Cizek (1977)
has laid emphasis on the so-called technique of gradation; and Gugel (1977)
has looked for 'Gestaltungsprinzipien' among the rubrics (Gugel 11ff. has a
good survey of the literature to date). There is, however, excellent sense in the
plea of Drexler (1969) to judge the author by his content not his 'art'.

33. The contrast of techniques with historiography is demonstrated by Sage
(1979).

34. The stylistic links between S's descriptions of appearance and the dry
'iconistic' style of the physiognomists is shown by G. Misener, 'Iconistic
portraits', *Classical Philology* 19 (1924) 97ff. On stylistic links with the jurists,
see below, ch.6, n.17. On Roman technical literature, see now the *Cambridge
History of Classical Literature: II, Latin Literature*, ed. E.J. Kenney (1982),
286-92 (Varro and Nepos), 493-4 (Vitruvius and Celsus), 667-73 (Pomponius,
Columella, the elder Pliny, Frontinus), 678-80 (Gellius). The stylistic aspirations of these authors vary considerably, from Varro's hasty impatience with
fine style to the clumsy flourishes of Pomponius or Pliny.

The author and his public

The *Caesars*, then, present historical material in a manner that the Roman would identify as non-historical. But to whom was the author addressing himself? It is impossible to determine who actually did read any given author, and no doubt works reached circles both wider and narrower than the writer hoped. But authors do betray something of their expectations. Historians saw themselves very largely as addressing men involved in public life. The theme of the practical utility of history was a common one: history was a tale of public life told by those with experience and understanding of it in order to improve the understanding of the reader. For the Romans, the utilitarian purpose was also a moral one. The past was a storehouse of *exempla*, and, by studying these, future generations would have models of what to follow and what to avoid. Tacitus felt that the record of Tiberius' reign, however grim and cloying, could benefit those living under autocracy. Philosophy on its own was inadequate as a guide to life. He could point with relief to a senator like Marcus Lepidus who found a recipe for survival under tyranny without compromising his self-respect. And because history had a practical and moral purpose, the historian adopted a didactic tone. The mordant epigrams of Tacitus drew attention to the lessons to be learnt from history. On a practical level the historian explained how things did work; on a moral level he commented on how people ought to behave.[35]

Suetonius' preface is lost. There, apart from addressing Septicius Clarus as 'prefect of the praetorian cohorts' he probably gave some indication of his purpose in writing. But even without this, we can infer something from the way he presents his material. His tone is anything but didactic. One of its most remarkable features is the rarity with which he intervenes to comment on his material. He does not speak *in propria persona*, except to comment on truth or falsehood. He offers no epigrams or *sententiae*. He does not even generally use value-laden adjectives to guide the reader towards

35. The moral and exemplary aims of Roman historians are explicit e.g. at Sempronius Asellio fr. 1 (Gellius *Noctes Atticae* 5.18.9), Sallust *Jugurtha* 4, Livy *Preface* 10, Tacitus *Histories* 1.3 and *Ann.* 4.33. On Lepidus as a model, *Ann.* 4.20. The conventional aims of historiography are neatly summarised in Lucian's essay *On how to write history*, on which see G. Avenarius, *Lukians Schrift zur Geschichtsschreibung* (1956). On the audiences of ancient historians, A. Momigliano, 'The historians of the classical world and their audience', *Ann. Scuol. Norm. Pisa* ser. 3 vol. 8 (1978) 59ff.

approval or disapproval. Value-judgments must often be implicit in the items he relates; yet he seeks to keep himself and his opinions in low profile. Again he quite deliberately avoids stepping into the historian's shoes.[36]

Tacitus' ideal reader is evidently a senator. Suetonius' is not; but nor is he the 'man-in-the-street'. It is particularly unjust to cast Suetonius as the author of a *chronique scandaleuse*, an exposé of the seamier side of palace life, which catered for that taste for 'the things behind the scenes which attract the ears and eyes of the curious because they are kept secret', as a late Roman potted history puts it. Scandal undoubtedly occupies a place in the *Caesars*, as for that matter it does in the historiographical tradition. But its place is a minor one. The author hardly waded through mounds of dull administrative detail as an excuse for tittle-tattle. At worst we may admit that he knew the value of the anecdotal in spicing up the dry and factual.[37]

Again, we might be inclined to see a 'mirror of princes' in the *Caesars*, a model laid before Hadrian of the behaviour a good prince should follow or eschew. The analytic presentation enables the reader to form a judgment of the performance of a series of rulers. Thus a picture emerges both of an ideal and of its opposite. But the ideal is not the conclusion so much as the presupposition of the *Caesars*. Suetonius does not seek to instruct a Caesar how to behave; rather he analyses how Caesars did behave against a background of assumptions about imperial behaviour. Hadrian could well have read the *Caesars* out of interest, but not to be taught lessons.[38]

Another suggestion is that he wrote for an equestrian bureaucracy

36. Virtues and vices in S are naturally value-laden; but elsewhere he avoids value-laden words. The neutrality of his style is shown by Ektor (1980).

37. The quotation is from *Epitome de Caesaribus* 48.18, cited by Flach (1972) 288. S's successor as imperial biographer, Marius Maximus, was notoriously more interested in scandal for its own sake: R. Syme, *Ammianus and the Historia Augusta* (1968) 89ff.; *Emperors and Biography* (1971) 113ff. The view of S as a gossip is epitomised by J.W. Duff, *A Literary History of Rome in the Silver Age*[3] (1964) 508: 'A great deal of it partakes of the nature of a *chronique scandaleuse* based upon tittle-tattle about the emperors and compiled by a literary man with the muck-rake, too keen upon petty and prurient detail to produce a scientific account of his subjects.' That S writes for 'the man of the street' is claimed by Paratore (1959) 341.

38. That S shares assumptions on how a ruler should behave with Pliny in the *Panegyric* and other Romans is argued below, particularly in ch.7. It does not follow that S shows Pliny's didactic purpose, made explicit at *Ep.* 3.18.2. On ancient 'mirror of princes' literature, see below, ch.7. n.7.

alienated from the traditional senatorial élite. The equestrian Septicius was distinguished by the dedication as an ideal reader. Yet, as will be seen, there is nothing in the Caesars at which a senator should take offence. Even if it contains much to interest the equestrian official, it is not such as to exclude the senator.[39]

The error is to make of the *Caesars* an alternative type of history to the *Annals*, written differently because for a different type of person. It is not history at all. It is biography, written by a scholar in the hellenistic tradition, composed neither to instruct nor to titillate but to inform. The neutral, non-committal presentation is that expected of a scholar: even details of sexual life are recorded without condemnation and without relish.

The scholar cannot write for everyone, and there are perhaps two interests in particular which Suetonius assumed in his reader: interest in the world of culture and literature, and interest in the world of imperial administration. They are interests that met in the scholarly *ab epistulis*. The combination was hardly rare at the court of Hadrian, a ruler noted both for his dedication to the administrative grind and for his fascination with hellenistic culture. But to form a clearer conception of the world to which Suetonius belonged and for which he wrote, we need to examine the place of scholarship in Roman society at large and at the imperial court in particular.

39. Against the argument of della Corte (1958) that S writes for an equestrian bourgeoisie, see below, ch.5.

Chapter Two

THE SCHOLAR AND SOCIETY

The sources create an accidental gulf between Suetonius the public figure – in his glory in the Hippo dedication, in disgrace in the life of Hadrian – and Tranquillus the scholar described by the *Suda* with his dismayingly long list of titles. Of the two, it is the scholar who is the less familiar figure. Only after the scholar and scholarship have been placed in their social context can we begin to make sense of the author and assess his output and the readership for which he wrote.

Studia in Pliny

The younger Pliny recommended Suetonius to Trajan as *probissimum honestissimum eruditissimum virum* – 'a perfect gentleman and an excellent scholar'. The phrase is neatly tailored for this gentleman scholar, or so it might seem until an eye is cast over the language of Pliny's other recommendations. Almost exactly the same string of superlatives (*probissimum gravissimum eruditissimum*) is applied to Sextus Erucius whose advancement in the senate Pliny backs (2.9.3). Sextus was the nephew of Septicius Clarus, and had an impressive enough career ahead: doubtless he was well-read, but there is no sign that he was an author as distinguished as Suetonius. Erudition and uprightness similarly recommend the young senator Asinius Bassus (4.15.7). Then there is a whole series of recommendations for preferment to equestrian military ranks, often the tribunate, and again and again Pliny points to their literary attainments: 'a great talent . . . erudite in pleading cases'; 'he loves learning'; 'I make use of his criticisms for my own writings'; 'his father was a great lover of learning'. In fact there are only three of Pliny's recommendations in which no mention of literary attainments is made, against a dozen in which it is.[1]

That is a fair reflection of the society evoked by Pliny's letters as a whole. Throughout Pliny is desperately concerned to foster *studia*, literary studies, and to secure promotion for *studiosi*, lovers of learning. Odd though it may seem to choose a soldier for his book-learning, military rank, like senatorial rank, was seen primarily as a token of public esteem. The poet Martial had been decorated by Domitian with the military tribunate: Pliny regrets the passing in his day of this old custom of rewarding poets for their praise with honours or money (3.21.3). But at other moments he is more optimistic. Studies flourish as never before under Nerva (1.10.1). Later the prestige of studies is maintained – because a young patrician endured discomfort to listen to Pliny speaking (4.16); though when the law-courts start to be businesslike in expediting the pleading of cases, he complains that studies have fallen into contempt and neglect (6.2.5). He has especial praise for the imperial procurator Titinius Capito: 'he fosters studies, loves cherishes and seeks advancement for *studiosi*' (8.12.1).

Of course there were also tough military men in Rome who neither understood nor cared about books. Trajan might have been among them, though Pliny vigorously denies it (*Pan*.47). But nothing could be further from the truth than to imagine a natural gulf between the intelligentsia and the military men and administrators. A series of vignettes is enough to dissolve that dichotomy. The general Vestricius Spurinna, veteran of the civil war of AD 69, is sketched in retirement: from dawn to dusk he is seldom without a book in his hand, or talking literature with his friends, or even composing Greek and Latin lyrics (3.1). Greek verses are also composed by another elder statesman, Arrius Antoninus, grandfather of the future emperor Pius (4.3). Pliny flatters him by turning his epigrams into Latin (4.18; 5.15). There is nothing amiss in

---

1. Recommendations for military posts at least partly on literary grounds are made by Pliny at: 2.13.7 (Voconius Romanus), cf. 10.4.4; 3.2.3 (Arrianus Maturus); 4.4.1 (Varisidius Nepos – P notes that he is learned, for him the most important thing: *disertum, quod apud me vel potentissimum est*); 7.22.2 (Cornelius Minicianus). P's backing for Iulius Naso for a magistracy includes reference to his father's support of *studia*: 6.6.3. The recommendations which make no mention of learning are addressed to Trajan: 10.26 (Rosianus Geminus), 86a (Gavius Bassus), 87 (Nymphidius Lupus). The anonymous and fragmentary recommendation 10.86b at least mentions *humanitas*. Consideration of the workings of patronage under the empire should now start from R.P. Saller, *Personal Patronage under the Early Empire* (1982) esp. 41ff.

writing light verse: Pliny can defend his own hendecasyllables by a host of worthy precedents, including Julius, Augustus, Tiberius, Nerva, as well as Verginius Rufus who refused the throne (5.3.5). Pomponius Bassus is a model of how a man who has achieved the highest honours and commanded armies should behave in retirement, engaging in learned disputes and reading avidly (4.23). But it is not necessary to wait until retirement for the opportunity for reading: Mamilianus, despite all his complaints of the pressure of military life, finds time for Pliny's epigrams, and qualifies for the accolade of a scholar, *viri eruditissimi gravissimi* (9.25.2). Pliny expects learning of a great man: the young aristocrat Calpurnius Piso proves himself worthy of his forebears by writing a poem on the constellations (5.17). He is also delighted to discover it in a lesser one. How the *eruditi* conceal their learning! He had visited Terentius Junior, a former officer and procurator, on his country estate, expecting the talk to be of agriculture, and found his host learnedly turning the conversation to Greek and Latin literature (7.25).[2]

   Literary accomplishment may have been little more than skin-deep in some of these characters whom Pliny praises. But there are two who demonstrate that it was possible to combine dedicated service of the emperor with an impressive literary output, and so provide useful comparison with Suetonius. The most impressive is the elder Pliny, procurator to the Flavians, and yet a man of encyclopedic learning and prolific output. His nephew describes his daily routine, which must have borne some resemblance to that of Suetonius. He reported for duty to Vespasian before sunrise and after the day's work returned home to give every moment to his books. A day's work can rarely have occupied more than the morning. He read as he ate, as he stripped for the bath, even as he travelled to and fro (3.5). The elder Pliny's writing shows a combination of two ingredients which also characterises Suetonius: hellenistic scholarship on the one hand (most of the numerous books he drew on for the *Natural histories* were works of hellenistic learning) and, on the other, interest in Roman public life. He wrote at almost equal length on scientific subjects and on contemporary history. The *Natural histories* are crammed with historical anecdotes as well as scientific learning; and we may perhaps surmise that

---

2. On literary patronage, see P. White, '*Amicitia* and the profession of poetry in early imperial Rome', *JRS* 68 (1978) 74ff., with the criticisms of Saller 28ff. Against the picture of a distinct class of 'military men', see B. Campbell, 'Who were the "viri militares"?', *JRS* 65 (1975) 11ff.

the *Histories* had their sprinkling of scientific or technical detail. Suetonius' works too divide between the scholarly and the historical; but in each, interest in the other shines through.

The second figure who bears comparison with Suetonius is Titinius Capito. Secretary *ab epistulis* to a succession of emperors from Domitian to Trajan, Capito was acclaimed by Pliny as a leading light in the renaissance of letters (8.12). Like Suetonius, he was not only secretary, but also biographer. He wrote verses on famous men, and also a work on *Deaths of famous men*. Martyrology was a fashionable genre. He caught the wave of the literary 'republicanism' that followed the murder of Domitian, just as he caught the public eye by his erection of a statue of Nero's victim Silanus in the forum and by his cult of Brutus, Cassius and Cato. He does not sound so learned a scholar as either the elder Pliny or Suetonius; but he amply illustrates enthusiasm for literature in an imperial official.[3]

The younger Pliny's picture of Roman society may well be one-sided. He had, after all, a vested interest in the advertisement and advancement of his own literary friends and protégés. But the assumption, which he expects to be shared by his addressees, is that literary accomplishments were the mark of a proper gentleman and constituted *per se* a claim for public respect and the conferment of positions of honour. This assumption can be put in perspective if we examine Pliny's concept of *studia*. The word is virtually untranslatable, at least into English; though it is itself an equivalent to the Greek *paideia*. It covers in the first place a literary education, the 'liberal studies' that were the making of a gentleman, and secondly the literary interests that were the continuing mark of one who had acquired the right education. For the orator Pliny, *studia* are often rhetorical accomplishments; but, as we have seen, they are also manifested in writing light verse or biography, in reading of any sort. The prestige of learning was a reflection of the prestige of the dominant literary education of the time. It is against the background of this educational system that Suetonius' scholarship must be considered.[4]

3. On Titinius, see Pliny *Ep*. 1.17 and 8.12. On the genre of martyrologies, above ch.1, n.18. On men of learning in the imperial entourage, Millar, *Emperor* 83ff. and below, ch.4.

4. On the transformation of Roman education, see the classic account of H. Marrou, *A History of Education in Antiquity* (Eng. trans. 1956) 229ff.; and recently S.F. Bonner, *Education in Ancient Rome* (1977). The most serious attempt to come to grips with the problem of the place and function of education in Roman society is J. Christes, *Bildung und Gesellschaft* (1975).

Suetonius and the history of education

Suetonius is described in the *Suda* as a Roman grammarian. Technically a *grammaticus* was a professor of literature, usually one who
taught for a living. With the property qualification of an *eques
Romanus*, Suetonius had no need of such an income, and there is
no evidence that he ever had pupils. But he wrote as such professors
wrote. Pliny dubbed him a *scholasticus*, a product of the schools;
John the Lydian calls him a *philologus*, a lover of learning. All
these terms are imprecise; but all are Greek, and the intellectual
context to which he belongs is that of Alexandrian scholarship.[5]

The best guide to his intellectual background is a work which
survives from his own pen: the slim but valuable essay *On grammarians and rhetors*. This consists of a series of lives, or rather brief
biographical sketches, first of the most notable Roman professors of
grammaticē ('grammar' is a misleading translation), and then of the
professors of rhetoric; the manuscript unfortunately breaks off
halfway through the second series. The essay has been read with a
certain impatience by modern literary historians. Although it preserves valuable pieces of information, for instance about Valerius
Cato who taught a generation of poets contemporary with Catullus,
it offers no overall framework for literary history. Anybody hoping
to find an account of the contribution of each professor to the
development of Roman thought and writing will be disappointed.
But this is to ask the wrong questions of the essay. Suetonius does
have a clear theme, which he states in the two prefaces: the rise in
prestige and social standing of the professions of *grammaticē* and
rhetoric and of their practitioners. What he describes is a remarkable
transformation in social attitudes, from the suspicion and rejection
of Greek-style education in the early first century BC to the

---

5. The best discussion of S's scholarly activities in relation to the *Caesars* is
still Macé (1900) 242ff. especially valuable for stressing the numerous links of
subject matter between the *Caesars* and the other works. However, Macé's
notion that S taught as a *grammaticus* (54f. discussing *Suda* s.v. *Trankullos*,
John Lydus *de Mag.* 1.34, Plin. *Ep.* 1.24.4) is rightly rejected by subsequent
scholars. The emphasis by Leo (1901) on the profound importance of the
traditions of Alexandrian scholarship for the understanding of the *Caesars* has
been played down by recent writers on S to their detriment. Important
discussions of the scholarly works from a purely philological angle are Funaioli
(1932) and Brugnoli (1968). For further details on the list of works see below.

lionisation of professors a century later. It is this transformation that helps to explain Suetonius' own scholarly career.[6]

Two prefaces, one to the lives of grammarians and the other to the lives of rhetoricians, sketch the general lines of development. The primitive and bellicose Romans of old had no use for *grammatice*. Though indeed there were sporadic signs of interest in culture earlier, Suetonius dates the beginnings of interest in the discipline to the mid second century BC when Crates, head of the library at Pergamum, broke his leg in the course of an embassy to Rome and offered lectures on his subject during his recuperation. Thereafter its reputation gradually increased until there were twenty schools flourishing simultaneously at Rome. Grammar became a commodity for which staggering prices were paid, and the fashion spread out from Rome to her provinces (*Gramm.* 1-3). The change of attitudes to rhetoric was even more startling. The official attitude at first was of sharp disapproval, and as late as 92 BC the censors issued a famous edict banning teachers of Latin rhetoric from the city. Yet half a century later the triumvirs Antony and Octavian were practising the schoolboy exercise of declamation in the midst of civil war; and thereafter rhetorical education became so much in vogue that it was possible, Suetonius claims, for a professor to advance from obscurity to the highest rank in the state (25.1-7).

Suetonius then documents his theme of the rise of repute of the arts by detailing the social status and origins of the successive professors. This interest in social status may have been a traditional one. At any rate, it was Cornelius Nepos, one of his sources, who observed that the former door-keeper Voltacilius Pilutus was the first freedman who dared to write history, until then the preserve of the high-born (27). Furthermore an approximate contemporary of Suetonius, the ex-slave Hermippus from Berytus (Beirut) wrote a work which may be regarded as a sort of Greek companion piece to the *Grammarians and rhetors*. This was a collection of biographies

6. The best text of the *de Grammaticis et Rhetoribus* is the Teubner edition of G. Brugnoli (1960); there is also an edition with useful complementary notes by della Corte (ed. 3, 1968). Disappointment at the absence of literary history is expressed by Funaioli (1932) 608, G.M.A. Grube, *The Greek and Roman Critics* (1965) 313, and elsewhere. Its value as an educational document is seen by all works on ancient education; as a social document it has been exploited by S. Treggiari, *Roman Freedmen during the Late Republic* (1969) 110ff.; and recently following the hint of J. Vogt, *Ancient Slavery and the Ideal of Man* (Eng. trans. 1974) 125, in the thorough investigation of freedman grammarians by J. Christes, *Sklaven und Freigelassene als Grammatiker und Philologen im antiken Rom* (1979).

of slaves who had won distinction in education (*paideia*) and is likely to be the source of the numerous notices about such Greek grammarians preserved in the *Suda* encyclopedia.

What Suetonius nowhere attempts is an explanation of the phenomena he documents. It is startling that as late as 92 BC, when the aristocracy was already so familiar with hellenistic culture, the appearance of teachers of Latin rhetoric on the Greek model caused such a reaction. One of the two censors responsible for the edict was the leading orator of his day, L. Licinius Crassus. Cicero reports that his objection was that these new schools taught young men *impudentia*, insubordination. The threat was of social mobility. According to the edict, 'our ancestors established what they wanted their children to learn and what schools they should attend'. In fact, aristocratic education took place largely in the family. From his father a boy learnt the *bonae artes*, the appropriate skills for a public figure of war, law and government as well as letters and public speaking. The adolescent learnt by imitating his father and his father's peers in the forum, in the senate, on the battlefield. The system was well suited to preserving the dominance of the aristocracy.

The danger inherent in the new schools of rhetoric was that they were public, open to anyone who could afford to pay the lecturer. Given the importance of public speaking in Roman political life, the acquisition of the art of rhetoric could be a potent instrument for promotion. Once the schools of rhetoric had been firmly established in the early days of the empire, it was well known that men rose to the top through rhetoric. Tacitus pointed to the example of two new men from Italian towns, Vibius Crispus and Eprius Marcellus, who rose to great power under Vespasian thanks to their rhetorical skills: 'the humbleness of their origin and the meanness of their financial circumstances only shows them to better effect as egregious instances of the practical utility of rhetorical training' (*Dialogus* 8.3).[7]

7. A. Gwynn, *Roman Education from Cicero to Quintilian* (1926) 59ff. argued that the ban on teaching was caused by the *popularis* sympathies of Plotius Gallus. Bonner, *Education* 71f. shows that this interpretation will not stand. The importance of the aristocratic ambience is seen by Christes, *Bildung und Gesellschaft* 136ff. The transformation of the social background of the leading Roman orators is neatly illustrated by W. Kunkel, *Herkunft und soziale Stellungen der römischen Juristen*[2] (1967) 287f.: under Augustus leading senatorial families (Paullus Fabius Maximus, M. Claudius Marcellus etc.) mix with new men like Cassius Severus. Under the Julio-Claudians, aristocratic orators disappear, giving way to provincials and new men.

Grammaticē was less dangerous than rhetoric. Grammarians taught the classics of literature and their interpretation: knowledge of literature was not so obvious a route to social promotion as rhetoric. Consequently, on Suetonius' showing, grammarians became established in Rome some time before rhetoricians, from the beginning of the first century BC. Yet they must have played a significant role in undermining old traditions of education in the family and in spreading the Greek style. The data assembled by Suetonius and Hermippus point to an enormous influx of teachers in the first century BC, predominantly from the Greek east. Paradoxically, the aristocracy encouraged the transformation it feared through its own competitive spirit. The pattern that emerges is of the powerful families competing to acquire scholars as tutors for their sons.[8]

The best source of scholars was of course the Greek east, and as Roman armies ravaged the East in the wake of the traumatic massacre of Romans by Mithridates of Pontus in 88 BC, the victorious generals returned with enslaved teachers among their precious booty. Cornelius Epicadus was the freedman of Sulla, presumably brought back from war; he taught Sulla's son and completed his master's unfinished memoirs (*Gramm.* 12). Sulla's lieutenant Lentulus bagged a grammarian trained by Crates, Alexander 'Polyhistor', who proved a writer of distinction on geography (*Suda,* s.v. Alexandros). When Sulla stormed Athens in 86 BC, the first man over the walls was a centurion called Ateius. He had his reward. His Athenian slave, later a freedman, L. Ateius Philologus, taught the Ateii, and the centurion's grandson Ateius Capito, one of the famous jurists of Augustus' reign, had high praise for this versatile teacher (10). In 70 BC, Amisos on the Pontus fell. One of the two most distinguished professors there was Tyrannion, a pupil of Dionysius Thrax, who wrote the first definitive systematic grammar. The general, Lucullus, is said to have been rather shocked

8. Particulars of Greek teachers in Rome were collected by A. Hillscher, 'Hominum litteratorum Graecorum ante Tiberii mortem in urbe Roma commoratorum historia critica', *Jahrb. f. class. Phil.* Suppl. 18 (1892) 355ff. For grammarians of servile status, Christes, *Sklaven und Freigelassene* gives a thorough discussion; many of the salient details appear in Bonner, *Education* 47ff. On the impact of Greek culture on late republican and Augustan Rome, see G.W. Bowersock, *Augustus and the Greek World* (1965). Since most of the information on teachers of servile/freedman status comes from Suetonius and Hermippus via the *Suda,* I give the reference to these in the text. On Hermippus himself, see Christes 137ff.

when his lieutenant Murena took the opportunity to acquire the professor as a slave. Freed, in Rome, Tyrannion became an authority on the building up of private libraries (*Suda*, s.v. Tyrannion). Of a later vintage was Timagenes, brought home captive from Egypt by Gabinius in 65, bought by the son of the dictator Sulla, under whom he rose, according to rumour, from cook to litter-bearer to teacher of rhetoric (*Suda*, s.v. Timagenes). The greatest of the eastern conquerors was Pompey; appropriately he had the largest number of professors in his train. But by now gentler methods were possible. On Rhodes Pompey attended the lectures of Aristodemus of Nysa, son of an academic, himself equally adept at grammar and rhetoric. Aristodemus had a brother, Sostratus, also a *grammaticus*, and Pompey induced his son, named after the uncle Aristodemus, to return to Rome to teach the young Pompeys Greek (*Suda*, s.v. Aristodemus). Nicias from Cos was another grammarian who enjoyed Pompey's patronage (*Gramm.* 14).[9]

The importation of Greek professors was necessary if the aristocracy wished to learn Greek literature and techniques. But it generally required a native Latin speaker to teach Latin; and one point which Suetonius' biographies illustrate is the parallel movement in the first century BC by which Latin-speaking slaves were trained up as teachers. Suitable material was provided by the towns of Italy: Crassicius came from Tarentum (18), Melissus from Spoletum (21), and Pompey's freedman Lenaeus is said to have run away back home (15) perhaps to Aurunca. Others came from Gaul (Cisalpine Gaul, presumably), like Antonius Gnipho, a foundling educated and then manumitted by his master (7). Spain was the likely origin of Augustus' freedman Hyginus (29). Slaves of eastern origin indeed could learn Latin if caught young enough. Staberius Eros was a Thracian bought as a boy from the slaver's stand (13). Epirota was

9. A few details above derive from elsewhere than Suetonius or the *Suda*. Ateius Philologus: that the grandfather of the jurist was a Sullan centurion is attested by Tac. *Ann.* 3.75; identification with the Ateius who stormed Athens in Plut. *Sulla* 14 is almost certain; I infer from Capito's praise of Philologus that he had been taught by him. Tyrannion: also familiar from Cicero's correspondence; the libraries he was involved with were those of the brothers Cicero (*ad Att.* 4.4A.1, 8.2; *ad Q. fr.* 3.4.5); the Aristotelian library of Apellicon plundered from Athens, Strabo 13.608f.; and his own of 30,000 volumes (*Suda*); on his capture see also Plut. *Lucull.* 19.7. Timagenes: the story of his rise from cook is given by Seneca *Contr.* 10.5.22; further, see Bowersock, *Augustus* 109f. and 125f.

home-born on Atticus' estate at Tusculum, but to judge from his name his parentage was Greek (16).

The readiness of aristocratic families to exploit the new availability of talented private tutors did most to undermine the traditional aristocratic system of education. Grammarians who started as private tutors might set up on their own: so Gnipho whose public lectures were attended in the mid-60s by Cicero (*Gramm.* 7). Staberius Eros offered free tuition for those unfortunates who had been deprived of rights and properties by Sulla's proscription of their fathers (13). Nor were all professors bound by servitude and manumission to particular patrons. Orbilius was a freeborn citizen from Beneventum who set up practice in Rome in 63 BC and there maintained a precarious existence on the proceeds (9). Similarly Valerius Cato was free, but left penniless by civil war. Although lionised as a teacher by a generation of young poets, he remained impoverished; this Roman Crates, as one pupil quipped, could clear up all questions grammatical but could not clear his own name of debt (11).

This influx of teachers resulted in a transformation of attitudes. By the end of the first century the Greek style of education in *grammaticē* and rhetoric had become the norm. Indeed it became so fashionable that the schoolboy exercise of declamation turned into a sort of public performance by the professionals to which the public flocked, as is documented for us at length by the enthusiast Seneca the Elder.[10] There was also a marked shift in official attitudes to education. Caesar as dictator granted citizenship to all professors and doctors at Rome (*Jul.* 42.1). Augustus similarly recognised professors and doctors as a privileged and protected group: they were exempted from an expulsion of foreigners during a famine (*Aug.* 42.3). Augustus also honoured a leading scholar of the day, Verrius Flaccus, by appointing him tutor to his grandsons at the handsome salary of 100,000 sesterces, a level of pay adequate for an equestrian procurator (*Gramm.* 17). His foundation of public libraries created further posts of honour for scholars. One such librarian whose name Suetonius records was the equestrian Pompeius Macer, son of Pompey's favourite, Theophanes of Mytilene;

---

10. The value of the elder Seneca's (not always accurate) history of the rise of declamation is carefully discussed by J.A. Fairweather, *Seneca the Elder* (1981) esp. 104ff. Seneca conceals the extent to which declamation was already established in Cicero's lifetime. See also S.F. Bonner, *Roman Declamation* (1949) and M. Winterbottom's introduction to the Loeb translation of the *Controversiae*.

Pompeius served Augustus in other roles as procurator. But two other librarians were grammarians from his own household, Julius Hyginus and C. Melissus (*Gramm.* 20 and 21). That a freedman could be employed in the same post as an equestrian is a token of the respect in which scholarship was now held.[11]

But the clearest official acknowledgment under the empire of the importance of education lay in the grant to teachers of grammar and rhetoric (as also to doctors) of immunity from local taxes and duties. The latest evidence suggests that their immunity goes back to the triumviral period when rhetorical education was already in high fashion at Rome. A later inscription shows Vespasian reaffirming the privileged status of teachers and doctors; Hadrian further extended the privileges, which were regularised in the form met in the legal codes by Antoninus Pius, who established a quota of tax-free grammarians and rhetors for each community. Emperors further promoted education by establishing official chairs. Vespasian led the way at Rome by creating chairs of Greek and Latin rhetoric, at the same salary of 100,000 sesterces that Augustus had paid Verrius Flaccus (*Vesp.* 18). Later emperors created other chairs in the provinces. Yet another privilege, established at an unknown date, opened for professors a special process for the recovery of unpaid fees.[12]

One vital factor in this dramatic reversal of Roman attitudes to education was the role which it could play in the empire. Education rapidly emerged as a prime instrument of Romanisation, invaluable for converting local aristocracies to a Rome-centred culture.[13] It is

---

11. On imperial librarians, see further below, ch.4. On the career of Pompeius Macer, Bowersock, *Augustus* 38f.

12. For the state and education under the empire see Marrou, *History of Education* 299ff., Bonner, *Education* 159ff., and G.W. Bowersock, *Greek Sophists in the Roman Empire* (1969) 30ff., especially on immunities for teachers. The main evidence is in the *Digest* 27.1.6, together with an edict of Vespasian; McCrum and Woodhead, *Documents of the Flavian Emperors* no.458. The new inscription, apparently dating the immunities back to the triumviral period, is published by D. Knibbe, *Zeitschrift für Papyrologie und Epigr.* 44 (1981) 1ff. For the special process for recovery of fees (*Digest* 50.13.1) see Christes, *Bildung und Gesellschaft* 1ff., discussing an old controversy among legal historians.

13. On the role of education in the social development of the empire, see the suggestive discussion of Keith Hopkins, *Conquerors and Slaves* (1978) 76ff. For the theme of 'Romanisation', see also A.N. Sherwin-White, *The Roman Citizenship*[2] (1973) 397ff.

amazing how quickly, after the tentative and unplanned emergence of a Roman literary education imported from the Greeks, this education was then exported to the provinces, as Suetonius himself notes (*Gramm.* 3.6). Spain led the way. Already in the early first century BC Sertorius is reported to have given the sons of the local nobility education in Latin. In the mid first century BC a Greek grammarian, Asclepiades of Myrleia, is recorded as active in Turdetania, the relatively advanced south-western tip of Spain. By the mid first century AD the region was producing the best Latin prose-writers and poets. Gaul was not far behind. In AD 23 the rebel Sacrovir was able to take hostage a class-room full of the sons of the Aeduan nobility at Autun. Three of Suetonius' post-Augustan rhetors came from Gaul, Statius Ursulus from Toulouse, Clodius Quirinalis from Arles, and Julius Gabinianus. Spain's products were even more distinguished: Quintilian, who was brought by Galba to Rome in AD 68, and Julius Tiro who rose through the senatorial career to the praetorship.[14]

The other western provinces followed suit; by the end of the first century AD Juvenal could couple Africa with Gaul as one of the main sources of orators (7.147ff.). In Antonine Rome in the mid second century the leading orator, Fronto, came from Cirta, and the leading grammarian, Sulpicius Apollinaris, from Carthage. If Hippo really was Suetonius' home-town, he would be of their company. Even Britain had its taste of education. Juvenal joked that *ultima Thule* at the ends of the earth was trying to hire a rhetorician. An inscription reveals that a Greek grammarian, Demetrius, was teaching in York in the 80s. Demetrius emerges from an essay of Plutarch as an academic of some distinction. Presumably he was there through the encouragement of Agricola, whom Tacitus describes as setting up schools for the sons of the local nobles. Tacitus comments acidly on the practical value of the policy: 'The innocent call it civilisation, when in truth it is an aspect of enslavement.'[15]

14. For the spread of education to the provinces, Marrou 292ff. On Asclepiades of Myrleia, Strabo 3.157. For rhetoric in Gaul, see Mayor's note on Juvenal 15.110 (382ff.). Parallels to Pliny's endowment to Comum are discussed by Sherwin-White on Pliny *Ep.* 4.13 (288). Some inscriptions recording *grammatici* in Italy and the provinces are collected in Dessau *ILS* 7761-7770.

15. See Tacitus *Agricola* 21.2; Ogilvie and Richmond in their commentary (32f. and 224) gather the evidence for Demetrius. Tacitus *Ann.* 3.43 shows the same process in action at Autun. Marrou 294 cites Plutarch *Sertorius* 14 as a precedent.

At the beginning of the first century BC literary education had aroused suspicion: it seemed to pose a threat to the established social order. Two centuries later it was deeply entrenched in a changed social order. For an élite drawn from a wide geographical range, literary attainment served as the mark of Romanness and gentle birth. It offered a passport to respectability. And in such a society, professors enjoyed corresponding prestige.

Grammaticē in the second century AD

Competition, fashion and practical advantage thus all conspired to elevate the prestige of grammarians, rhetoricians and the studies they promoted. The rhetoricians took the first pickings, as befitted the practical, political value of their art. It was a rhetorician, Quintilian, not a grammarian, who was honoured with the rank of consul. The most fashionable literary movement of the second century AD, termed by its historian Philostratus the 'Second Sophistic', was a rhetorical one. The élite both Greek and Roman streamed to the lecture halls to hear the 'sophists' perform their model declamations, and emperors held them in high honour.[16]

The abundant self-advertisement of this movement has tended to distract attention from *grammaticē* in the same period. Grammarians were paid less well than rhetors, and enjoyed less status. But it is an unjustifiable assumption that because the republican grammarians whom Suetonius records were mostly freedmen, those of the imperial period will have been freedmen also. Suetonius only records two post-Augustan grammarians. One, Remmius Palaemon, was an ex-slave, who made a fortune from teaching and from a shrewd investment in a vineyard (23). The other, Valerius Probus, was a freeborn citizen from the veteran colony of Beirut (24). It is likely enough that, at least by the second century, many were freeborn provincials like Probus. Nor were they without distinction: the names of three grammarians are preserved from Italy who were honoured with membership of their local councils. Another, Helvius

16. The historical importance of the Second Sophistic has been amply demonstrated by Bowersock, *Greek Sophists*. G. Kennedy, in Bowersock (ed.), *Approaches to the Second Sophistic* (1974) 17ff., stresses the basic but forgotten point that these sophists were essentially professors of rhetoric, and that the educational system lies at the root of the movement.

Pertinax, pupil and for a time successor of Sulpicius Apollinaris, was to rise to emperor.[17]

More telling is the evidence that interest in grammatical questions was carried past the schoolroom and was alive among the educated at large. This can be seen best in the *Attic nights* of Aulus Gellius, who was younger than Suetonius by a generation. As a young man in the reign of Antoninus Pius he took his education from the grammarians, rhetors and philosophers of Rome (later he went to Athens for the final polish). Not unlike the young Boswell in London, he cultivated the most brilliant figures of the intellectual scene, and took notes of some of the conversations he heard (though with less honesty and accuracy than Boswell). His Johnson was Favorinus of Arles, once a friend of Hadrian's, technically a philosopher, but showman enough as a speaker to qualify as the only westerner among Philostratus' sophists. Other luminaries were the grammarian Sulpicius Apollinaris and Cornelius Fronto the Latin orator, tutor of Marcus Aurelius. Gellius' own interests (he himself always remained an amateur) were those of the grammarian: above all the meanings and usages of words, particularly in old and little-read texts, and secondly antiquarian lore about matters social, legal and religious. It is therefore on the whole only the grammatical parts of conversations that are filtered through his hotch-potch of anecdotes and learned notes, the *Attic nights*. But selective though they are, they illustrate vividly the interest in matters grammatical among the intelligentsia.[18]

17. That Latin grammarians were freedmen is assumed as a generalisation (for all periods) on the basis of S's lives e.g. by Bonner, *Education* 58. However, M. Rutilius Aelianus, *grammaticus* at Beneventum, belonged to the local curial class (*ILS* 6497); P. Atilius Septicianus of Comum was freeborn and an honorary member of the local council (*ILS* 6729); though Q. Tuticanus Eros who enjoyed the same distinction at Verona was probably a freedman (*CIL* 5.3433; see Christes, *Sklaven und Freigelassene* 152). The names of the following leading *grammatici* of the second century AD show no signs of servile origin: L. Caesellius Vindex, Q. Terentius Scaurus, Velius Longus, Aemilius Asper. Scaurinus son of Scaurus was naturally freeborn; as was Pertinax, temporarily the successor of Apollinaris, though his father was a freedman. This is not, however, to obscure the fact that teachers of rhetoric always enjoyed more prestige than grammarians.

18. On the life and times of Gellius, see Friedländer, *Sittengeschichte* 4, 284ff. (*Life and Manners* 4, 322ff.). Though Gellius is much exploited as a source of fragments, his value as a witness to contemporary culture (apart from the phenomenon of 'archaism') is little noticed. See, however, E. Champlin, *Fronto and Antonine Rome* 46ff.

A characteristic scene is set in the forecourt of the imperial palace (4.1). A crowd is awaiting the emperor's levée; it includes a group of scholars, to whom a grammarian is holding forth in a dull and pompous manner on the gender of a word. Favorinus is provoked into showing him up; and a request for the meaning of a word reveals that he is capable neither of a proper philosophical definition nor understands its literary usage. The grammarian should know better, for the word occurs in a disputed passage of Virgil familiar to every schoolboy. In another episode set in the Palace the orator Fronto argues with Sulpicius Apollinaris and an unnamed grammarian, who distinguishes himself by an apt off-the-cuff quotation (19.13). Most frequently Gellius is found in the little crowd of followers behind the great Favorinus. He strolls in the Forum of Trajan waiting for his friend the consul to finish judging a case; the conversation, as often, involves the discomfiture of an anonymous grammarian on a grammatical point (13.25); or he strolls in the baths of Titus where one of the company, who must be a man of considerable years, recalls sitting at the feet of Valerius Probus, the outstanding grammarian of the Flavian age (3.1). Usually Favorinus likes to show up the professionals; but there is a strange reversal when they meet the grammarian Domitius 'the Madman' in the street. When asked about the meaning of a word, Domitius launches into a tirade on the futility of philosophers: if Favorinus really wants to know, he will send a book on the topic; but what a tragedy that philosophers interest themselves in footling lexicographical questions, when the grammarian is interested in Life and Manners (18.7). Domitius' rebukes were only partly unjust. Favorinus (like Fronto) was obsessed with words. At his dinner table there were regular readings of literary works. These included Gavius Bassus' *On the origin of verbs and substantives*, and Favorinus was alert enough to controvert false etymologies (3.19).

Throughout one receives the impression of a Roman intelligentsia fascinated by learned questions; by no means are their interests confined to the schoolroom and lecture hall. Not only philosophers, rhetoricians, poets and anonymous bystanders but the great men of the state breathed this air. Favorinus' friend the consul is not likely to have escaped the battle of wits and learning; the city prefect Erucius Clarus, nephew of Septicius Clarus, took an obscure point of priestly law to Apollinaris (7.6.12). But above all, we should consider those learned conversations in the ante-rooms of the palace: did they cease when the doors were opened and the learned admitted

to the imperial presence? We shall see later (ch.4) that they did not.
Here then is the society to which Suetonius belongs: one in which
a literary education has come to assume a cardinal role, and in
which many carried away from their schooldays a taste for the
professors' game. Well enough off, as an *eques Romanus*, to be able
to dispense with the unpredictable income of a professional, he
immersed himself in the techniques and writings of the learned.
Perhaps, like men whom Gellius knew, he had drawn inspiration
in the reign of Domitian from Valerius Probus, who as he relates
did not so much take pupils as regale a small circle of followers
from his deep store of learning.

Against this background, can we come to any closer understanding
of his scholarly output as a whole? We are hampered here by the
meagreness of the fragments of his *corpus* – it is always salutary to
remember how small a proportion of this the *Caesars* formed.
Tranquillus, as they call him, is much cited by later scholars: by
commentators on Virgil and Horace, compilers of word-lists, or
authors of monographs on similar topics like Roman games or the
calendar. But such fragments are no more than enticing glimpses:
they give no idea of a work as a whole, nor of the purpose and
drive behind it. Indeed, there is little agreement as to how much
'Tranquillus' survives. The two German collectors of his fragments,
Carl Roth and Augustus Reifferscheid, produced within two years
of each other in the mid nineteenth century collections of his
'Remains' of startlingly different proportions: Roth's filled forty-five
scant sides, Reifferscheid's three hundred and sixty. There had been
no new discoveries in the intervening years; that came a few years
later in the shape of a Byzantine epitome of the essays *On words of
insult* and *On Greek games*, written in Greek and easily the best
preserved of the non-biographical works.[19] The contrast lay in the
principles of fragment collecting. Roth austerely restricted himself
to the sentences where a view was explicitly attributed to the author.
Reifferscheid worked on the principle that such direct citations form
the tip of an iceberg where a later author dealing with the same
subject has based himself on one authority, but only names him for
disputed points; and thus he printed out in full works like Macrobius
On the Roman year. Reifferscheid has been justly criticised as

19. Discovered in a monastery on Mount Athos in *c*.1865 by Emmanuel
Miller and published in 1868, these Byzantine extracts have now been edited
by Jean Taillardat (1967) and the text conveniently amplified from later
derivative works, in particular the Homer Commentaries of Eustathius.

suffering from 'elephantiasis'. In particular there is little to be
said for his assumption that a hypothetical encyclopedic work of
Suetonius called *Pratum* or *Prata* lies beneath the *Etymologies* of
Isidore, bishop of Seville in the seventh century. A leading authority
on Isidore compares his work to a Romanesque church: there may
be fragments of classical columns embedded in the structure, but
the building as a whole belongs distinctively to the seventh century.[20]
Yet both collections have their uses: Roth's for showing at a glance
what is certainly Suetonian, Reifferscheid for gaining a more general
impression of what Latin grammarians were interested in and how
they handled their subjects. Scholarship is by nature tralaticious,
each writer taking over and passing on the accumulated learning of
the last, and Suetonius must be seen within the framework of a
tradition running over eight centuries from Aelius Stilo and Varro
to Isidore and beyond.

More damaging than the uncertainty about what is Suetonian is
the lack of an authoritative study of this Latin tradition of
scholarship. A study is needed not only collecting the facts of who
wrote what, but relating these scholars to the changing world in
which they wrote, from the disintegrating republic that made Varro
so anxious to recapture ancestral traditions, to the Christian and
increasingly barbarous world in which a Servius fought to preserve
the pagan literary heritage. For lack of such a work, no more than
a few hints can be offered here.[21]

First, a negative point. No edition or commentary on a text
features among Suetonius' writings. Edition and commentary were
the original form and backbone of Alexandrian scholarship; the
establishment and elucidation of the classics – Homer, comedy,
tragedy and lyric – were the first care of authors like Aristophanes,
Zenodotus and Aristarchus. Latin scholars followed suit, commenting on Ennius and the early dramatists at first, and on Virgil and

20. The most effective demolition of Reifferscheid's use of Isidore is that of
Wessner (1917). On Isidore, see Jacques Fontaine, *Isidore de Séville et la
culture classique dans l'Espagne wisigothique* (1959) 16 and 748f. The notion
of S's *Prata* as a great encyclopedia will hardly survive the sceptical survey of
G. Brugnoli (1968) 137ff., who sees in it a collection of miscellaneous essays,
possibly gathered after the author's death.
21. For the great Alexandrian tradition, R. Pfeiffer, *History of Classical
Scholarship from the beginnings* (1968) is invaluable. But for the Roman
tradition one must fall back on the bare sketch of J. Sandys, *History of Classical
Scholarship* 1 (1903). See also A. Gräfenhan, *Geschichte der klassischen
Philologie im Alterthum* 4 vols (1843-50). On early Latin scholarship, F. Leo,
Plautinische Forschungen[2] (1912) 23ff. still breathes life.

Horace from very shortly after their appearance. This activity is linked with the basic exercise of Greek and Roman education: the reading of the literary classics, and their elucidation through a word by word question and answer exchange between master and pupil. The scholar's commentary differs only in sophistication, not in method, from the schoolboy's. The problem (*zētēsis, quaestio*) is put, an answer (*lusis, solutio*) suggested, whether lexical, mythological, historical or whatever is appropriate. Suetonius, free from the practice of teaching, spared himself the grammarian's standard fare. Nor did he write on grammar in our sense, the *ars grammatica*, which, once systematised by Dionysius 'the Thracian' of Rhodes, maintained its tyranny over the schoolchild unchallenged until the present generation.

The next point is about his methodology. Though no commentator, Suetonius could not escape the scholarly methods that were the product of commentary. Because the problem-and-answer process centred on individual words (or names), the discussion of words is the central and obsessive topic of ancient scholarship. Almost all the works that now survive, when they are not commentaries ('scholia'), are lexica, either of words only, or like a Larousse including proper names (the *Suda* is one such). We may broadly divide Suetonius' works into three categories; lexicographical (on 'words for things'), antiquarian (essays on institutions), and biographical.[22] In all three

22. Macé (1900) 243 divides the works into four categories: 1. grammar and literary history; 2. archaeology and institutions; 3. historical biography; 4. natural history. 'Literary history' is a misleading description of the literary biographies; 'natural history' depends on dubious assumptions about the nature of the *Prata*. My own division is an approximate one designed to illustrate the author's methods. For convenience I list known titles.
(i) Lexicographical. *On names and types of clothes* (Roth 281); *On physical defects* (Roth 302); *On insults* (Roth 282); *On weather-signs, On names of seas and rivers, On names of winds* (all from the *Prata*, Roth 304f.). Against the authenticity of the *Differentiae Sermonum* (Roth 306ff.), see G. Brugnoli, *Studi sulle differentiae verborum* (1955).
(ii) Essays on institutions: *On Greek games* (Roth 275); *On Roman spectacles and games* (Roth 278); *On the Roman year* (Roth 281); *On Rome and its customs and manners* (Roth 282); *On the institution of offices* (Roth 302).
(iii) Biographical. *Illustrious men* (Roth 287); *On famous courtesans* (302); *On kings* (Roth 303).
Miscellanies, the *Prata* and *de Rebus Variis* (Roth 303), naturally elude my categorisation. (The two titles might, I suggest, refer to the same work; it may indeed have been no more than a collection of the above-named essays.) *On signs in books* (Roth 281) on critical signs and possibly shorthand is a variant on lexicography, following the usual listing process. One work falls into a class of its own, *On Cicero's Republic* (Roth 281); we only know that it was not a commentary, but polemical, a reply to Didymus Chalcenterus.

the method of commentary on a word is apparent. *On words of insult* is the best surviving example of the first: insulting names are assembled, divided into types (according to the sort of person being insulted: lecherous men, women, fools, old men, etc.); and for each word there is an entry, explaining its meaning and citing the passages of literature where it occurs. 'Kēlon. One inclined to sex. Metaphorically from a rutting donkey. So Archilochus, "I flowed over like the *kēlon* of the donkey of Priene".' (The entry is probably much abbreviated.) At the start of the essay is a short preface dealing with the history of the topic ('goes back to Homer . . .') and analysing the types of word-formation involved in coining an insult.

The method, to be expected in anything lexicographical, is also apparent in his other types of work. An essay on customs or institutions, as the surviving *On Greek games*, lends itself to subdivision and quotation of examples. There are board games, party games and children's games. 'Dicing: the oldest game, invented by Palamedes (see Sophocles' *Palamedes*) . . . A throw scoring one used to be called a "die": this explains the problematic line of Aristophanes, "Achilles threw two dice and a four" . . .' The same procedure could be applied to Roman customs, official posts and the like. No different is the biographical method. The *Grammarians and rhetors* are the only literary lives that survive as a group. Just as in the *Words of insult* we find an introduction (when grammar or rhetoric was introduced and how it progressed, what it consisted of) and then a series of entries; only here the words commented on are proper names. Ample quotations illustrate the facts of the lives. We may note too that 'illustrious people' are divided into categories (grammarians, rhetors, poets, historians . . .) like games or insults.

The *Caesars* is the same thing on a large scale. The introduction is lost. But we have a series of lives, all the available specimens (up to a point) of a particular phenomenon, 'Caesars'. Even within the lives the construction is often around rubrics, topic after topic, though since this is consecutive prose, the reader is normally spared the abruptness of a one word heading at the top of a paragraph. But always the old method shows through: Suetonius' thought runs not in consecutive narrative like a historian's, nor in developing argument like a philosopher's, but in word-heading and commentary with instances. The virtues possible within the limitations of this method are clarity of division, and learning and accuracy in commentary on the rubric. These are the author's distinctive virtues.

Thirdly, Suetonius is not isolated from his contemporaries,

especially in Greek scholarship. His essays on *Insults* and *Greek games* were written in Greek. He is evidently using the methods of contemporary Greek scholarship; and we may be confident that most of the learning derives from the Greek tradition. In the passage cited above on dicing he would have been able to refer to the commentary on Aristophanes' *Frogs* by Didymus Chalcenterus ('Brassguts'), the formidable polymath of the Augustan age. Perhaps, however, he already found the information processed in the lexicon of Pamphilus, another Alexandrian of slightly later date.[23] We possess no external evidence on the order of composition of his various works, but it might be a fair guess that he learnt his trade, so to speak, on Greek words, and gradually progressed to the accumulated learning evident in the *Caesars*.[24] To illustrate the fact that his choice of subjects is by no means peculiar, we may take as an example the writings of one Greek scholar. Telephus of Pergamum was a generation younger than Suetonius; having established a reputation, he was summoned to Rome by Antoninus Pius to be tutor to Verus. His writings include the lexicographical (*On names and types of clothes and other garments*, almost identical in title to Suetonius' *Names and types of clothes*); the antiquarian (*On Athenian courts, On Athenian ways and manners, On official posts*) and the biographical (*Lives of dramatists*, and *On the kings of Pergamum*). It is a pity that no fragments survive to allow closer examination of the parallel.[25]

Suetonius, then, was not a pure scholar, editing and commenting for school use, but he harnessed the methods of the grammarian to questions of contemporary interest. He has been dismissed in the

23. Taillardat in his introduction (22ff. and 36ff.) argues confidently for Pamphilus as the immediate source of S in both works, drawing ultimately on Didymus; any similarities between S and Pollux *Onomasticon* which groups words, in the fashion of Roget's Thesaurus, according to topic, are thus explained by derivation from a common source. To accept this with confidence one needs a demonstration that Pamphilus also grouped by topic; if that could be shown, it might help explain S's monographs on words for particular types of things. But in that case what was left for S to do?

24. No help on the question of relative chronology is offered by Pliny *Ep.* 5.10 urging S to publish his first work (in 105/6 according to Sherwin-White's book date). Macé (1900) 66, like several others, assumes that this was the *Illustrious men*, quite without warrant, and in my view without probability; see below, ch.3.

25. The list of Telephus' works comes from the *Suda*. For discussion, Wendel *RE* V A (1934) 369ff.

past as a collector of curiosities; and indeed his disparate list of titles gives the impression of an omnivorous and unselective pursuit of odd information.[26] Yet if there is a thread that holds his work together, it is surely an interest in what one might, with Domitius the Madman in Gellius' anecdote, call 'Life and Manners'. This is best apparent in his antiquarian works, those on games, Greek and Roman, or on Roman customs. But it is also discernible to a lesser extent in the lexicographical compilations. These are not pure linguistic studies, like Verrius Flaccus *On correct usage*, so much as monographs on various aspects of life seen through their vocabulary. Words for clothing will have involved discussion of archaic Roman customs – a fragment survives on priestly caps. Physical defects, apparently a medical subject, might have touched on the old Roman fascination for physical oddities reflected in their mercilessly frank *cognomina*. Investigation of words of insult meant ransacking sources like old comedy and invective, rich in details of ordinary life. These monographs are too poorly attested to allow certainty; but the interest in life is manifest in the biographical works. The lives of authors, as we shall see, are not so much about literature as about the public standing of the authors. The *Caesars* too are written by one with an eye to the daily life of emperors and their impact on the daily life of others. The viewpoint is distinctively that of the antiquarian, not the historian.[27]

But the clearest sign of the way that Suetonius' interests hang together is the enormous extent to which he draws on previous works in the *Caesars*. These were the culmination of former interests as well as a new departure. The *Illustrious men* prepared much of the ground for writing biographies of emperors; we will see that many of the interests of the biographer of literary personalities shine through in the *Caesars* (ch.3). Of his other scholarly works, none was so frequently cited or drawn on in antiquity as that *On games*.

---

26. The classic statement of the case that S was driven by idle *curiositas* is by Funaioli (1947). Steidle and his followers have combated this view with reference to the *Caesars*; it is a pity that nobody has tried to make sense of the scholarly works. The implied assumption that there is no more to scholarship than fact-collecting is an odd one.

27. It is not suggested that all S's monographs can be subsumed under the head of 'life and manners'. Fragments on names of winds and waters suggest an interest in natural history; this has been blown up out of proportion by seeing in the *Prata* an encyclopedia of natural history (above n.21). A solitary hint of pure grammatical interest is the fragment on prepositions from the *de Rebus Variis*: Roth 303, Reifferscheid fr.205.

This book, comprising one volume on the Greeks and two on the Romans, must count as a major achievement, and if we are to lay stakes on which publication Pliny was awaiting in AD 105, this should be a favourite. Correspondingly, discussion of games and shows bulks large in the *Caesars*: details of the performances put on by each emperor in their full variety, gladiatorial, equestrian, theatrical, athletic, the names of gladiators, tragedians and pantomimes all betray the scholar's expertise. One stray fragment offers an illustration. Commenting on the description of the 'Troy game' (*lusus Troiae*) in the *Aeneid*, Servius notes that 'the game commonly called pyrrhic is named Troia, and Suetonius Tranquillus explains its origin in the book on boys' games'. Servius has garbled his Suetonius here, as elsewhere; the Troy game was not called pyrrhic, and the two are distinct. But it is not unlikely that Suetonius sought the origin of the *lusus Troiae* in the pyrrhic. The Troy game was an exception in that it involved aristocratic young Romans performing on horseback in public; the pyrrhic was a type of dance popular in Asia Minor, but it too was performed by young men of high birth. Suetonius will have seized on the Asian link offered by the name of Troy. In the *Caesars* both performances of the Troy games (under six Caesars) and of pyrrhic dances are carefully noted, and the author shows himself interested in the issue of whether it is proper for young aristocrats to perform in public.[28]

In addition to public games there were private ones. Suetonius describes how Augustus relaxed by fishing, a popular imperial pursuit, or by playing knucklebones or 'nuts' with dwarf children (83). He has also much to say about the Greek game of dicing, traditionally regarded as depraved at Rome, but popular in this period. A precious series of quotations from Augustus' letters gives a vivid picture of the innocent amusement offered in the imperial household by the gaming table (71). Claudius shared this passion, had a special travelling board made for his carriage and wrote a book on the art of dicing (33.2). Perhaps Suetonius, who certainly

28. For the essays *On games*, see Reifferscheid frr.181-98. The more austere collection of Roth 275-80 shows at a glance how much more frequent citations of this work are than of other scholarly essays. The best notion of the scope of the *Roman games* is given by Tertullian's essay on the topic; for a judicious discussion of the extent of its debt to S, see the edition of E. Castorina (1961) 97-104. The links with the *Caesars* are described by Macé 317ff. On the Troy game, see Roth 278 = Reiff. fr.197; performances of the game in the *Caesars* at *Jul.* 39.2, *Aug.*43.2, *Tib.* 6.4, *Cal.* 18.3, *Cl.* 21.3, *Ner.* 7.1; the pyrrhic at *Jul.* 39.1 and *Ner.* 12.1-2. See further below, ch.6.

discussed dicing in detail in his own book on Greek games, had used Claudius' essay. But not all dicing was innocent: Caligula played for profit and cheated heavily (41.2), Nero played for extravagant stakes of 400,000 sesterces per point (30.3).

Because the evidence for the essays *On games* is relatively good, we can go quite far in establishing links with the *Caesars*. It is likely enough that if the other antiquarian works were better attested the same could be done for them. At least it is possible to demonstrate that the *Caesars* draws on the *Institution of offices* (ch.4) and on the *Roman year*, and it will be argued that much of the antiquarian interest of the *Caesars*, in military, religious and civil institutions, goes back to such essays as that *On Rome and its customs* (ch.6). The links are not limited to the biographical and antiquarian works; in fact there are hardly any attested Suetonian titles which do not suggest some connection with the *Caesars*. The *Physical defects* does much to explain the precise information on the physical ailments and debilities of each Caesar. Suetonius may also have drawn on it for the same purpose in his literary lives; at least he could describe how the orator Messala Corvinus died from an ulcer on his *spina sacra*, a technical term which, as Fronto (who suffered from a similar affliction) tells us, Suetonius himself coined. The interest in *Names for clothes* is apparent in the *Caesars*, whether in the description of Nero's adoption of the Greek lyre-player's uniform (51), or of Domitian's regalia at his new festival (4.4), or even in the observation that Augustus wore slightly raised heels (73). Its antiquarian dimension is reflected in the report of Augustus' indignant enforcement of the wearing of the toga by citizens; the toga was the traditional sign of the Romans, 'lords of the world and people of the toga' (40.5). Hadrian was to reinforce this enactment in the author's own day, according to his biographer (22.2). Another topic on which Suetonius wrote (where is unclear) was that of signs and ciphers. He duly reports on the ciphers of Julius and Augustus. Finally, even the *Lives of the courtesans* (a subject familiar also to a series of distinguished hellenistic scholars) may conceivably be detected behind the information that Caligula had a notorious *affaire* with a prostitute called Pyrallis (36.1) or behind the knowledge of Domitian's sexual diversions (22.).[29]

29. Many of these links are noticed by Macé: on dicing, 282-4; on offices, 300-2; on the calendar, 307-10; on physical defects, 331-5; on clothes, 306. Athenaeus 13.567a cites essays on Athenian prostitutes by Aristophanes of Byzantium, Apollodorus of Athens, Ammonius, Antiphanes and Gorgias.

Disparate and petty the subjects of Suetonius' researches may indeed appear. Yet even on the fragmentary evidence that survives, a degree of internal consistency emerges. There is a perceptible continuity of interest from the lexicographical and antiquarian works through the literary lives to the *Caesars*. If we would isolate a single unifying factor, it is an interest not in pure scholarship, linguistics, textual or literary criticism, but in life. What the epigrams of Martial, the letters of Pliny and the satires of Juvenal do in their various ways to illuminate the society and culture of the early empire, the scholarship of Suetonius likewise does. If the merit of the *Caesars* lies in the picture evoked of imperial society and culture, it was the author's scholarly curiosity that laid the foundations for his achievement.

Chapter Three

THE SCHOLARLY BIOGRAPHER

Suetonius came to the *Caesars* already an experienced biographer. The *Lives of illustrious men* was a classic in its own right; but it also in many respects laid the basis for the *Caesars*, determining the author's method and approach. It was, we may well feel, a strange background for a biographer of emperors. To Suetonius, as to his many Greek and Roman predecessors, 'the illustrious' meant primarily notable authors. He named the most important of his predecessors in his preface: Hermippus, who wrote 'lives of distinguished literary figures'; Antigonus, biographer of philosophers; Satyrus, part of whose life of Euripides has been discovered on papyrus; and Aristoxenus, an authority on music as well as a literary biographer. His Roman predecessors are named as Varro, Santra, Nepos and Hyginus. It is true that Nepos included generals in his series of famous men (it is primarily the section on Greek generals that happens to survive), and Hyginus at least wrote on Scipio Africanus. Still, on the whole it was authors of whom they wrote, and Varro restricted himself to poets.[1]

Literary lives

Many have regretted the loss of Suetonius' *Illustrious men*, and with good reason. Much scholarly energy has been expended on attempts to 'reconstruct' the lives, above all the lives of the poets. Some of the most important can be partly salvaged, for it is clear that some of the biographies of poets prefaced to the ancient

1. The names of S's predecessors are preserved in Jerome's preface to his own *de Viris Illustribus* = Reifferscheid fr.1. All are discussed by Leo (1901). The Greek tradition is discussed by Momigliano (1971) esp. 73ff. For Satyrus' *Life of Euripides*, see Italo Gallo, 'La vita di Euripide di Satiro e gli studi sulla biografia antica', *Parola del Passato* 113 (1967) 134ff. On the title of S's work, see Brugnoli (1968) 41ff., arguing that it may have been *Catalogus virorum illustrium*.

commentaries derive substantially from Suetonius' collection. This is certain for the life of Terence, beyond reasonable doubt for Horace, probable for Lucan, and highly likely for Virgil, though controversy still surrounds his various lives. All four make interesting reading, and they offer numerous points of contact with the *Caesars*. But in order to put the *Caesars* in their proper perspective, the study and 'reconstruction' of individual lives is not nearly so important as an attempt to grasp the scope of the series as a whole. This problem has suffered relative neglect. Yet enough can be said to cast light on the intellectual horizons of the author and explain some notable features of the *Caesars*.[2]

Two main sources combine to give us a fairly reliable idea of the scope of the *Illustrious men*. Of prime importance, of course, is the surviving section on grammarians and rhetors, though critics have scarcely been able to veil their disgust that it is the dull academics not the poets who have been preserved. The second source is the learned Church father Jerome. It was 'Tranquillus' on whom he modelled his own series of lives of Christian authors. More important, he turned to the *Illustrious men* in order to supplement Eusebius' chronological tables which sought to align the major historical and literary events of the Jewish and Greek peoples. Suetonius was Jerome's only source for Latin literary data, at least until Jerome could draw on his own knowledge for the figures of the fourth century. Jerome made heavy use of Suetonius: some ninety or so entries give data about seventy or more authors (doubt about marginal figures means that the numbers are only approximate). As a result, we have something like a content list of Suetonius' lives.

Unfortunately Jerome did his job in a hurry. Apart from committing chronological howlers, he missed out many of Suetonius' authors, and we may guess that the original total was well over a hundred. An idea of the extent of his omissions is given by the comparison of his data on grammarians and rhetors with the original. He mentions only five of the twenty grammarians, cutting out everyone before Verrius Flaccus; he does better by the rhetors,

---

2. Recent scholarship has focussed on the lives of the poets. Rostagni (1944) produced a new edition of these lives. Paratore (1946, revised 1950) is an extended criticism of Rostagni's edition. H. Naumann (1974 and 1979) has argued for the authenticity of the surviving lives of Terence, Horace, Virgil and Lucan. E. Fraenkel, *Horace* (1957) 1ff. is a valuable commentary on the Suetonian life.

naming ten, but dropping six. Perhaps his manuscript of the grammarians was mutilated; even so, it is obvious that he was selective. Scholars therefore have felt at liberty to assume that names missing from Jerome were included in Suetonius.[3]
Which then were the authors who featured? To judge from the labels Jerome attaches to names, they fell into several main categories: the poets in their many varieties, epic, lyric, tragic, satiric and so on; the orators, historians, philosophers; and of course the grammarians and rhetors. These in fact are the categories Juvenal enumerates in his satire on literary patronage (7). Patrons are so mean, he complains, that unless the emperor intervenes, literary men are reduced to poverty, whether poets, historians, orators, rhetors or grammarians (he omits philosophers). Juvenal may well have written the satire in the wake of the publication of the *Illustrious men*. At any rate, Suetonius evidently arranged his authors in their separate categories.[4]
The natural assumption is that within these categories Suetonius enumerated all the authors of consequence down to his own lifetime. It is agreed that there was a cut-off point. The dreadful muddle Jerome makes between the two Plinys, uncle and nephew, indicates clearly that there can have been no Suetonian life of the younger Pliny, his own patron. It has variously been supposed that this was because Pliny was still alive when the *Illustrious men* came out, or because Suetonius adopted the same terminus as in the *Caesars*, the death of Domitian. Yet a closer look at the names on Jerome's list shows that there is no reason to suppose that Suetonius' lives were

3. Attempts to reconstruct S from Jerome move from Mommsen's paper of 1850 'Ueber die Quellen der Chronik des Hieronymus', *Gesammelte Schriften* 7 (1909) 606ff. Roth 287-301 and Reifferscheid 3-144 with discussion at 363ff. offer alternative reconstructions based on Jerome. A thorough examination of Jerome's notices name by name was undertaken by R. Helm, *Hieronymus' Zusätze in Eusebius' Chronik* (*Philologus* Suppl. 21,2, 1929). Brugnoli (1968) 57-60 shows how little progress has been made since. For the circumstances and methods of Jerome's compilation, see J.N.D. Kelly, *Jerome, his life, writings and controversies* (1975) 72ff. That Jerome worked from a mutilated manuscript is argued by Brugnoli (1968) 131ff.
4. G.B. Townend in an unpublished paper, of which Townend (1972) is a brief report, makes the attractive suggestion that Juvenal's seventh satire draws on the *Illustrious men* in cataloguing ill-rewarded literary types, poets, historians, orators, rhetoricians and grammarians; cf. also *JRS* 63 (1973) 152. He goes on to suggest that S's order was the inverse of Juvenal's, and that it was because Jerome had before him a progressively more mutilated manuscript that his own list is so lacunose. I am grateful to Professor Townend for showing me the full text of his paper.

complete even as far as the death of Domitian. On the contrary, a marked pattern emerges, of concentration on the age of Cicero and Augustus, with waning interest in the Julio-Claudian period, and almost complete neglect of the Flavians. It is worth looking at the list in some detail, for there are many surprises. We must remember, of course, that Jerome offers only a selection; but if his selection is at all representative, there are some very odd points that demand explanation.[5]

Take the poets first. The list opens as it should with a galaxy of poets of the middle republic: the epic poets Ennius, Livius and Naevius, the comedians Plautus, Caecilius, Terence and Turpilius, the tragedians Pacuvius and Accius, and the satirist Lucilius. Here Suetonius could draw happily on the collections by Varro and Nepos. But once in the first century BC, the density of names increases greatly. Most of the big names are here: Lucretius, Catullus, Gallus, Horace, Virgil, Varus, Ovid. The obvious absentees are Propertius and Tibullus: Jerome must have nodded. But more impressive is the profusion of names of minor, some very minor, figures: Furius Bibaculus, Varro of Atax, Cornificius, Varius and Tucca (Virgil's executors), Aemilius Macer, all outshone by their more talented contemporaries; the mime writers Laberius, Publilius the Syrian and Philistio; the authors of local Italian-style drama, Quintius Atta and Pomponius of Bononia; and even those negligible brothers Bavius and Maevius, whose only claim to fame was that Virgil pilloried them in the *Eclogues*. Then, after the age of Augustus, the fall-off is startling: only Persius and Lucan, both of Nero's reign. There is total silence not only as to the lesser Julio-Claudian poets (Manilius, Phaedrus, Calpurnius for instance) but also about all the poets of the Flavian period, Statius, Silius Italicus, Valerius Flaccus and Martial, let alone those who do not survive but were well thought of by contemporaries, Serranus,

---

5. Roth lxxviii inferred that the *Illustrious men* must have appeared before Pliny's death, and is generally followed, e.g., Macé (1900) 69ff., Funaioli (1932) 598, Brugnoli (1968) 59. Rostagni (1944) xi is more cautious. But the worthlessness of this argument was seen already by Reifferscheid 422: one might as well suppose that the *Caesars* must have been written before the death of Nerva in 98. The only life likely to have transcended the limit of Domitian's death is that of the rhetor Julius Tiro. However, even this is to assume that he happens to be identical with the Julius Tiro whose disputed will came up before Trajan in AD 105, Plin. *Ep.* 6.31.7f., a possibility not even considered by Sherwin-White, *The Letters of Pliny* 394.

Saleius Bassus or Maternus. Is this Jerome's selection? If so, why exclude Martial and include Bavius?[6]

The list of orators is even more limited. It starts with Cicero and ends with the accuser Domitius Afer who died in AD 59. The cluster of names around the very late republic is striking: Calidius, taught by the same Greek rhetor, Apollodorus of Pergamum, as Augustus; the younger Curio; Atratinus, rival to Cicero's pupil Caelius (Jerome has missed the latter); the Furnii, father and son, who fought on opposite sides at Actium; Asinius Pollio, Munatius Plancus and Messala Corvinus, notable figures of the reign of Augustus; Q. Haterius, Asinius Gallus, Cassius Severus and Votienus Montanus who survived Augustus to meet their ends under Tiberius; then only Passienus Crispus, the stepfather of Nero who died under Caligula, before Afer. Suetonius only had to read Cicero's *Brutus* (which he certainly knew) to see that Cicero was the culmination of a long Roman tradition, and to find the names of dozens of orators before him. Nor did eloquence die with Afer, and Tacitus' *Dialogus* could have provided the names of many notable figures, including the sinister pair Vibius Crispus and Eprius Marcellus. Then there were famous orators in the reign of Domitian, of whom Pliny's letters supply details, like his own rival Aquilius Regulus, to say nothing of Tacitus and Pliny themselves.[7]

The orators, at least on Jerome's showing, were thus restricted to a brief period centring on the reign of Augustus. The other prose writers fall within the same general limits, but they are not even completely represented within their limits. The historians are a very odd selection. Sallust and Livy, the classics of the later republic and the Augustan age, are there, but apart from them are only four names: Nepos the biographer, Fenestella the Augustan antiquarian, Asconius Pedianus, the learned commentator on Cicero who died under Vespasian; and we may add from other sources the elder

---

6. The gaps in the list of poets are discussed by Rostagni (1944) xix-xxiv who concludes, in my view rightly, that S's coverage was very uneven. Quite different is the list of 'classics' given by Quintilian 10.1.85-100. That Jerome made some omissions is certain, and Rostagni 133ff. rightly attributes to S the manuscript life of Tibullus with its typically Suetonian quotation of Domitius Marsus.

7. Scholars are divided as to whether the orators before Cicero were included by S: thus Reifferscheid 406 supposes that they were not, but Funaioli (1932) 606f. challenges this. That S knew Cicero's *Brutus* emerges from *Jul.* 5.1 and 56.2. The question must remain open.

Pliny, historian, scientist and philologist. Here we miss not only the republican annalists who preceded Sallust, from Cato and Calpurnius Piso to Licinius Macer and Valerius Antias, but even the main historians of the early empire, Servilius Nonianus, Aufidius Bassus, Fabius Rusticus, Cluvius Rufus and others. The philosophers too make a queer bunch: Seneca is there, a famed orator as well as a philosopher. But instead of the philosophers whom Quintilian (10.1.123-5) thought worth mentioning, the Sextii and their pupil Cornelius Celsus, the Stoic Plautus and the Epicurean Catius, Jerome mentions only two names, and of men we would hardly associate with philosophy: the antiquarian Varro, and his learned contemporary, the savant and divine Nigidius Figulus.[8]

Nor is this all. The confusion over the historians and philosophers is added to by the presence of a medley of displaced persons who appear to fit into no category at all. Pylades the Augustan pantomime star can at least be accounted for: he will have been mentioned along with Roscius in the prefatory remarks on the Roman stage. But what of Tiro, Cicero's freedman, who invented the first Roman shorthand system, Artorius, the doctor of Augustus who died not long after Actium, Servius Sulpicius the jurist, or Servilius Isauricus who like Sulpicius was honoured with a public funeral, but is not credited with writing of any genre? It is surely too much to suppose on this slender basis that Suetonius also wrote a series of lives of doctors and jurists – where are the others? – and many scholars prefer to forget this embarrassing evidence.[9]

The lazy solution to all these difficulties is to play down the value of Jerome's evidence. Jerome was hasty, muddled and quirkish, but of course Suetonius was thorough and without prejudices, and we must imagine him wading efficiently through the main poets, orators, historians and philosophers down to Domitian's death. What gives the lie to this solution is the internal evidence within Suetonius. The

8. Macé 262f. simply assumes that the early imperial annalists must have been covered by S. Similarly Reifferscheid 407f. assumes the philosophers must have been there. In fact the majority of notices in Jerome are about expulsions of philosophers from Rome: this is a likely enough Suetonian theme, see below.
9. Reifferscheid 375 puts Pylades in the preface to the *Poets*, but is not followed by Rostagni 5ff. Mommsen 613 included Tiro in the life of his master Cicero; but this fails to accommodate the clearly Suetonian history of stenography which Reifferscheid frr.105-7 associates with Tiro. Following Mommsen 616f. all scholars reject the possibility of series of lives of jurists and doctors; Sulpicius and Artorius are variously disposed of, by subterfuge or neglect.

names in Jerome's list, for all the oddities of their distribution, do in fact correspond remarkably well with the kind of authors in whom Suetonius manifests interest elsewhere. The list constitutes precious evidence of the sorts of authors Suetonius did and did not read, was or was not interested in.

In the first place, the chronological distribution makes perfectly good sense. Jerome, who was trying to fill out his chronological list for the whole Roman period, had no interest in creating an artificial cluster of information round the lives of Cicero and Augustus. But for Suetonius, writing at the start of the second century AD, the closer he got to the present, the more things were a matter of common knowledge. Many of his contemporaries will have known Statius or Martial better than he. Their biographies required interviews with friends, not book-learning, and it was research in the libraries that was his forte. Nor was the middle republic such an attractive period for research. Varro and Nepos, probably also Santra and Hyginus, had gone over this ground very thoroughly. It was the age of Cicero and Augustus, when his four predecessors were themselves alive, that offered the best opportunities for breaking new ground.

This pattern is borne out by the surviving lives of grammarians. Suetonius believes that philological studies reached Rome in the mid second century; yet he deals with the earliest scholars very rapidly in the preface. Lampadio, Vargunteius, Aelius Stilo and others of the second century merit no full biographical notices (2.4-3.3). The list of famous professors starts with the first century; eleven belong to the lifetime of Cicero, who is frequently named or cited; six to that of Augustus; two to the Julio-Claudian period; and one to the Flavians. The early empire must certainly have produced more professors of distinction than are here named. The balance with rhetors is a little different: four are Ciceronian; five or six were active in Augustus' lifetime; four flourished under the Julio-Claudians, and three under the Flavians. Here at least the first century AD is better served, necessarily so since it was in this period that declamation was at the height of fashion. But at least we can see here that Jerome has no bias against the post-Augustan period: he has entries for three Julio-Claudian rhetors, and two Flavian ones.

So it looks as if the massive concentration of detail, much of it minute, on the Ciceronian and Augustan period does reflect Suetonius' area of expertise. Though he does not completely neglect the second century BC or the post-Augustan age, he does not show the same inclination to dig out recondite material. He simply was not so well read in these periods.

We can go further. The literary lives hang together as a group, and not only in the sense that they are conceived of as a coherent series rather than as a collection of individual lives (this is particularly clear with the grammarians). They are also a group in that the authors relate to each other and are used as sources for each other. Grammarians and rhetors, after all, were the teachers of poets and orators. Grammarians wrote commentaries on earlier poets, and could be used as sources for their lives; while poets who were pupils of grammarians provided information for their teachers' lives. Suetonius is generous in citing his authorities (it was part of scholarly style), and again and again the authorities he cites are themselves authors whose biographies he wrote.

The orators are a good example of this. At least half the orators who appear in Jerome's list are mentioned by name in the lives of the grammarians and rhetors. Cicero of course is both named and quoted frequently. Pollio is quoted as criticising Sallust for using Ateius Philologus to collect archaisms for him (10). A letter of Messala Corvinus is quoted speaking dismissively of Valerius Cato (4). Asinius Gallus wrote an epigram about Pomponius (22). Plancus took Albucius Silus under his wing (30.2). Famous trials are mentioned involving Curio (25.4), Atratinus (26) and Cassius Severus (22). The orators also appear in the *Caesars*. Messala was responsible for a complimentary decree in favour of Augustus which Suetonius quotes (58); Cassius Severus libelled the ancestor of Vitellius (2.1); Haterius had a sharp exchange in the senate with Tiberius (29); and Passienus Crispus left his money to his stepson Nero (6.3). Thus it is just the orators named by Jerome with whom Suetonius elsewhere displays acquaintance. Conversely he rarely shows acquaintance with the orators Jerome does not mention, Cicero's predecessors and Afer's successors. There are no citations from the elder Cato or the Gracchi.[10]

The same observation can be applied to Suetonius' 'historians'. Nepos, Fenestella and Asconius sound to us an odd group. Yet it was these learned antiquarians who were most useful to the author

10. Though S does not cite pre-Ciceronian orators, he does occasionally betray knowledge of their existence: Julius modelled his style on Strabo Caesar (55.2), Galba's ancestor Sulpicius was one of the leading speakers of his day (3.2). He also knew of Licinius Crassus (*Ner.* 2.2) and Hortensius (*Tib.* 47).

of the *Illustrious men*, and not the annalists who concentrated on military and political events. Nepos and Fenestella are cited in the life of Terence: Fenestella had shown that some of Nepos' assertions were chronologically impossible. Asconius is twice cited in the life of Virgil: he had written an essay against Virgil's critics. All three must have featured together in the life of Cicero. Gellius in the *Attic nights* (15.28) reports a dispute over the age of Cicero when he made his defence of Roscius. Nepos, though a personal friend of Cicero's, committed a howler, asserting that he defended Roscius at 23; Fenestella controverted Nepos, changing the age to 26; it took Asconius to hit on the correct age of 27. Jerome duly reports from Suetonius that Cicero defended Roscius at 27. Gellius, ever a magpie, must have lifted the controversy direct from the Suetonian life.

Suetonius' close familiarity with learned authors like these three, as well as Varro, the elder Pliny, Santra and Hyginus, manifests itself again and again. Why suppose that he wrote biographies of the annalists in whom he shows no interest and ignore the evidence of Jerome who confirms his inclination to the men of learning? While we can never be confident that an author not named by Jerome was therefore not the subject of a Suetonian biographical notice, we should be most wary of supposing that Suetonius dealt with any group not represented in Jerome. Another such group is that of the fashionable 'Stoic' biographers of the early empire, familiar from the letters of Pliny. Arulenus Rusticus had written a life of his master Thrasea Paetus, and Herennius Senecio of Helvidius Priscus; both biographers met their ends, allegedly in consequence, under Domitian. Pliny's friend Titinius Capito wrote on the deaths of some of Domitian's victims; while Fannius had completed three volumes on the fates of Nero's victims when he himself died in AD 105-6. But despite Pliny's effusive praise for these biographers, there is no sign that Suetonius interested himself in them. Indeed the one reference he makes to Rusticus reveals his ignorance: he attributes to him the life of Helvidius.[11]

It is best to avoid forming too fixed an idea of the layout of the *Illustrious men*. More important is to grasp its character, learned and idiosyncratic; not at all after the style of a modern handbook of literary history, dealing with everything that *ought* to be there, but following where the author's interests and reading led, and packed with recondite information. Perhaps we should envisage the collection growing by a process of crystallisation, and not in a straight

11. On these biographers, see above, ch.1, n.18. On Rusticus' biographies, Tacitus *Agricola* 2.1 is to be preferred to *Dom.* 10.3.

line. Bavius and Maevius, even Varius and Tucca, may owe their place (if indeed they enjoyed entries of their own) to an attempt to explain things about Virgil. Other misfits could owe their mention to similar reasons. Servilius Isauricus, listed by Jerome, is not otherwise known as an author. But he does, as it happens, feature in an anecdote in the life of the rhetor Epidius (28). Octavian and Antony were told by a political opponent that it was better to be a follower of Isauricus than of the slanderous Epidius, as they were.

If we seek to extend Jerome's list, we should think in the first place of authors Suetonius knew and used: Domitius Marsus the epigrammatist, who had things to say about Orbilius, Epirota, Bavius and Tibullus; Ticidas, a follower of Valerius Cato; Ateius Capito, the Augustan jurist, warm supporter of the family grammarian Philologus. Another candidate might be the grandfather of Galba, more famous for his studies than for political achievement, who wrote a history which Suetonius describes in terms so well applicable to his own work, *multiplex nec incuriosa*, 'manifold and not lacking in scholarship' (3.3). Above all we miss the name of Santra, antiquarian and biographer, who is to us no more than a name, but a name known from Suetonius.

Literary lives and Caesars' lives

It is worth lingering over the *Illustrious men* simply because it explains so much about the *Caesars*. It was a work of very considerable learning. Suetonius needed to be at home in at least part of the work of each author about whom he wrote. Of course, it was not all original research. Inevitably he owed much to a succession of predecessors, criticising each other in turn, as did Nepos, Fenestella and Asconius, and also to the commentaries of his master, the formidable Probus. Even so, the sheer range of the work meant that there could be no simple dependence on forerunners. It is most implausible that this should have been his first publication, which Pliny awaited so impatiently in AD 105. The book is the fruit of long years of scholarly study, and ought to follow the bulk of the less demanding philological and antiquarian essays. In its wake, Suetonius could approach the *Caesars* with a mind already stocked with information; and this is surely what he did, moving more or less directly from the lives of authors to Caesars.

The progression was a natural one in more than one sense. Nepos, and probably Hyginus, had included generals or politicians alongside literary figures in their biographies. Twelve Caesars formed a series in much the way that poets or grammarians did, only the scale was rather different. But there is another way in which the *Illustrious men* naturally drew the author on to the *Caesars*. One of the features of the literary lives one cannot miss is the acute awareness of the relations between the authors and the outside public world. This comes across markedly, as we have seen, in the *Grammarians and rhetors*. The essay is primarily about cultural history, not literary history. It is concerned with the absorption by the Romans of Greek education, and with the rising public esteem of the arts and their practitioners. The same is true of the *Poets*. The life of Terence revolves round the relations between the playwright and his aristocratic patrons. Scipio, Laelius and others – were they contemporaries of Terence? Is it true that his patrons wrote his comedies for him? There is no literary criticism here, no attempt to assess Terence's contribution to the Roman comic tradition. The lives of Virgil and Horace are equally obsessed with the patronage of Maecenas and Augustus, and perhaps the most valuable feature of either of them is the citation of letters from Augustus. The life of the orator Passienus Crispus describes the way he earned approval in succession from Tiberius and Caligula (when the latter asked whether he had committed incest with his sister, he tactfully answered 'Not yet'). This reads very much like the account of Vitellius' courtier father (2.4-3.1). The life of Lucan concerns his rise and fall in Nero's favour; at first rewarded with a quaestorship, he quarrelled when Nero walked out of a recitation, and signified his contempt for Nero's verse by citing it aptly in a public latrine; eventually, he turned conspirator.

Even in the fragments preserved by Jerome, one is aware of the presence of Augustus and his successors. The orator Atratinus committed suicide in the bath, and left Augustus his heir. Asinius Gallus was horribly punished by Tiberius. Quintilian was brought to Rome from Spain by Galba. The fragments referring to philosophers suggest that Suetonius was largely concerned with persecutions and expulsions of philosophers and astrologers. Nigidius died in exile. Anaxilaus, Pythagorean and magus, was expelled from Italy by Augustus. Seneca was exiled by Claudius and driven to death by Nero. Vespasian exiled all philosophers. Titus recalled them: Musonius Rufus returned from exile in AD 80. Domitian expelled philosophers yet again. We may recall the struggle rhetoric had for recognition at Rome in the face of censorial and consular edicts: for philosophy the struggle against public opinion went on much longer, and Suetonius surely was interested in tracing it.[12]

The author of literary lives was thus already familiar with the Caesars. One thing led to another. Writing the life of a poet like Furius Bibaculus led to the life of the grammarian Valerius Cato he said so much about (or perhaps the other way round). Writing of the Augustan poets or the early imperial orators and rhetors led to lives of the Caesars themselves. In fact 'Caesars' was an ingenious choice, given Suetonius' chronological predilections. It allowed him to handle the late republic as well as the early empire.

How did the scholar set about equipping himself for his new task? The writing of history is a time-consuming undertaking. Cassius Dio tells us that it took him ten years to do his reading before he put pen to paper. Cicero himself would have liked to have become Rome's first real historian, but he frankly admitted that history, unlike philosophy, could not be written as a hobby in odd moments. The younger Pliny too shied off the onerous task of collating variant versions. It is easy to imagine that Suetonius had a hard grind of historical research ahead of him before he could write his *Caesars*. Yet it may be quite wrong to suppose he ever undertook it.[13]

One feature of the *Caesars* is, to our sorrow, only too palpable. The quality falls off sharply as the work progresses. The *Julius* and *Augustus* are in a class apart for length, minuteness of focus, abundance of documentation and liberal citation of authorities. The Julio-Claudian lives are still substantial, but they lack the freshness and sharpness of the first two. The citation of original documents falls off, and is largely limited to the early parts of the *Caesars* which actually fell in Augustus' reign. Authorities are no longer named; the detail becomes cruder; and the regrettable habit of covering up for lack of information by generalising from single instances emerges. The next three, civil war, lives are sketchy indeed. There is interesting material on the background and early careers of Galba, Otho and Vitellius, but the handling of their reigns and

12. Macé 256ff. notes the frequency of allusions to Caesars in the *Illustrious men*. He also observes that S failed to make use of most of these items in the *Caesars*, surely because it was the authors, not the Caesars, on whom these anecdotes cast light. Macé's observation undermines the argument of Brugnoli (1968) 33f. that the *Grammarians and rhetors* must have been published later than the rest of the *Illustrious men* and later than the *Caesars* on the grounds that the *Caesars* ignores information contained in the *Grammarians*.

13. So Dio 72.23.5, Cicero *de Legibus* 1.8-9, Pliny *Ep.* 5.8.12.

even their private lives is cursory in the extreme, hardly amounting to a couple of paragraphs. Perhaps the brevity of their reigns may excuse this; but the sad decline continues with the Flavians where there is no such excuse. The *Vespasian* is an interesting and sympathetic life, but its detail is extraordinarily thin. The *Titus* is closer to romance or panegyric than biography. The *Domitian* is an improvement, and contains some precious details; but it must be a matter of lasting regret to the historian that the biographer who spent his early life in Domitian's Rome and who knew so many people, inside the palace and out, who could remember the same period, dealt with this life in the same number of chapters as the *Galba*.

The explanation for this decline may be sought partly in the author's disgrace. We know that at least the first instalment of the *Caesars* was dedicated to Septicius while still in office. He and the biographer were dismissed early in Hadrian's reign (as we have seen), and it is quite possible that the *Caesars* still awaited completion at the time of the dismissal. It is nice to think of a dispirited Suetonius, out of favour, mechanically completing his most ambitious undertaking without the old zest and energy. But even if this happens to be right, the dismissal was no more than a psychological excuse for neglecting what the author had little appetite for in the first place. The pattern of decline of interest corresponds so exactly with what we have observed in the *Illustrious men* that there can be no doubt that the same predispositions of the author lie behind both.[14]

This should provoke further reflections on the scholarly author's methods and sources. He did not transform himself from scholar to historian, but set about his new task in his old way. What did he read? Writing on authors, he read their works. He did the same for the Caesars. He may have made direct use of Julius' *Commentaries* for his analysis of his generalship. He read Augustus' private correspondence with great care. He also used his autobiography, and the letters of Antony to or against him. He read Tiberius' brief autobiography, and was shocked to discover him laying the death of Germanicus' children at Sejanus' door, despite the fact that one

14. The decline was observed by Macé 361ff. and attributed to S's decline in interest. Townend (1959) 286ff. further documented the extent of the decline and connected it with his dismissal from office; the idea is supported by Syme (1980) 116ff. But J.A. Crook (1969), in a review of della Corte advocated a return to Macé's explanation.

was executed after Sejanus' fall (61.1). Claudius also wrote eight volumes of memoirs that displayed his lack of tact (41.3); the biographer could quote his indignant complaint at the brutishness of his pedagogue (2.2). Nero was famous for his poetical aspirations: Suetonius used Nero's poems to condemn his charioteering from his own lips (24.2), and to identify a senator who claimed to have compromised the young Domitian (*Dom.* 1.1). Domitian wrote a light essay *On looking after hair*: the biographer cited it to illustrate the emperor's sensitivity about his own baldness (18.2). All these works were private, literary, products. It seems not to have crossed his mind to make an analysis of the public official documents of each emperor as a modern historian would. But then, maybe the secretary knew too much about the circumstances of composition of official documents to think that worthwhile.

Then there were contemporary documents. Julius' friend Oppius wrote a useful biography: the author recalled an incident on a journey when he had a sudden attack of fever and Julius gave up his own bed (72); or how Julius ate a dish dressed with bad-tasting oil rather than embarrass his host (53); and doubtless he provided many other details. Julius' other close friend, Cornelius Balbus, described the discovery of prophecies of doom immediately before his murder (81.2). Augustus' freedman Julius Marathus could similarly supply intimate details of his physique (79.2), and had wild messianic tales of a proposed slaughter of innocents at his birth (94.3). To balance these friendly accounts were contemporary invectives. Julius was plentifully slandered; for involvement with Catiline by his colleague Bibulus, the orator Curio, the historian Tanusius Geminus and by a certain Actorius Naso (9); and for sexual misconduct by (among others) the orators Dolabella, Curio father and son, and Cicero (49-52), by Bibulus, Memmius and Pompey, and by the poets Calvus (49.1), Catullus (73) and Pitholaus (75.5). Augustus was libelled in his youth by open 'letters' of Antony, Cassius of Parma and doubtless others including anonymous lampoons (2-4 and 68-70). Suetonius also produces lampoons against Tiberius (59), Nero (39.2), Otho (3.2) and Domitian (14) and records the appearance of a pamphlet under Claudius arguing that nobody ever pretended to be a fool, despite the emperor's public claims to have done so (38.3).

There is much more in this vein. The important point is that the vast majority of sources whom Suetonius names, or cites verbatim, which he does with considerable frequency in the first two *Caesars* and only exceptionally thereafter, are not the standard historical sources or indeed works in general circulation, but just the kind of sources he had drawn on in the *Illustrious men*, obscure, ephemeral or distinctly 'literary'.

This is not to say that he makes no use of historians. He quotes them when they provide first-hand evidence. Asinius Pollio could vouch for the words of Julius immediately before the battle of Pharsalus: 'They would have it so' (30.4). The disloyal Cremutius Cordus, whose works were banned by Tiberius (61.3) but taken off the black list by Caligula (16.1) described the tense atmosphere in the senate when Augustus conducted his purges (35.2). An anonymous consular historian, most likely Servilius Nonianus, witnessed the incident when Tiberius was prompted by a dwarf jester to hasten a condemnation (61.6). Finally he cites the elder Pliny once in order to refute him: Pliny reported seeing an inscription in Germany which proved Caligula was born there, quite wrongly (8).

Ancient historians were habitually shoddy, by our standards at least, about citing their authorities. Predecessors are rarely named except at points of disagreement or error. Silence is no argument for ignorance. Inevitably Suetonius must have based himself on standard historical accounts of the principate. The numerous correspondences of detail between him and Tacitus, Plutarch and Dio demonstrate that he drew on some of the same sources as they did. It is even possible on the basis of such comparison to come some way towards reconstructing which these sources were. But though this exercise is important for understanding the relationship between the Caesars and other surviving historical accounts, it should not be allowed to overshadow what is special and unusual about Suetonius.

Suetonius had to use historians; but there is little sign that they excited him. The proper procedure of the ancient historian was to read through his predecessors, comparing and judging their accounts, and to seek to produce a version that was more accurate and more elegant. Here lay the labour and the challenge. It was not a challenge Suetonius rose to. The fact that the sources he names and quotes are not historians, except when they happen to be conveying personal anecdotes, reflects his very unhistorical approach. The obscure, out-of-the-way, antiquarian details were the ones he was capable of contributing and enjoyed contributing. We should be very cautious of overestimating the amount of time and effort he put into reading and digesting the historians, though undoubtedly he did use them. It is relevant to recall which 'historians' appear on Jerome's list.

Sallust and Livy were the grammarian's favourites, and he may be expected to have known them well. The elder Pliny was a kindred spirit, and surely appealed to him. But, these apart, we cannot assume that he had any special familiarity with historians as opposed to antiquarians and writers of memoirs, nor that he undertook more than the inevitable minimum of investigation in this direction for the *Caesars*. At any rate, he covered his traces, and he cannot now be caught out.[15]

The investigation of oral sources was the second main element of the historian's craft. It may be imagined that the closer Suetonius came to his own times, the more he relied on non-written sources, and that this contributed to his failure to name authorities in the later lives. Again, the matter is very hard to control. The prevalence of what we regard as 'gossip' in some of the lives has led many to suppose that Suetonius made use of orally-circulated stories and rumours. Yet the labour involved in collecting oral accounts was considerable, even for those not so conscientious as Thucydides. The very lack of detail in the *Domitian* is a strong indication that Suetonius took little pains on this score. It is safest to imagine him continuing with his philological methods, which involved essential reliance on the library supplemented by the occasional personal anecdote. The grammarian Nisus, as Suetonius reports, used to say that he had heard from his elders that Varius in editing Virgil's epic changed the order of two books, and deleted four prefatory lines. Suetonius' own personal contributions are very much along these lines. He recalled at the end of the *Lucan* that the poet's works used to be lectured on at school. In the *Grammarians* he remembered how the one called Princeps used to declaim rhetorically and dispute grammatically on alternate days (4.9). In the *Caesars* he reminisces to similar effect. His grandfather used to report the inside palace story about Caligula's Baiae bridge – it was all to frustrate an astrologer's prediction (19.3). His father used to describe the final, glorious, moments of Otho which he witnessed (10.1). He himself remembered the appearance of a false Nero (57.2) and an anti-semitic trial under Domitian (12.2). Perhaps too it was he who had seen inscriptions celebrating Vespasian's father in Asia (1.2) and statues of Titus throughout Germany and Britain (4.1); or even

15. Macé's chapter on the sources of the *Caesars* (357ff.) is judiciously restrained. There can however be little doubt that S used Cluvius Rufus, as Townend has shown in a series of papers: Townend (1960), *Hermes* 89 (1961) 227, *ib.* 92 (1964) 467, *Am. Journ. Phil.* 85 (1964) 337.

the golden dice thrown by Tiberius in the fountain at Padua (14.3).[16]

The scholarly biographer had no need to transform himself into a historian in order to tackle his new subject. He could draw on his old expertise, especially his familiarity with writings of all sorts from the ages of Cicero and Augustus. He could use his old methods: little more than a reading of the standard period histories would be necessary to provide the essential historical backbone. He could also indulge old interests. Caesars were not totally different from orators. Julius had claims to a ranking as one of Rome's leading orators, as Cicero's testimony showed; a comparison of texts indicated that Strabo Caesar was his first model (55.2). Augustus had firm views on rhetorical style, pungently expressed, and had mocked Antony as falling between two rival schools (86). Tiberius was nothing if not a self-conscious speaker: his style was that of Messala Corvinus, but marred by excessive obscurity (70.1). Caligula too had a ready tongue, and criticised the style of the fashionable Seneca as sand without cement (53). Claudius spoke in public often enough, but his total lack of a sense of propriety undermined his efforts (39-40). Nero, still a student in age at his accession, declaimed in public to general approval (10.2). Suetonius had already observed in the *Grammarians and rhetors* what good this did to the profession (25.6). Galba at least came from a family of accomplished orators (3). Vespasian made up for a lack of educational polish by his lively sense of humour (22-3). Titus' early promise as an orator was considered remarkable (3). Domitian is criticised for his neglect of style; yet Suetonius had to admit that he could put things remarkably neatly. It was he who said it was the misfortune of a prince that nobody would believe a conspiracy had been discovered unless he was killed (20-1).

Biographical form

In the *Caesars* we see emperors not only as orators, but as historians, poets, grammarians, critics and essayists. The *Illustrious men* leaves its unmistakable stamp. But it should not be invoked to explain everything. In particular it is necessary to tread warily in the question of biographical form. The problem is how far the literary

16. Della Corte (1967) 143-52 stresses S's character as 'memorialista' with his love for the anecdotal. If the anecdotes and sayings in the later lives are of oral provenance, they are of a different type from the oral evidence historians collected. Syme (1981) 111f. conjectures that certain items are the fruit of the author's own travels.

lives provided a ready-made formula which could be applied without further ado to the *Caesars*. Fragmentary though the preservation of the poets' lives may be, enough survives to show that there were many striking formal similarities with the *Caesars*. Yet it is essential to bear in mind the question of scale. Even the shortest of the *Caesars* exceeded the longest of the *Poets* (undoubtedly Virgil) by an order of magnitude. The vast majority of the literary lives were no more than thumb-nail sketches. In one case the author was crippled by the paucity of his information, and needed to deploy all his learning in order to say anything: in the other there was an *embarras de richesse*. It would be a remarkable formula indeed which could cater for both.

What, first, is 'biographical form' and what is special about that met in Suetonius?[17] There is, as we have seen, an otiose sense in which any biography has a form which makes it instantly recognisable as such. Certain features are common to numerous types of biographical record. Parentage, date of birth, details of education, nature of main achievements, date and circumstances of death, names of spouses and offspring, value of estate and other details of this order can naturally be found in any Suetonian life, as in any other ancient life, or any modern one. The presence of this basic framework, though it instantly alerts the reader to the fact this is biography, can indicate little more. But when it comes to describing character and personality there is much wider scope for variation, and it is here that Suetonius may be felt to impose his sign manual.[18]

His characterisation of Claudius may serve as a specimen (30-42). Once the analysis of Claudius' rule has reached its climax in the description of the way his wives and freedmen dominated him, the biographer turns to the personal details. First his appearance, the impression of dignity conveyed by his build and grey head, counteracted by the absurdity of his body and features when in movement, his spluttering laugh, running nose and stuttering tongue (30). This is followed by a comment on his state of health, which with the exception of a bad attack of the gripes was good (31). Next we are given an account of his way of life. His style of entertainment

17. Ancient biographical form has been much discussed since Leo (1901). The most substantial contributions have been Stuart (1928), Steidle (1951), A. Dihle, *Studien zur griechischen Biographie* (1956), Momigliano (1971).

18. The occurrence of these topics on the ancient gravestone is nicely illustrated by R. Lattimore, *Themes in Greek and Roman Epitaphs*[2] (1962) 266ff.

is described as lavish, though it is observed that he had quaint theories about flatulence (32). Then some details of his routine: he had a marked appetite for food and wine (he once left his seat of judgment tempted by the smells of a nearby sacerdotal dinner), slept very little, but tended to nap while at work; had a strong, but strictly heterosexual libido; and amused himself by dicing, for which he had a passion (33). We now move to an account of his salient traits of character: he had a marked sadistic streak, evinced in his fondness for death-sentences and for gladiatorial duels (34); he was exceptionally timid and gullible, which led to his manipulation by palace staff (35-7); he was given to outbursts of wrath, which he admitted openly, and he failed to convince the public that his folly was put on (38); and he was exceptionally absentminded (39). Finally the biographer turns to his intellectual side: his conversational style (40), his activities as an author (41) and his accomplishments in Greek (42).

No two of the *Caesars* are exactly the same, but a corresponding group of personal details is found in almost every one, composed of the same basic items (appearance, style of living, characteristics, intellectual pursuits) or a selection of them, in this order or in a variation on it. The same formula shines through in the more substantial literary lives. Horace was short and fat, and Augustus wrote teasingly to him to say that so voluminous a man should write more voluminous poems. His sexual appetite was intemperate: his bedroom was lined with mirrors. He lived mostly in his country hideout which was still pointed out near a grove at Tibur. (This last is a most Suetonian aside: the house where Augustus was nursed was also 'still pointed out' – 6.) The biography then went on to discuss Horace's poetry. Virgil was tall and dark, but suffered from bad health, stomach pains, headaches and blood-spitting; he had little appetite for food and wine, was mildly homosexual, but in general was wholly proper in behaviour, and painfully shy. After some notes on his properties and family, the *Life* goes on to examine his studies, not proceeding to his poetry before observing his interest in medicine and mathematics, and his lack of gift for oratory.

Among the *Illustrious men*, Horace and Virgil were evidently treated at exceptional length. The majority of the sketches will have included at most one or two details of this sort. Terence was of medium height, slender and dark. That is all in a relatively full life. Nothing is said of the physique of any of the surviving grammarians and rhetors, except that Sextus Clodius had bad eyesight (29).

Remmius Palaemon is the only one of that series about whose personal life much could be said: he was very arrogant, called Varro 'the pig', was so luxurious in his life-style that he bathed several times a day and outspent a considerable professional income, while his perverse sexual tastes gave him a bad name (23).

On this basis, can we say that Suetonius used the same biographical formula for the Caesars as for authors? It is helpful to consider how Plutarch approached the same problem, for comparison throws up both similarities and contrasts. Plutarch's formula for personal details is very similar in that he gives exactly the same sort of details. He describes Sulla's appearance, his complexion blotched like a mulberry, and his style of life, his fondness for entertainers and actors, his behaviour at dinners, and his proneness to sexual indulgence (*Sulla* 2). We hear about Pompey's character, his charm and tact, his majestic appearance, enhanced by the swept-back hairstyle modelled on Alexander's, his relationships with mistresses, and his simple tastes in food (*Pompey* 1.3-2). Again, Crassus' way of life was very moderate and restrained, and accusations of adultery were untrue; but this millionaire was certainly avaricious when it came to money; his hospitality was generous and he was a man of high culture, a very able orator, well read in history, and a dabbler in philosophy (*Crassus* 1-3).

These examples are enough to show that Plutarch drew on the same group of topics as Suetonius: appearance, character, way of life, physical appetites and cultural interests. But there are also considerable contrasts. The style has a completely different feel. Suetonius is factual and compact, as if he were rattling off a list of prescribed items. Plutarch is much more relaxed and flowing, and the reader is led along from one point to another without noticing the transitions. The information emerges so naturally from the course of the discussion, and the illustrative anecdotes are told with such charm, that it is not easy to recognise the presence of a schema. Plutarch's treatment of this aspect of a biography is in line with his approach as a whole. He writes as an essayist, treating a man's life as a story worth telling for the interest of the tale, and worth discussing for the improvement to be derived from its morals. He narrates and ruminates where Suetonius lists, analyses, informs.[19]

The value of the contrast is to show what extraordinarily different

19. For a comparison between Plutarch and S, see A. Wardman, *Plutarch's Lives* (1974) 144ff.

use could be made by contemporary authors of the same biographical framework. Yet Friedrich Leo, in a study of the ancient biographical tradition of fundamental importance, drew wider conclusions from the contrast. He wrote at a period, at the turn of the century, when classical philology was much affected by Mendelian biology. It seemed that literature could be scientifically categorised in the same way as plants, divided into genus (genre) and species, each variant being traced back to its original descent. Leo saw in Suetonius and Plutarch two branches of the same family, biography; one branch scholarly and informative, the other philosophical and reflective. He argued that the two species had already split off from each other in the third century BC. Suetonius was the descendant of a long line of scholarly biographers writing lives of literary men, Plutarch of philosophical ('peripatetic') ones writing about men of action.

Leo's genetic classification never fitted the surviving specimens. Nepos' *Lives* and Tacitus' *Agricola*, the main Latin biographies apart from Suetonius, cannot be usefully interpreted in these terms: the *Agricola* is neither philosophical nor scholarly, but historical, being in its core section concerned with the conquest and government of Britain. Worse, when a papyrus fragment of the *Life of Euripides* by the peripatetic Satyrus was discovered, it proved a complete surprise: it is in dialogue form. But then, a work of literature is not a plant. The form of a plant is determined by its genetic make-up: it cannot choose. But an author can make what he will of a work of literature, and though ancient authors liked to place their works in a recognisable tradition, they did so as a conscious act of will, and made their own decisions about where to follow tradition and where to part from it. The great value of Leo's book was to show that Suetonius' biographies do indeed belong to a long scholarly tradition. The discovery of an Alexandrian collection of *Bioi Endoxōn Andrōn* ('Lives of Illustrious Men') would cast invaluable light on the *Illustrious men*. But the fallacy is to suppose that because the *Caesars* was written by one deeply versed in this tradition, its fundamental features were predetermined: the plant had its genetic make-up, and, once Roman emperors had been crossfertilised with literary biography, they would automatically grow up in a certain form.

In fact there are vast areas of the *Caesars* for which the *Illustrious men* can offer no precedent. They could offer, for example, no possible framework for handling the public administrative life of an emperor. Suetonius set about this in what was certainly a scholarly way, and I shall suggest that he was here much influenced by the Roman antiquarian tradition (chapter 6); but this had nothing to do with literary biography. It is also important to realise how little the literary lives explain about an area where they might have provided a model, that is the description of character.

The biographical schema common to Suetonius and Plutarch offered an opportunity for describing character. Traits of personality, whether the avarice of Crassus or the idiosyncrasies of Claudius, could be enumerated along with other personal features, most naturally directly after a description of physical appearance. But though both authors make occasional use of this method, it is exceptional. It is only really suitable for a short biographical sketch. In a full length portrait, character is much too important for such perfunctory treatment. The two biographers go different ways. For Plutarch the interpretation of *ēthos* is so central that he prefers to let it emerge from the whole narrative of a man's life: his actions over a long period of time gradually reveal his true character. In the *Caesars* character is also of great importance, but in a different way. Virtues and vices form a large part of what makes an emperor good or bad, and Suetonius sets about documenting them in a scholarly way. Each vice or virtue is taken separately, and exemplified by a list of actions and anecdotes (below, chapter 7).

Suetonius' method here has no more to do with literary biography than does Plutarch's. The approach he has adopted is that of encomium, in which it was strongly recommended that actions should not be narrated chronologically, but distributed under virtues. Xenophon's encomium of the Spartan king Agesilaus set the model. After a brief chronological survey of Agesilaus' career and campaigns, Xenophon offers a series of chapters that document his virtues: piety, justice, temperance, courage and wisdom, and then some less definable qualities. This is a method designed for handling men of action, particularly kings. It is merely perverse to suggest that when Suetonius employed the same scheme on emperors, because it was a non-narrative method it must have been the product of the scholarly biographical tradition.[20]

Imperial biography was a much more demanding project than anything Suetonius had yet undertaken. He needed to draw on all

20. S's debt to encomium was seen by Steidle (1951) 129ff., accepted by Momigliano (1971) 87. For an introduction to the ancient encomiastic tradition, see D.A. Russell and N.G. Wilson, *Menander Rhetor* (1981) xiff. The practice of panegyric under the empire and its influence on S is discussed below, ch.7.

his resources of learning and experience in order to rise to the challenge. The lives of literary figures offer an essential clue as to how he contrived to write biographies that were more than potted history. They explain much about his intellectual horizons, his methods and his interests. They should not be asked to explain everything. He drew extensively on all his previous scholarly work, on Games, the Calendar and other antiquarian subjects. He enriched the scholarly biographical schema from other sources, encomium and native Roman tradition. In consequence, the *Caesars* is very much *sui generis*.

Chapter Four

THE SCHOLAR AT COURT

The *Caesars* was dedicated by Hadrian's secretary *ab epistulis* to his praetorian prefect. Between them, the two men held two of the most important posts in the emperor's service. It is fair to speculate that it was through holding this post that Suetonius was emboldened to turn his pen to the Caesars. Certainly these biographies are not simply the product of armchair scholarship out of touch with the realities of public life. On the contrary they are written by one with experience of emperors and their business, and for readers no less experienced. But where does this show?

Suetonius the official is not so readily pinned down as Tranquillus the scholar. It is not easy to establish what views and mentality characterise the imperial official. We are beguiled into supposing that we understand the imperial service by the innumerable career inscriptions that survive like the Hippo inscription on Suetonius himself. The limitations of this sort of evidence are formidable: inscriptions tell us what posts people held, not why they were given them, what they had to do, how the system worked or how those within the system viewed life. It is all too tempting to operate by analogy from other bureaucratic systems. Too often the assumptions derived from analogy prove deceptive.[1]

Two alternative approaches to the question may be conceived. The first, adumbrated in the imaginative book of della Corte, is to work from a preconceived notion of what the views of an official ought to have been, and look for traces of them in his work. It is a

1. The most comprehensive survey of the imperial administration remains O. Hirschfeld, *Die Kaiserlichen Verwaltungsbeamten*[2] (1905). The epigraphic evidence for officials is collected in the massive studies of H.G. Pflaum, *Les Carrières procuratoriennes équestres* (1960-1) for equestrians, and G. Boulvert, *Esclaves et Affranchis Impériaux* (1970) for freedmen. Strong pleas have been made by a series of scholars against inferring a systematic and bureaucratic nature for the imperial service. See particularly Millar, *Emperor* 59ff., and R.P. Saller, *Personal Patronage under the Early Empire* (1982) esp. 79ff.

method fraught with dangers, the more so if the preconceptions are themselves erroneous. It is safer to start from what we know about Suetonius the scholar, and ask what place the scholar had at court, what was the nature of the offices he held, and how it is reflected in his work. But let us start by testing the first approach.

Offices in the Caesars

At first sight there is something in Suetonius' attitude that suggests the ideal modern bureaucrat: self-effacing, matter-of-fact, dry, precise, unambiguous. One senses a contrast of personality with Tacitus not unconnected with their different public roles. The ex-consul, independent, proud, acerbic, does not hesitate to deliver his *sententia*, in praise or condemnation; the civil servant hides behind an official *persona*, offering up a barrage of information without explicit comment, but with strong implicit presuppositions.[2]

There may well be something in this impression; though we should remember that Suetonius may not have spent even a decade in office, and that what is distinctive in his style is at least as likely to derive from his scholarly background. But the real danger comes when we attempt to isolate a political viewpoint that distinguishes the official. A seductive case can be made. Hadrian has acquired a reputation as something of a bureaucratic reformer. He was certainly not the first emperor to use equestrians rather than freedmen in his secretariat, as his biographer alleges: that custom, as will be seen below, goes back to earlier emperors. But he does seem to be the first who made consistent use of equestrians in all the top posts. The temptation therefore is to imagine an equestrian bureaucracy, confident in its new-found influence, and contemptuous of the senate which only in name administered the state.[3]

---

2. The classic modern analysis of the bureaucratic type is by Max Weber, *Economy and Society*, ed. G. Roth and C. Wittich (1968), 3,956ff. The contrast between S the bureaucrat and Tacitus the senator is built up by della Corte (1967) 196ff., a stimulating discussion, even if overstated. Cizek (1977) 156ff. lays stress on S's use of apparent objectivity, but the methods he uses to extrapolate S's real opinions are too crude.

3. For the view of Hadrian as a reformer, B. d'Orgeval, *L'Empereur Hadrian. Oeuvre législative et administrative* (1950) 205ff. The exaggerated claims of the *Epitome de Caesaribus* 14.11 are dealt with by J.A. Crook, *Consilium Principis* (1955) 56ff. and 135ff. The claim of *SHA Hadr.* 22.8 that he was the first to appoint *equites* as secretaries is manifestly wrong.

Moreover Suetonius himself, so the case runs, was one of the first new-style equestrian secretaries. It happens to be known that he wrote an essay entitled *de Institutione Officiorum* ('On the institution of offices'). Just as the equestrian officer Pliny wrote a work on javelin-throwing, and the curator of aqueducts Frontinus a manual on aqueducts, it is nice to think of the secretary Suetonius writing an official history of the imperial bureaucracy.[4]

Sadly this work *On offices* does not survive: it is only mentioned once casually by a grammarian, and then only for an etymological point. But Suetonius has a habit of drawing on his scholarly works in the *Caesars*, and in fact the etymological point which Priscian cites occurs also, in abbreviated form, in the discussion of Caligula's birthplace (8.3), suggesting strongly that *On offices* did precede the *Caesars*. Enough traces survive, and enough observations about offices are made in the *Caesars*, to demolish the picture of the self-important equestrian bureaucrat.

In the first place, we must abandon the misconception of institutional rivalry between bureaucracy and senate. Senators as well as equestrians served emperors, in more prestigious if less intimate positions than the secretariat. Suetonius, quite properly, applies the word *officia* indiscriminately to senatorial, equestrian and freedman positions. There is no sense that senatorial offices are a class apart. Suetonius does draw a distinction between offices and republican magistracies: the latter he terms *honores*, never *officia*. In practice, the emperor, at least by Suetonius' day, might be no less responsible for appointments to magistracies than to offices. Both types of appointment could be made on the system of patronage illustrated in Pliny's letters. But magistracies were based on the statute book, strictly limited in tenure; offices were additional duties created by the emperor to which he appointed directly and in which service lasted until the appointment of a successor.[5]

4. The fragments of the *de Institutione Officiorum* are gathered by Reifferscheid frr.199-201. Macé (1900) 300ff. stressed the links with the *Caesars*. Della Corte (1967) 18 saw in it a preparatory study to ·Hadrian's reforms of the service.

5. S speaks of both senatorial and equestrian *officia* at *Galb.* 15.1, of both equestrian and freedman *officia* at *Oth.* 7.1 and *Dom.* 7.2. For senatorial *officia*, cf. also *Tib.* 63.2, *Vit.* 5 and presumably *Dom.* 1.3 where Domitian makes twenty appointments in a single day. For the distinction between magistracies and offices, cf. Pliny, *Ep.* 3.1.12, *obiit officia, gessit magistratus*. The same distinction is maintained on legal grounds in Pomponius' *Enchiridion* in *Digest* 1.2.2.33: magistracies are *legitimi*, offices extraordinary.

Next, there is an astonishing observation to be made about reports of the institution of offices in the *Caesars*. There is only one extended passage reporting the creation of new offices by any of the Caesars, and that is of Augustus' creation of new jobs for senators. 'To give more senators a share in the administration, he designed new offices, curatorships of public buildings, roads, aqueducts, the riverbank and corn-distribution; the city praefecture; and occasional boards to review membership of the senate and equestrian panels' (37). There is no suggestion of a gulf between these new offices and republican magistracies. Suetonius goes on to describe other new ways in which senators were given jobs: the censorship was revived, the praetorships were increased in number, and Augustus even had a plan for a supernumerary consulship for himself to avoid blocking the way for others.

On the other hand, there is only one equestrian office he describes being instituted, and he does so to cast an ugly light on an emperor's debauchery. Tiberius instituted the post *a voluptatibus praepositus*, a sort of Mastership of the Revels, which he gave to the *eques* Caesonius Priscus (42.2). It is hardly a glorious moment in the history of the equestrian bureaucracy. By an extraordinary coincidence, the only epigraphically attested equestrian holder of this post served Hadrian. Whether Suetonius was pulling Hadrian's leg, or whether a perverse sense of humour led the emperor to revive the post after reading the *Tiberius*, or whether this is simply coincidence, we cannot say. But it is clear that Suetonius had no intention of using the *Caesars* to emphasise the importance of the equestrian offices.[6]

He certainly had ample opportunity. There is a section on Augustus' relations with the equestrian order immediately after the one on the senatorial order in which the new offices are mentioned: but no hint of offices for equestrians is to be found (38.3-40.1). He reports that Egypt was reduced to a province, but omits to mention that it was put under an equestrian prefect (18.2). He describes the creation of the fire-guard, *vigiles*, but makes no mention of the new

6. The (probably) Hadrianic *a voluptatibus* was Ofellius Maior Macedo: Pflaum, *Carrières*, no.112. There is, however, plenty of other evidence for freedmen in this office, cf. Hirschfeld, *Verwaltungsbeamten* 295, n.3. It is amusing to note that the astrologer Firmicius Maternus suggested that those born under the sign of the planet Venus might become *praepositi voluptatum* (*Math.* 3.6.3). Nero's use of the senator Petronius as his *elegantiae arbiter* (Tac. *Ann.* 16.18) is of course another, and less 'official', matter.

praefectus vigilum (30.1). He lists various measures to remedy a crisis in the corn-supply, but omits the *praefectus annonae* (42.3). He knows about the adaptation of the praetorian guard as a police-force but is silent about that most powerful of equestrian posts, the one held by the dedicatee of the *Caesars*, the praetorian prefecture (49.1).

It is another work that gives a glimpse of his views on the institution of his own secretaryship, *ab epistulis*. The life of Horace quotes a letter of Augustus to Maecenas in which the emperor tries in vain to persuade the poet to come and join him to help with his correspondence. There is no doubt that Suetonius saw this as an attempt to institute an office: he describes the offer as of the *officium epistolarum*. He also reveals ample knowledge of Augustus' first officials *a bibliothecis* (see further below): it is too easily forgotten in discussions of the 'bureaucracy' that a librarian too was an official drawing a salary, and that already Augustus had appointed an equestrian, Pompeius Macer, to the post. Suetonius could doubtless also have said something about Augustus' treasury secretaries *a rationibus*, who will have been responsible for the balance-sheet, *rationarium*, which he mentions (28.1).[7]

We may speculate in vain about the reasons for the absence of this material from the *Caesars*. Perhaps, for once, he felt he had written enough on the topic already. Perhaps he thought it did not matter. Perhaps he thought it mattered too much. But what must be abundantly clear is that he did not use imperial biography as an opportunity to underline the historical importance of the equestrian service. And if we may guess at the contents of the essay *de Institutione Officiorum*, it is unlikely that he had such a purpose there either. Its appearance might well give the reader of Pflaum's massive volumes on equestrian procurators a shock. One thing we can be sure of is its antiquarian character. The author found space for a list of archaic quotations that demonstrated that *puerperium* could refer to the birth of a girl (to which office can this have possibly been relevant?). He probably made much of librarians, and of a false start in the poet Horace. Even the title *de Institutione*

---

7. The *officium epistolarum* offered to Horace is supposed by some to be a purely private post, distinct from the 'official' post (E. Fraenkel, *Horace* (1957) 17); a view challenged by Millar, *Emperor* 85. Further evidence that S knew about the *a rationibus* comes from *Aug.* 101.4: Augustus left behind at his death a statement of the finances of the empire, together with the names of the freedmen and slaves who could provide an account (*ratio*).

spells out the interests of the antiquarian, as in the essay *On games* where he detailed 'which festivals were instituted in what order to which gods by whom'.[8]

Scholarship at court

The alternative approach holds out more promise, and this is to inquire into the role of the scholar at court. The position of the scholar in educated society was examined in an earlier chapter (2). Aulus Gellius implies that the discussions of grammatical questions among the intelligentsia went on inside as well as outside the palace. There is abundant evidence elsewhere that the court was not cut off from the intellectual currents of its day.

The emperor Trajan was a tough soldier not otherwise known for his learning. Yet his panegyrist Pliny insists on the cultivated atmosphere of his court. 'How princely is the moulding you give to the upbringing and morals of the young. How you honour the teachers of rhetoric and distinguish the doctors of learning. *Studia* have recovered their breath and blood under you, and returned to their homeland ... Is there anyone who professes humane learning who does not reckon among your prime merits the ease of access you allow?' (47.1-3). The dinner-table reveals what sort of man the emperor is. No gambling, no extravagance, no gross gourmandising, no obscene jokes in ill-taste. In their place are found kindly invitations, educated wit and respect for learning (*liberales ioci et studiorum honor*: 49.8).[9]

The picture Pliny paints is a general one, and is hard to substantiate. But the description undoubtedly fits the court of Trajan's dilettante successor, Hadrian. The sources leave no doubt about his obsession with intellectuals, and his mercurial relations with them. According to his life, behind which the pen of the biographer Marius Maximus may be suspected, he surrounded himself with 'philosophers, grammarians, rhetors, musicians, geometricians and astrologers'. The list is only partial. He appears in the physiognomical analyses of his friend Polemon of Laodicea, who saw a sign of

---

8. See below, ch.6, for indications that the creation of equestrian posts was deliberately suppressed; also there n.30 for S's antiquarian interest in institution.

9. Despite Pliny's praise, there is little sign that Trajan had literary attainments beyond the minimum requisite of his class: H. Bardon, *Les Empereurs et les lettres latines* (1940) 341ff.

excellence in his flashing grey eyes. He exchanged playful doggerel with the poet Florus. He provoked the architect Apollodorus by his experiments with domes, and tried to prove his independence in designing a temple for the forum. He claimed competence in sculpture and painting, and indeed all other arts. When he claimed so much, no wonder he proved himself a grammarian too. One anecdote has Favorinus arguing with him about the usage of a word (as usual), and caving in on the grounds that none could challenge the learning of the master of thirty legions. Suetonius tells a rather different tale of how Tiberius was flatly told by the grammarian Pomponius (an ex-pugilist) that his authority over citizenship did not apply to language (*Gramm.* 22).[10]

Hadrian actually published on questions of *grammaticē*, in two books of *Sermones*. Later grammarians quote them to describe two incidents in which he fences with Terentius Scaurus, described by Gellius as the noblest grammarian of the reign, and father of the Scaurinus who was tutor to the emperor Verus. In one Hadrian rebuts Scaurus' opinion on the scansion of a word by writing for a second opinion to a rival authority. In the other he overthrows the opinion of Scaurus that a word is not good Latin usage by citing a letter of Augustus in which it is discussed (of this, more later).[11]

The scholarly atmosphere of Hadrian's court may have been taken to extremes. But Pliny's praise of Trajan confirms that encouragement of culture and education was expected of the court. The same expectation is seen later in the second century in Lucian's satirical sketch of an illiterate book-collector who hopes by his ostentatious book-buying to come to the notice of the emperor, being a 'friend of studies'.[12] Against this background, men of learning had an obvious place at court. Suetonius was not alone as a scholar official. In fact he is only one, if the most distinguished, of a group

10. The intellectual interests of Hadrian are described at *SHA Hadr.* 14.8-16 and Dio 69.3-4. For his astrological interests and his friendship with Polemon, see below, ch.8, n.28. On his relations with Favorinus and other intellectuals, G.W. Bowersock, *Greek Sophists and the Roman Empire* esp. 50ff. In general on his cultural tastes, Bardon, *Les Empereurs* 393ff., and R. Syme, 'Hadrian the intellectual', in *Les Empereurs Romains d'Espagne* (1965) 243ff.

11. The two incidents are reported by Charisius, (*Grammatici Latini*, ed. Keil, 1.209) and Priscian (ibid. 2.547). Bardon, *Les Empereurs* 413f. comments very briefly on Hadrian's grammatical work.

12. Lucian *Ignorant book-collector* 22. The work is translated in the Loeb Lucian vol.3. On the importance of culture in the emperor's relations with his subjects, Millar, *Emperor* 491ff. is basic.

of academic characters who held one or more of the three offices of libraries, studies and letters at this period. Of the others, just enough is known to give an idea of their similar backgrounds. Dionysius of Alexandria was a pupil of Chaeremon, also known as the tutor of Nero, and was Chaeremon's successor as head of the Museum in Alexandria; Dionysius held office probably under Trajan in charge of libraries and letters (as well as embassies and 'responses'). A later head of the Museum, Julius Vestinus, held precisely Suetonius' combination (or succession) of posts, libraries, studies and letters; he served Hadrian, and so perhaps was Suetonius' successor. Later, under Hadrian, Valerius Eudaemon had charge of libraries and letters. Nothing is known of his qualifications, but Hadrian quarrelled with him, as with Suetonius and a string of other intellectuals. Volusius Maecianus under Pius supervised studies, libraries, and petitions. He was a voluminous writer on legal matters; as with Pomponius and Gellius his learning was also antiquarian.[13]

Other secretaries *ab epistulis* have rather different backgrounds. Particularly notable is the group of Greek sophists, professors of rhetoric, who had charge of Greek correspondence under the Antonines. They are well-known from Philostratus' *Lives of the Sophists* which makes clear the reason for their employment: as sophists were chosen by Greek cities as their mouthpieces in approaching emperors, so emperors found it convenient to employ sophists as their mouthpieces in responding. Like Suetonius they were intellectuals rather than military types; but Suetonius was no sophist, for he had no talent for display oratory. He was much closer to Dionysius and Vestinus; though not a Greek, his intellectual background was in Alexandrian scholarship. He was the Roman counterpart to a head of the Museum. Why then did Trajan and Hadrian appoint these scholarly types to offices?[14]

13. On the literary attainments of members of the emperor's entourage, see Millar, *Emperor* 83ff. I follow him (see 90-1 for his account of S) except in placing greater emphasis on the scholarly (and not rhetorical) accomplishments of those like S. On this group see Townend (1961b), and Pflaum, *Carrières* no.46 (Dionysius), no.105 (Vestinus), no.110 (Eudaemon), no.141 (Maecianus). On Hadrian's quarrel with Eudaemon, see Syme (1980) 74. On Maecianus, Millar 103.

14. The sophistic secretaries are discussed by Bowersock, *Greek Sophists* 43ff. His views are now modified by E.L. Bowie, 'The importance of sophists', *Yale Classical Studies* 27 (1982) 29ff.

Librarians

The common factor is surely the library. When the Ptolemies sought to make Alexandria the cultural capital of the civilised world, they established the Mouseion, the temple of the Muses, and an associated library, containing the first systematic collection of Greek texts. Among its first librarians were the founding figures of hellenistic scholarship, Zenodotus and Eratosthenes. The link between scholarship and libraries remained close from then on. Romans in acquiring Greek literature and education necessarily turned to the collecting of books. The Greek scholar Tyrannion and others like him were much in demand in the late republic for helping aristocrats to collect their private libraries. Lucullus, according to Plutarch (42.1), had a particularly fine library which he threw open daily to Greek scholars, so that his house seemed a 'resort of the Muses'. In his leisure hours he would stroll in his cloisters discussing points with the scholars. And from the beginning of the empire, the provision of public libraries was one of the most important contributions of the Caesars to the promotion of learning and culture. For the facts, we must turn, characteristically, to the former librarian, Suetonius.[15]

Julius was the first to plan a public library in Rome, and one of the unfinished commissions of his dictatorship was the appointment of the scholar Varro to assemble and arrange the books, both Greek and Latin (44.2). The plans were dropped, and it was an old lieutenant of Julius', the historian Asinius Pollio, whose Atrium Libertatis in fact provided the first library (fr. 102 Reiff.). Augustus rapidly outshone Asinius: he built two public libraries, at the very start of his reign the temple of Apollo adjoining his house on the Palatine, and a little later the portico of Octavia (29.3-4). The corollary of libraries was librarians; and it should be remembered that *a bibliothecis* was one of the earliest 'offices' Augustus must have established (undoubtedly it will have featured in Suetonius'

15. S's interest in libraries was appreciated by Macé (1900) 220ff. His views are amplified by Gomoll (1935). There is little to be learnt from any writer other than S about Roman libraries: see the account in Hirschfeld, *Verwaltungsbeamten* 298ff. Tacitus nowhere so much as mentions libraries. The suggestion by N. Reed, *CQ* 26 (1976) 309ff. that Tacitus was Titus' librarian is incredible. I find the attribution by Reifferscheid fr.102 of Isidore's passage on libraries to S in principle convincing, despite the scepticism of Brugnoli (1968) 209f. But fr.102 surely belongs to the *de Institutione Officiorum*. On Ptolemaic patronage and the library at Alexandria, P.M. Fraser, *Ptolemaic Alexandria* (1972) 305ff.

monograph). The first librarian was Pompeius Macer; Suetonius cites a letter to him from Augustus forbidding the publication of some slight literary works by Julius (*Jul.* 56.7). Pompeius was an *eques Romanus*, but of Greek origin; his father or grandfather was Theophanes of Mitylene, friend and historian of Pompey from whom he derived vast wealth and prestige; his son entered the senate later in Augustus' reign, and father and son were forced to suicide under Tiberius. Macer will surely have been a capable scholar. Two other librarians under Augustus were distinguished grammarians, though of servile origin: Hyginus, author of important grammatical works and friend of Ovid, was a Palatine librarian; Melissus, a freedman of Maecenas, was the first librarian of the Porticus Octaviae (*Gramm.* 20 and 21).

Later emperors will necessarily have appointed librarians, but Suetonius only betrays the odd glimpse of their interest in libraries. Tiberius insisted that his favourite poets, the obscurantist Euphorion, Rhianus and Parthenius should be included in the collections (70.2). Caligula perversely wanted Virgil and Livy removed from all shelves (34.2). Under Domitian one of the libraries was seriously damaged by fire, and this otherwise allegedly philistine emperor took great care to make good the losses, sending to Alexandria for replacement copies (20). Trajan and Hadrian, then, needed scholars in the first place because they needed librarians. Trajan's addition to the public libraries of Rome was magnificent. He celebrated the final conquest of Dacia in AD 107 by building a great new forum and market complex, the centrepiece of which was the Column, flanked by two libraries, the *bibliothecae Ulpiae*. The building was at least partly complete by around AD 113; and by the same date Pliny was probably dead and Suetonius returned from Bithynia. Perhaps it was Suetonius, like Varro, Macer or Melissus, to whom the emperor delegated the job of ordering the new library. A later biographer was to vaunt the usefulness of the *bibliotheca Ulpia* in composing his lives of Aurelian (1.7-10) and Probus (2.1). Suetonius may have been able to make a similar claim in his now missing preface, and with greater justification. This is only a guess; the important point is that the emperors whom he served were as keen as any to rival Alexandria.[16]

16. Pflaum, *Carrières* 267f. believes that the librarian of the Ulpian libraries was called *a bibliothecis divi Traiani*; but this title is only once attested, and even here a second inscription on the same man simply calls him *proc. Aug a bybliothecis*. The librarian was surely responsible for all libraries, cf. Hirschfeld

Studies

As with Vestinus and Volusius Maecianus, Suetonius' career linked librarianship with the post of *a studiis* – whether both posts were held simultaneously or one after the other is in each case obscure. Were scholars needed in this post too? The difficulty is that there is no agreement as to what the duties of the *a studiis* were. Various guesses have been made. Perhaps he did the research for imperial decisions; but the only sign that such learned 'research' was needed is a story of Hadrian who decided on the legitimacy of a baby born ten months after its father's death 'after investigating the views of ancient philosophers and medical writers'. Few cases turned on such technicalities. Another possibility is that this official kept the imperial archives; this is conceivable, but it is more likely that each office kept its own records. The latest suggestion is that the *a studiis* acted as ghost-writer for the emperor's speeches. If that is right, scholars like Suetonius and Vestinus were an odd choice in preference to accomplished rhetoricians. It is made stranger still by the strong disapproval with which Suetonius, an old hand at the job, notes that Domitian neglected 'even basic style' and got others to write his speeches (20).[17]

The best evidence has been neglected, and that is what Suetonius himself has to say about the 'studies' of emperors. In nearly every life he includes a chapter or more on the 'liberal studies' of the emperor.[18] The assumption behind these chapters is that an emperor ought to interest himself in literary matters. Thus the item on Domitian cited above comes from a chapter that opens: 'he neglected liberal studies from the beginning of his reign'. The degree of education and the range of literary interests he documents in the

Verwaltungsbeamten 303. If S did organise the Ulpian libraries, we must assume that he combined the posts of *a studiis* and a *bibliothecis*, as did Volusius Maecianus. This is perfectly possible; see van't Dack (1963). If the *SHA* is to be trusted, the *bibliotheca Ulpia* became the repository for official documents (cf. Tac. 8.1). Certainly Gellius consulted old praetors' edicts there (*Noctes Atticae* 11.17). It is suggested below that it was the imperial libraries which gave S access to unpublished letters of Augustus.

17. For various conjectures as to the functions of the *a studiis*, see Macé 110f., Hirschfeld *Verwaltungsbeamten* 332f., Millar, *Emperor* 205.

18. See also above, ch.3. The relevant passages on the *studia* of Caesars are: *Jul.* 55-6, *Aug.* 84-9, *Tib.* 70-1, *Cal.* 53, Cl. 40-2, *Ner.* 52, *Tit.* 3.2, *Dom.* 20. Cf. *Vesp.* 22-3 on his wit.

Caesars is astonishing. Of only three Caesars does he have nothing in this line to report, and since these are the mayfly emperors of the civil war his silence is probably due to lack of information. All the others show some degree of accomplishment, quipping with citations of Greek poetry, or themselves producing occasional works. Some are substantial or at least prolific authors. Julius of course was a major literary figure (55-6) and Claudius could employ his long years of enforced idleness in composing many-volumed histories (41-2). But even the supposedly philistine Domitian wrote an essay complete with a quotation of Homer (18.2), while the busy Augustus' productions ranged from polemic, philosophical protreptic and auto-biography to epigrams tossed off in the bath (85). Nero's ambitions as a poet were notorious: Suetonius goes to the trouble of vindicating the authenticity of his attempts against the sceptics. The biographer had personally handled his first drafts, scored with deletions and second thoughts (52).

Emperors with literary interests naturally surrounded themselves with men of literary talent. A vivid picture of grammarians at court is conjured up by his account of Tiberius. The philhellene who in exile on Rhodes had attended the lectures of rival professors (11.3) and who took umbrage when the grammarian Diogenes would not lecture for him except on the sabbath (32.2), still as emperor relished the company of grammarians. He delighted in plaguing them with abstruse questions drawn from his daily reading – What name did Achilles take when disguised as a girl, or what songs did the Sirens sing? (70.3). He was much put out when he caught a certain Seleucus cheating by making discreet enquiries after his current reading (56).

Tiberius' taste for the grammatical was certainly not the rule. But Hadrian, as we have seen, had the same taste, and one of the citations from his grammatical *Sermones* gives a possible glimpse of the secretary *a studiis* at work. Wishing to establish whether the word *obiter* is good Latin, Hadrian cites an array of sources, the mime-writer Laberius and other 'ancients' and finally a letter of Augustus in which Tiberius is ticked off for avoiding the word. Of course, comments Hadrian in a tone of superiority, Augustus was not a perfect scholar, and may only be speaking as a layman. It is a curious coincidence that an *a studiis* of Hadrian had made something of a corner in the letters of Augustus. Hadrian employs the letters just as Suetonius might. It does not follow that Suetonius had provided him with the citation, nor that his job as *a studiis* was to do so. But at least it gives a hint of why an emperor like Hadrian valued the expertise of a scholar like Suetonius.[19]

The modern assumption that the role of an imperial official was necessarily a public one can be misleading. An emperor might simply like to be guided in matters cultural. The line between public and private is blurred. Domitian supposedly read nothing but the minutes of Tiberius (20), but Augustus shared the fruits of his leisure-reading with his staff and governors, to whom he circulated improving extracts (89.2). But there was one point at which an emperor's literary interests had considerable public significance. Emperors were great patrons of literature. The cultured and learned were rewarded by privileged access to the imperial presence and by grants of money and other favours. Augustus did everything to encourage the talents of his age. This involved enduring recitations, of poetry and history, oratory and philosophy (89.3). Naturally it also involved dispensing money, as he did twice to Horace (recorded in the poet's life). Tiberius did likewise, though Suetonius clearly regards 200,000 sesterces as a reward to Asellius Sabinus for a gastronomical debate between a mushroom, a figpecker, an oyster and a thrush as going too far (42.2). Vespasian's support of the arts was notable: he rewarded poets handsomely (the figure of 500,000 sesterces for Saleius Bassus is attested), along with rhetoricians, architects, engineers, actors and musicians (18-19.1). The negligent Domitian established competitions, private and public, for prose and poetry (4.4).

The tastes of emperors affected others. Under Nero, musicians flourished: the lyre-player Menecrates carried off the fortune of a conquering general (30.2). Tiberius' penchant for certain minor Greek poets provoked a rash of scholarly studies, designed to catch his eye (70.2). The emperor's disfavour was to be feared: though one does not know if Seneca's popularity was affected by Caligula's dismissive verdict (53.2). But even an emperor with marked tastes of his own might welcome guidance in the distribution of benefits to the budding talents of the reign.

The patronage of the emperor was still crucial for literature in Suetonius' day. The younger Pliny attributed a revival of literature to Trajan's benign concern. Juvenal a little later left the emperor (Hadrian, it is assumed) in no doubt as to what was expected of

19. The quotation from Hadrian's *Sermones* is from Charisius in *Grammatici Latini*, ed. Keil, 1.209.

him: 'On Caesar alone hang the hopes and *raison d'être* of studies', and he goes on to demonstrate at length the inability of literary men to make ends meet, whether poets, historians, orators, rhetors or grammarians. It has already been suggested that Juvenal had read Suetonius' *Illustrious men*. One of the main themes of that work was the extent of the dependence of culture upon patronage, particularly that of the Caesars. The theme would have sounded well from the pen of an *a studiis*.[20]

The best route to the emperor's purse was by dedication of writings. But how many emperors had time to read the smallest fraction of what was offered? 'When you shoulder such a burden of business unaided, protect the security of Italy with arms, adorn it with morals, and improve it with laws, I would commit an offence against the common welfare if I wasted your time with protracted talk'. So Horace opens his poetic letter to Augustus: a highly favoured poet addressing an emperor famous for his patronage. What then are we to infer of Domitian, who, Suetonius claims, read neither poetry nor history after his accession? Statius and Martial bombarded him with indifferent *pièces d'occasion*, and periodically they must have reaped their reward (Martial was granted the tribunate and the rights of fatherhood, Statius the right to draw a private supply from a public aqueduct). So long as emperors made an issue of 'promoting talents' and yet were pressed for time, they needed subordinates to mediate their contacts with the literary world. There was enough here to keep a studies adviser busy.

Only one of Suetonius' predecessors in this post is known by name, and that is on Suetonius' own evidence: Polybius the freedman of Claudius. He was the addressee of an understandably sycophantic essay of consolation by Seneca, then in exile. It is surely no coincidence that it was to the *a studiis* the literary exile turned his flatteries.[21]

---

20. Tacitus *Agricola* 3.1 believed literature to have been suppressed by Domitian. Pliny *Ep.* 1.10 and 13 acclaimed its revival under Nerva. At *Pan.* 47 he gives the credit to Trajan, but at *Ep.* 8.12 Titinius Capito's patronage also takes credit. Such talk of literary renaissance has a strong propagandistic element: but it is taken seriously by Gordon Williams, *Change and Decline* (1978) 284ff. On Juvenal and S, see above, ch.3.

21. Millar, *JRS* 57 (1967) 16f. observes that though Polybius is depicted by Seneca receiving petitions, it does not follow that he was *a libellis*. The petitions that kept him busy might have been from literary men. Another possible *a studiis* is the Sextus to whom Martial addresses blandishments (5.5): cf. Hirschfeld, *Verwaltungsbeamten* 333, n.2.

Correspondence

The posts of librarian and studies adviser were, it emerges, ones that called for a professional scholar. The same was not true of the secretaryship *ab epistulis*, or at least not to the same extent. Rhetoricians are found in the post more frequently than scholars. The crucial requirement was some sort of gift for composition; such as might be found in Horace, author of verse epistles; Julius Secundus, one of a family of orators from Gaul; Titinius Capito, author of the *Deaths of Famous Men*; or, less ostentatiously, imperial slaves manumitted for their literary gifts, *ob studia*. We cannot form a very precise idea about the nature of the Secretary's job: how much was decision-making, how much stylistic aid in the composition of letters, how much honorific. We can only say he 'assisted' in dealing with the multifarious imperial correspondence. Statius, writing in praise of a freedman secretary of Domitian, Abascantus, gives an impression of the range of topics: reports to and from the front, letters of appointment, communications with the cities of the empire.[22]

Imperial secretaries can have possessed little or no technical expertise in the topics of their correspondence (notably on military affairs). Their skills lay in handling letters, and it is on this side of the job that Suetonius casts light. He is interested in the physical aspects of the letter. Julius wrote to the senate not on scrolls like former proconsuls but on pages 'in the form of a memorandum', thereby setting a precedent (56.6). He also used a simple cipher when communicating on confidential matters; so did Augustus, though he substituted B for A and so on, not D for A like Julius (*Aug.* 88). Augustus put the time as well as the date on his letters, and sealed them, after various experiments, with the signet-portrait by Dioscurides used by all subsequent emperors (50). Suetonius also comments on his spelling (properly, for orthography was the province of the grammarian): Augustus seems to have adopted the Shavian principle of spelling according to sound (88). Banal though it may sound, orthography must have been one of the concerns of the *ab epistulis*; misspelling gives the impression of lack of education,

---

22. On the functions of the *ab epistulis* see Millar, *Emperor* 213ff. He shows that the main concern of the *ab epistulis Graecis* was with style; he seems to me too sceptical in denying the same concern to the ab *epistulis Latinis*. There is sense in the attempt by Sherwin-White to detect the hand of the secretary in Trajan's replies to Pliny: *The Letters of Pliny* 536ff. For Statius on Abascantus, *Silvae* 5.1.81ff.

and there was a rumour (which Suetonius discredits) that a provincial governor had been 'sent his successor' in consequence of a spelling mistake.

Suetonius also interests himself in the circumstances of handling correspondence. He describes how Vespasian had a regular session reading letters and departmental minutes before dressing (21), and how Titus, when he took over these responsibilities, dictated answers (6.1). Domitian, he alleges, relied on others to write his letters (20); though in another incident, he is found at work dictating an official circular in the name of his procurators when he commits the blunder of referring to himself as 'Our God and Master' (13.2). Julius used to deal with his letters while watching the games, a tactless practice avoided by Augustus (*Aug.* 45.1). Nero, by contrast, was so negligent that for eight days after the news of Vindex's revolt he sent not a single reply or instruction (40.4).

Of secretaries themselves Suetonius only gives two examples, both cases of corruption. Augustus had an amanuensis called Thallus, who betrayed the contents of a letter for a price: Augustus punished him by having his legs broken (67.2). Thallus was only a minor secretary, but the sale of 'smoke', inside information from the palace, was a notorious form of corruption in later reigns. The severity of Augustus towards his subordinates contrasts with Claudius' total lack of control. His freedmen not only exercised undue influence over his decisions, his appointments, grants and judgments, but they even reversed the emperor's decisions by forgery or alteration of documents (29.1). The letters patent (*codicilli*) here mentioned were certainly the province of the *ab epistulis*.

The impression this last passage gives is that Suetonius thought it no business of the secretary to make decisions. Of course it would be possible to tender advice with more tact and on less blatantly corrupt grounds than Claudius' freedmen did. But the employment of scholars and rhetors makes more sense if their primary concern was supposed to be with form rather than content. For the distinction we may compare his surprised observation on Tiberius: he consulted the senate not only on how to reply to letters from foreign powers (that was odd enough) but on the form in which to put it (30).

The use of documents

Suetonius, it seems, does in fact betray signs of his official activities. One possible product of his official career has attracted particular interest and is worth looking at closely, and that is his attitude to and use of documents. The issues are neatly summed up in a remarkable passage, where he discusses the birthplace of Caligula (8). There are three possibilities: a contemporary of the emperor claims he was born at Tibur, near Rome; the elder Pliny argued for Koblenz on the Rhine frontier, adducing local inscriptions (Pliny served in the army in that area) and some popular verses; and Suetonius has discovered that the official records name Antium, on the coast south of Rome. Clear and vigorous argumentation follows, which establishes the truth beyond doubt. Pliny had already refuted the claims of Tibur; it was a different Gaius who was born there. But Pliny's own arguments for a German birthplace fall down; chronological considerations show that the father, Germanicus, had not yet left for the frontier at the time of the birth. Suetonius confirms this by quoting a letter of Augustus to the mother Agrippina, dated two years after the birth, showing Caligula to be still in Rome, and about to be taken off to Germany. Against this, Pliny's evidence has no weight: the inscriptions are vague, referring to an unspecific 'childbirth', and the verses are anonymous and therefore undependable. Which leaves, Suetonius concludes, the evidence of the Records, which have the authority of an official document, and which are plausible enough in view of Gaius' fondness for Antium.

There is no passage comparable to this for its display of learning and careful evaluation of evidence in any surviving ancient historian, though indeed it emerges again that Pliny was unusual among historians, citing epigraphic evidence from his own experience. Suetonius' method here is not that of the historian, but that of the scholar. His own scholarly expertise can be seen at one point, for his discussion of the meaning of *puerperium* in Pliny's inscription draws, as we have seen, on the earlier monograph *On offices*. But apart from the scholarly side, can we not also detect an 'official' side, both in his respect for the authority of public records, and in his ability to quote from a private letter of an earlier emperor?

Suetonius' respect for documents manifests itself both in the frequent use he makes of them and in the occasional expression of enthusiasm. In the civil wars of AD 69 fire swept the Capitol, destroying (along with the great temple) the numerous bronze tablets recording decisions of the senate and plebiscites on treaties, alliances and privileges from the beginning of the city. These, to the number of 3,000, Vespasian had restored. Suetonius, characteristically reserved, allows himself an enthusiastic comment: 'a most fine and ancient instrument of empire' (8.5). The word he uses both here and in the *Caligula* passage for a collection of records, *instrumentum*, is unknown to literary language, but is the correct legal and bureaucratic expression – an official is attested with the title 'Assistant to the Collection of Proceedings' (*ad instrumentum commentariorum*). It is hard to resist the impression that Suetonius' enthusiasm is connected with his experience as an official.

As an imperial secretary, he will certainly have known the value of such an *instrumentum*. The nature of its work made it essential that the office *ab epistulis* keep a file of past imperial correspondence. Letters conveyed benefits, privileges, decisions, grants, promotions or whatever; and the only way to substantiate a claim that the present or a past emperor had granted a 'benefit' was to produce the relevant letter. Particularly this became necessary after Titus started the practice of ratifying his predecessors' decisions *en bloc* (8.1). Suetonius presumably appreciates the significance of this innovation. Thenceforth emperors were in some degree bound by the decisions of those before them. A nice illustration of this process comes in the correspondence between Trajan and his governor of Bithynia, Pliny (*Ep.* 10.65-6). The governor is faced by disputes about the status of foundlings who have been brought up by their finders as slaves. He has been shown an imperial edict and several letters, but feels unhappy about their authenticity, and applies to Trajan for guidance, in the confidence that authentic records will be to hand in his files. Trajan replies that after research nothing has been found of general application which covers the case of Bithynia. Evidently officials, surely including the *ab epistulis*, have been required to look into their files. The task must have been a formidable one: the corpus of imperial letters was extensive, and the references that Pliny offers are of the vaguest sort - 'letters of Vespasian to the Spartans', but no date, let alone modern-style reference code.

It may be, then, that we catch the accents of the *ab epistulis* when Suetonius speaks the language of archival research: thus various allegations had been made about the background of Vespasian's grandfather, 'but personally, despite adequately detailed research, I have been unable to find any trace of this' (1.4). But this is also the language of scholarship. It could hardly be claimed that Suetonius owed his awareness of the value of documents exclusively to his office. Scholars had used documents long before him. We only see again how the roles of scholar and official reinforce each other:

a scholar was ideally equipped for answering tricky questions about the status of foundlings.

The letters of Augustus

But perhaps the most intriguing question is how far his office gave Suetonius privileged access to the documents he drew on in the *Caesars*. At the heart of this problem lies his use of the letters of Augustus, as instanced in the discussion of Caligula's birthplace. Over fifty fragments of Augustus' private letters survive, the vast majority preserved by Suetonius. There is no more valuable contribution he makes to our understanding of the Caesars; and the free quotation of authentic letters is also one of his best contributions to the genre of biography, foreshadowing Boswell (the letters that appear in ancient historians are usually fictional compositions like the speeches). The range of questions he illuminates by using this one source is impressive. Primarily, of course, the letters illuminate the private life of Augustus: his exchange of polemic with Antony (7), his views on treasonable slander (51.3), his care in educating his family (64), his fondness for dicing (71), his simple tastes in food (76), much about his views on style and his own practices in writing (86-7), and a glimpse into his superstitions (92.2). No less effective is their deployment to illuminate the lives of those who came into contact with him. We hear of Julius' minor literary ventures and their suppression by Augustus (*Jul.* 56.7). By the citation of six letters to Tiberius he quashes the unworthy allegation (found also in Tacitus) that Augustus designated Tiberius his successor against his better judgment (*Tib.* 21). We have seen his contribution to the question of Caligula's birthplace. Perhaps most illuminating of all are the three letters to Livia about the young Claudius (4). Quoted at length, they give a penetrating account of the boy's mixture of talent and gaucherie, and at the same time a fascinating insight into Augustus' manipulation of his family.

The question, then, is whether it was as imperial secretary, or perhaps in an earlier office, that Suetonius had access to the letters of Augustus. There is another question that arises from this one: why does he not go on to quote the letters of Augustus' successors? Did he have the opportunity or desire to do so? Was it his disgrace and removal from office that cut him off from his best source of information?[23]

23. The fragments of Augustus' correspondence are collected by E. Malcovati, *Imperatoris Caesaris Augusti Operum Fragmenta*[5] (1969). There are two

There is little doubt that he consulted at least some of these letters in the palace. He had seen autograph copies, on which he could base comments on Augustus' orthography, and as most of the letters in question were to members of the imperial family, it was probably somewhere in the palace that they were kept. There is no doubt that in his official capacity he will have been accustomed to searching through at least the public letters of Augustus for past judgments and precedents. (A document of Domitian survives in which he bases a decision on a letter of Augustus to his veterans.)[24] But there is a great danger of sliding into modern preconceptions of confidential government archives and their use by historians. There is another vital side to this question, and it brings us back to Suetonius the scholar.

It was not as an imperial biographer that Suetonius discovered the value of Augustus' letters. He had already used them to effect in his literary lives. He describes how Virgil received letters expressing the anxious interest of the emperor in the progress of the *Aeneid*, and quotes from four bantering letters to Horace, in addition to the invitation to become his secretary. Nor is this all. It is likely enough he had drawn on this correspondence in the monograph *On offices*: the invitation to Horace and the letter to Pompeius Macer as librarian would have been very pertinent here. Moreover, he used the correspondence in philological works which, unlike a life of Augustus or of the poets he patronised or a work on posts he established, had no obvious link with Augustus. One passage from his *Prata* quoted by Isidore in his *Etymologies* is a discussion of different words for seas and rivers. Isidore gives little more than a précis, omitting the citations which would substantiate the usages;

---

distinct schools of thought about S's use of the letters of Augustus. Macé 110ff., 'Le secrétaire ab epistulis aux archives impériales', argued that S used privileged access to unpublished documents; Townend (1959) 286ff. pushed his case further, proposing the hypothesis that it was S's dismissal that cut off access to the archives which he would otherwise have used in the later lives. But already Rostagni (1944) ix was sceptical about privileged access; Levi in his *Divus Augustus* commentary (1951) xlivf. raised powerful arguments against Macé, not wholly disposed of by Townend. Now Malcovati (1977) has demonstrated S's use of the Augustus letters in his scholarly works. Syme (1980b) 115 has made the important observation that S as secretary must have accompanied Hadrian on his travels: were the archives available?

24. For Domitian's letter, see Woodhead and McCrum, *Select Documents of the Flavian Emperors* no.462, lines 21f.

but he does happen to include them for the expression 'blind swell', meaning a heavy sea swell without white horses: Augustus wrote 'we reached Naples in a blind swell'. When the grammarian Charisius quotes a letter of Octavian to Antony to illustrate the word for 'straits', it is clear that he too is drawing on this passage from Suetonius. So Suetonius not only read the correspondence between Antony and Octavian out of interest in their mutual slanging; it served as an authority for lexicographical points.

This is not an isolated instance. Another late grammarian, Priscian, cites a letter of Augustus to Virgil in which he used the reduplicated perfect *excucurristi*. The likelihood that this derives from Suetonius is increased by a comparable fragment in which he discusses whether *decurrit* or *decucurrit* is correct Latin. The rule he gives is that the reduplication is dropped in compounds; so Augustus' *excucurristi* will be an example of a solecism. As Hadrian knew, Augustus was not a perfect scholar.[25]

The question thus changes its complexion. Why did Suetonius first read Augustus' letters to Antony or Virgil: out of historical, or out of philological, interest? Because there is no chance of establishing a secure chronology of his works, we cannot answer that question with certainty. But it is very relevant to observe that Suetonius was not the first scholar to cite these letters. Suetonius comments that Augustus' spelling was unorthodox (88). Quintilian had already made a similar observation, and from inspection of autographs: Augustus had an odd spelling of *heri* ('yesterday'). Suetonius was not the first to read the correspondence between Virgil and Augustus: Tacitus in his *Dialogus* (a work of literary criticism, not of history) observed that Virgil had been held in high esteem by the emperor 'as his letters witness'. The implication is that people generally knew these letters; perhaps they were familiar with them from an earlier biography, such as that of the grammarian Probus. Moreover, the elder Pliny knew about Augustus' letters: quite apart from those which publicly bemoaned the scandalous behaviour of his daughter Julia (probably addressed to the senate and thus public knowledge), he could use the correspondence for odd scraps of information: a procurator sent Augustus a head of corn with an incredible four hundred grains; and he bore witness to the medicinal powers of vetch.[26]

25. On both these passages see Malcovati (1977) 194. The passages concerned are collected in Malcovati, frr. 45, 31, 35.
26. See Malcovati frr.46-9; cf. 36.

Should we conclude that the letters of Augustus were published and in circulation like those of Cicero and so well known to the reading public? Surely not. Suetonius produces his quotations with the air of one who is certainly not handling well-known material. True, he also cites some of Cicero's letters; yet one has the impression that with Augustus' letters he is offering one of his rare collector's items, like the portents reported by Asclepiades of Mendes (*Aug.* 94.4) or the statuette presented to Hadrian (*Aug.* 7.1). The error is to reduce the issue to black-and-white alternatives: either the letters were published or they were in secret imperial archives. But the fluid conditions of the ancient book-trade allow for grey areas. A text might enjoy limited circulation or limited availability without being formally 'published'. One might, for instance, imagine that Vespasian had made at least some of Augustus' letters available to scholars by placing them (or a copy) on the shelves of the imperial library. Thence copies might be taken privately.[27]

Certainly Augustus was known as a letter-writer to a limited number of *cognoscenti* before Suetonius. Already in his life-time he was known as a prodigious correspondent. Nepos in his *Life of Atticus* records that the young Augustus kept up an almost daily correspondence with Atticus, quizzing him about antiquarian lore or problems in poetry. Learned and witty, it was just the kind of correspondence to attract those with antiquarian or philological tastes, like the elder Pliny, Quintilian, Suetonius, Hadrian or subsequent grammarians. This is nicely illustrated by a chapter of Aulus Gellius. He describes reading one night a volume of letters by Augustus to his grandson Gaius, and being captivated by their unaffected and simple elegance. 'My dear Gaius, my sweetest little ass, heaven knows how I miss you when you are away . . .' Even in their fragmentary state, the letters show their charm, their human touch and their liveliness of expression, in the peppering of *bon mots* from Greek or colloquial language. In fact, quite apart from

---

27. It is generally accepted that the letters to Gaius were published (Malcovati frr.21-4), and presumably those to Atticus which Nepos knew were also (fr.43). It is perfectly reasonable to assume that others were not in general circulation: Townend (1959) 287. It does not follow, however, that they were locked away in secret palace archives: they might have been available in one of the imperial libraries, like the minor works of Julius (56.7). The connection between the dismissal and the decline of the post-Augustan lives should probably, in my view, be abandoned; see also above, ch.3.

historical interest, there was something special about these letters which the *cognoscenti* naturally relished.

We need not rule out the possibility that Suetonius had some sort of privileged access to some of the letters. His librarianship may have helped him in this respect as much as his responsibility for 'studies' or letters. But the conclusion which should be resisted is that it was because he was an imperial official that Suetonius had the impulse to use this source. The company Suetonius keeps is that of contemporary men of learning, not of modern archival researchers. It follows that we cannot attach much significance to his failure to quote the correspondence of Augustus' successors. Here too he keeps company with his contemporaries. None of them cite the letter of any Caesar from Tiberius to Domitian, whether for philological, biographical or historical purposes. Either their correspondence was unavailable; or it lacked the special qualities that set Augustus' epistolary style apart. In any event, there is no evidence that it crossed Suetonius' mind to employ it.

The essential truth is that behind the official we should never forget the antiquarian and philologist. The 'official in the archives' conjures up a picture easily recognisable to modern eyes; we have to strain to see the more unusual, but more revealing picture of a grammarian reading the letters of an emperor who cared about literature and scholarship, and whose style ranked him as a minor classic.

Overall, a rather different conclusion emerges about the relationship between Suetonius' official career and his writings from what might be expected. Certainly the interests of the official leave their mark on his pages: he has an unusual amount to say about offices at large, and those he held in particular. But this does not tempt him to write a new kind of history. He does not, for instance, take the opportunity to rewrite imperial history as an account of the development of a centralised bureaucracy. If anything he used his official experience to give him a better insight into the private matters that interested the scholarly biographer.

But the way a scholarly biographer sees emperors, though only one of many possible angles, is not a quirkish one. It was his scholarship that made Suetonius and others like him useful to emperors. Because the society in which they operated placed a high value on literary culture of the hellenistic type, emperors played an important role in the world of culture, providing public libraries

and promoting by their support the talents of the age. They liked
to be seen themselves as men of education, in their conversation and
their public letters and pronouncements. For these reasons learned
men had a place in their entourage. There is no gulf between
Suetonius the secretary and Tranquillus the philologist.

PART TWO

THE SUBJECT

Chapter Five

EMPERORS AND SOCIETY

There is little problem in recognising the social standpoint from which Tacitus or the younger Pliny write. They were senators, and the senate occupies the centre of their universe. A disproportionate amount of the *Annals* (many have felt) is given to what went on in the senate. In the assessment of a ruler, his attitude to senate and senators is crucial: to be 'good' is to be good by senatorial lights. 'What is more civil, more senatorial than the title we (senators) gave you – Optimus, the Excellent?'[1]

Suetonius was not a senator, and his viewpoint is not so easy to identify. At least, there has been widespread disagreement among modern scholars as to the social standpoint he does represent. Many were content to recognise 'the familiar illusions of the senatorial circle', until a book appeared under the title *Svetonio: eques Romanus* with the vigorously argued thesis that the *eques Romanus* had a distinctive approach. Representative of the *piccolo equestre* (the phrase suggests *petit bourgeois*), Suetonius had broken free from the senatorial influence of his patron Pliny and wrote as the spokesman of a new generation of civil servants, convinced of the practical advantages of autocracy and free from the traditionalism that hankered after the republic and senatorial government. The thesis is controversial, and met with little approval. One scholar even countered with the suggestion that Suetonius represents the 'man in the street', the reader of the gutter press with a taste for the sensational and sordid.[2]

---

1. On the traditional senatorial domination of historiography, see e.g. E. Badian, 'The early historians', in T.E. Dorey (ed.) *Latin Historians* (1966) 1ff. On the senatorial ideology summed up in Pliny's *Panegyric*, see the edition of M. Durry (1938) 21ff.; also F. Trisoglio, *La Personalità di Plinio il Giovane* (Mem.Ac.Sc.Torino. Cl.Sc.Mor.ser.4, vol.25, 1972) 78ff.

2. A senatorial viewpoint is detected in S by H. Peter, *Die geschichtliche Literatur über die römische Kaiserzeit* 2 (1897) 70, followed by Macé (1900)

The eques on society

What sort of views, social and political, should we expect of an *eques* in the emperor's service?[3] There is no use in trying to make a Whig of Suetonius. The Roman world lacked, so far as can be seen, the deep divisions of ideology between the progressive and the conservative, familiar since the early modern period. In no sense did the *equites* form a social 'class', separate from the senate in economic background, social intercourse or ideological stance. Drawn from the landowning aristocracy of the empire, *equites* and senators mingled on easy terms. There was nothing in his background to set Suetonius apart from Tacitus or Pliny. Tacitus was son of an equestrian procurator; and his father-in-law Agricola was descended on both sides from procurators, 'the equestrian nobility' as he proudly observes in his biography. Pliny's background was comparable: nephew and heir of Pliny the procurator, he married into the equestrian élite of his native Comum. Pliny's letters show no gulf between the senators and the numerous *equites* of his acquaintance; they went to the same dinner parties, applauded the same poetry and forwarded their careers by means of the same network of patronage.[4]

'Class' is the wrong word to describe the *equites*. Like members of the senate and their families, they formed a rank, *ordo*, a legally defined status within the hierarchy of the citizen body. Under the republic, membership of the senatorial and equestrian ranks had been conveyed or confirmed by the censors in their periodic reviews of the citizen-rolls. After Augustus the censorship lapsed and the

---

84f. and Ailloud (Budé translation 1931) xxxiii. The thesis of an equestrian-oriented S was put forward by della Corte (1958, revised 1967). The misapprehensions and insights of this work are distinguished in a review by Crook (1969). For the 'man in the street' thesis, Paratore (1959). Cizek (1977) 167ff. rejects della Corte but compromises unhappily with a picture of a senatorial-equestrian alliance led by Septicius. For effective demolition of della Corte and a just appreciation of S, see Gascou (1976).

3. On the same question, see now the paper of Alföldy (forthcoming). He uses the *Caesars* as a test-case for analysis of the Roman conceptions of the structure of their own society. I am grateful to Professor Alföldy for sending me a copy of this paper in advance of publication.

4. The modernising view of the *equites* under the republic was exploded by P.A. Brunt, 'The equites in the Late Republic', in *Second International Conference on Economic History, 1962* (1965) 117ff., reprinted in R. Seager (ed.), *The Crisis of the Roman Republic* (1969) 83ff. The same arguments can be extended to the empire with the help of the thorough documentation in A. Stein, *Der römische Ritterstand* (1927) esp. 345ff. on social links.

emperor absorbed their functions, and though on occasion emperors conducted 'reviews' of the *equites*, as Suetonius records, it seems that the rank was taken for granted by men of free birth and the requisite property qualification. More important was the grant of marks of dignity within the bracket of equestrian rank – membership of the jury panels, army rank, and for the élite procuratorial posts.[5]

As an *eques* and moreover one honoured with high office, Suetonius enjoyed a place of high standing in society, albeit inferior to that of a senator. In practice, of course, the *ab epistulis* was in a position of greater influence than many a senator. That produced the paradoxical situation of inverted ambition – the preference of a traditionally lower rank for the positions of power it could open. Nevertheless the fiction of the superiority of the senator was sustained. Both the possibility of tension between senator and *eques* and Suetonius' acknowledgment of the proprieties are illustrated by an anecdote he tells of Vespasian. A senator and an *eques* had quarrelled, and brought their dispute to the emperor. His ruling was that while an *eques* might not insult a senator, to *return* an insult was his right as a citizen. Thus, the author comments, Vespasian demonstrated that the two ranks differed not so much in liberty as in dignity (9.2). The story suggests how touchy the Romans might be about their *dignitas*; we may be surprised that Vespasian found a squabble like that worthy of his attention, and almost equally surprised that Suetonius thought it worth telling as his sole concrete illustration of Vespasian's restoration of social order.

There can be no doubt that Suetonius not only acknowledged the traditional hierarchy of status, but positively approved of it. Perhaps the clearest indication of this is his use of the social hierarchy as a principle for the organisation of facts. The central core of his discussion of the administration of Augustus (35-40) examines the ranks in their due order. Suetonius has much to say about the senate, the control of its membership and its organisation (35-38.1). A transitional paragraph considers Augustus' treatment of the sons of senators, whom he prepared for senatorial life and even awarded

5. The nature and recruitment of the *ordines* is expounded by C. Nicolet, *The World of the Citizen in Republican Rome* (trans. 1980) 49ff. Also of value is B. Cohen, 'La notion d'ordo dans la Rome antique', *Bull.Ass.Budé* ser.4. vol.2 (1975) 259ff. The precise definition of an *eques* has long been controversial; see Millar, *Emperor* 279ff. for the debate and for the recruitment of the order under the empire.

an army rank later normally reserved for equestrians, the prefecture of a cavalry brigade (38.2). Next comes a paragraph on his supervision of the dignity of *equites* – he revived the old ceremony by which they trooped past the censor on horseback (38.3-40.1). Any belief that Suetonius thought more highly of the importance of his own order than the senate's must founder at this point: he omits to breathe a word of the new 'offices' Augustus created for *equites* despite having listed the new senatorial ones. As we have seen, he was certainly very familiar with the facts he suppresses. Next we find a brief paragraph on the *populus Romanus* (conduct of the census and of elections) (40.2). Finally a discussion of his policy of enfranchisement and manumission leaves us on the margin between citizens and their free subjects and slaves. The whole section is then rounded off by a suitable anecdote: Augustus made citizens wear the traditional mark of citizenship, the toga, and he cited Virgil in his support (40.3-5).

In this life the hierarchical arrangement is easy to detect, and is an obvious enough principle of arrangement given the emperor's censorial activities. In others the reader must be fairly alert to notice what is happening. So in the life of Julius, the traditional paragraphing of the manuscripts and modern editors obscures the hierarchical section. Censorial supervision of the senate is tacked on to the end of one paragraph (41.1-2), and the census of the *populus* and grants of citizenship to professors and doctors forms the beginning of a new one (41.3-42.1). Yet there is a linking sentence, the last of the former paragraph: Julius divided membership of the juries between members of the senatorial and equestrian orders. The *equites* are almost, but not quite, forgotten. The run senate-*equites*-citizens-slaves-foreigners is also palpable in the *Claudius* (23.2-25.3: as the numeration suggests, the modern paragraphing is again haywire) and fleetingly in the *Caligula* (16.2-3) where items on magistrates, *equites* and *populus* follow each other duly. It is curious that only in the life of this last, disreputable ruler has he more to say about *equites* than about senate.

Hierarchy is a habit of thought for Suetonius. The pattern recurs in numerous other passages as well as these sections on administration (more examples will be given below). Of course, he adopted this pattern for tidiness of analysis, not because he was an *eques*. It was a traditional pattern, used by Tacitus in reviewing Tiberius' early government, or by Valerius Maximus collecting anecdotes of old Roman institutions. But it reflects an underlying belief in the continuing relevance of the traditional social order.[6] Imperial society was acutely status-conscious. Certain new developments in Suetonius' own day illustrate the point. One is the hardening of the distinction in legal texts between the respectable and the humble – *honestiores* and *humiliores*. There was certainly nothing new in the assumption that the propertied classes merited differential treatment before the law; but it is only under Hadrian, it seems, that the distinction was being formally articulated in these terms. We may compare the tone of indignation in which Suetonius records that Caligula punished many men of respectable rank, *honesti ordinis*, by branding, forced labour in the mines, being thrown to the lions or even more degrading tortures (27.3). Caligula's contemporaries will also have been shocked; but by Suetonius' day such penalties were explicitly reserved for the humble.[7]

Another sign of pride in rank is the growing use of status epithets in inscriptions. Towards the end of the second century a growing number of *equites* describe themselves as 'splendid'. Suetonius seems surprised that Claudius struck from the jury panels a leading Greek provincial, *vir splendidus*; his only offence was ignorance of Latin (16.2). In refutation of allegations of the modesty of Vespasian's social background, he points to evidence of the *splendor* this equestrian family enjoyed locally (1.3). A further rank indication that emerges in second-century inscriptions is the distinction between procurators according to their salary grade. Differential salary levels were surely established at an early stage; but only later were thousands of sesterces per annum advertised like pips on the shoulder from *sexagenarii* (sixty thousanders) through *centenarii* (one hundred thousanders) to *ducenarii* (two hundred thousanders). Suetonius provides the earliest attestation of the term *ducenarii*: he notices that Claudius rewarded even two-hundred-thousanders with

6. Gascou (1976) 269 well speaks of 'une conception hiérarchique de la société romaine'. Similarly Alföldy (forthcoming). Tacitus uses a hierarchical pattern twice in reviewing the Roman empire. *Ann.* 4.6 orders the *rei publicae partes* under Tiberius: senate, magistrates, equestrian *publicani*, equestrian procurators, plebs, provinces, imperial household (freedmen and slaves). *Hist.* 1.4-11 reviews the empire in January 69; senate, leading equites, people (divided into the 'good' and the *plebs sordida*), urban troops, provinces. The anecdotes of Val.Max. 2.2-6 are ordered thus: senate and magistrates (2.2.1-8), *equester ordo* (2.2.9), *populus* (2.3-5), foreign peoples (2.6).

7. On the distinction between *honestiores* and *humiliores*, see A.N. Sherwin-White, *The Roman Citizenship*[2] (1973) 313, and P.D.A. Garnsey, *Social Status and Legal Privilege in the Roman Empire* (1970) esp. 103ff.

consular decorations (24.1). A *ducenarius* himself, he hardly expected such distinction from Hadrian, and he surely thought Claudius' action excessive. Similarly there are status implications when he specifies that Vespasian was the first to pay state salaries to Greek and Latin rhetors – at a hundred thousand per annum (18). This put them on a level with centenary procurators.[8]

Splendidus and *ducenarius* are status indications that were treasured by high-ranking *equites*. But it is not from the *amour propre* of an equestrian that Suetonius uses them. He is lavish with status indications at all levels. One notable habit of his is to tell an anecdote in which a character is indicated only by status and not by name. When Claudius made marriage between uncle and niece legal and non-incestuous, none could be found to follow his example but a *libertinus* and a *primipilaris* whose weddings he actually attended (26.3). How bizarre for the ruler to attend the social functions of any so humble as a freedman, or even a top-ranking centurion. Claudius had embarrassing experiences in court: he was called an old fool by a *Graeculus* (*petit Grec*); and sustained a flesh-wound when an *eques Romanus* in indignation that common tarts should be allowed to give evidence against him, hurled his pen and papers at the judge (15.4). The story was told that Tiberius had a man condemned after being asked by a dwarf jester over dinner why the accused had been allowed to get away with it; Suetonius notes the status, not the name of the eye-witness authority, a *vir consularis* (61.6). His high status presumably establishes his credentials.

These anecdotes all show the author sensitive to gradations of status. This sensitivity is not merely occasional: rise and fall in social dignity is an important theme in his work in general. It will be recalled that his *Lives of grammarians and rhetors* had as its central theme the rise of literary education and its practitioners in Rome. The status aspect is basic. Grammar was once despised and taught by semi-Greeks, then given a boost by two *equites*, and finally so rose in popularity that even the most prominent, *clarissimi viri*, put their hand to it (1-3). Similarly rhetoric, once harried by the censors, gradually became decent, through practice by a praetor, consuls, triumvirs and finally emperors (25.2-6). As the arts themselves rose, so did their professors: rhetoric so flourished that 'some

8. On procuratorial grades, H.G. Pflaum, *Les Procurateurs équestres* (1950) 230ff. The use of the label *splendidus eques Romanus* is discussed by S. Demougin, *Epigraphica* 37 (1975) 174ff., challenging the idea that this was a formal title.

rose from the lowest fortune to senatorial rank and the highest honours' (25.7). Not enough of the lives of rhetors survive to illustrate the point precisely. But Voltacilius Pilutus was once not merely a slave, but a chained door-keeper, yet he rose through manumission to teach Pompey and to storm the senatorial bastion of historiography, the first freedman to do so; 'history had never previously been written except by the most respectable, *honestissimi*' (27). Epidius had been censored for calumny, though he boasted an ancestor locally worshipped as a god at Nuceria (28). Sex. Clodius was a mere Sicilian, and was rewarded by Antony with an estate of a size that horrified Cicero (29). Albucius Silus was an erstwhile dignitary of Novaria but left for Rome in umbrage when the defendants in a case pulled him foot-first from his seat of judgment (30). If the manuscript continued, we should doubtless hear how Quintilian was awarded an honorary consulship, and how Julius Tiro, the last of the book, rose to praetorship.

The background of grammarians is almost universally servile (above, chapter 2). Suetonius' lives of them illustrate the power of literary studies to bring manumission and social promotion. They also illustrate more generally the unpredictability of life, in downs as well as ups. Antonius Gnipho (7) was born free but exposed and eventually manumitted by his foster parent. Melissus (21) too was exposed, because his parents quarrelled, and later was claimed by his mother; but he preferred to remain in service to Maecenas, which brought its rewards. Valerius Cato was not a freedman, as alleged, but an orphan stripped of his patrimony by the chances of civil war (11). Orbilius (9) was another orphan, his parents foully murdered by enemies and his inheritance taken. He climbed through service as a magistrate's attendant and in the army, and in early retirement took up schoolmastering in his home town of Beneventum. Valerius Probus, doyen of Flavian scholarship, was also freeborn: but it was only in desperation at his failure to secure a posting as centurion that he took to studies (24).

Suetonius carried the same interest in status to his *Caesars*, though of course at a very different social level, and on a grander scale. Most of his Caesars were descendants of the highest nobility. The biographer is scrupulous about establishing the precise degree of nobility of an emperor's family. How many consuls and trium-phators could the *gens Claudia* muster? (*Tib.* 1.2). Who was the first Sulpicius to confer fame on the family? (*Galb.* 3.2). Suetonius clearly respected noble birth; but pride of nobility was not always a good thing. Julius boasted descent from the kings and Venus: 'our family has both the sanctity of kings and the reverence of gods, the protectors of kings' (6.1). It was an ominous boast from one who seemed to aspire to kingship. Caligula's arrogance verged on the pathological. He was ashamed at his descent from the ignoble Agrippa, and preferred to believe his mother a bastard child of Augustus, begotten in incestuous union with his own daughter. He denounced his grandmother Livia to the senate as low-born on the grounds that she had an ancestor who was a mere town-councillor at Fundi – a monstrous suggestion, considering that public records showed he held office at Rome (23.1-2). The aristocratic Domitii were another arrogant lot: Nero's grandfather produced *equites* and Roman matrons on stage, and his father drove a coach without stopping over a boy on the Appian Way, and struck out the eye of an *eques* who reproached him too frankly in the forum (*Ner.* 4-5). Nero was to be no better.

Four of the Caesars were no aristocrats; and the scrupulous care with which Suetonius details their family backgrounds provides us with rare and precious documents of family mobility in the Roman world. Mark Antony scoffed at Octavian as the descendant of a rope-maker and a silversmith. Suetonius knows the value of such invective, and shows the Octavii to be the cadet branch of the dominant local family of Velitrae who preferred the peace of local distinction, while the senior branch pursued the highest honours at Rome (1-2). Vespasian came from a similar Italian municipal background, though not quite so distinguished (1.2-4). His grandfather was a centurion from Reate, his father an equestrian tax-collector (Suetonius cites epigraphic evidence of his activities). But it was his mother whose family conveyed the greater distinction: monuments to the Vespasii were still to be found at the little hill-top village that bore their name six miles out from Nursia on the Spoleto road. The use of documentary evidence (twice) makes for a trustworthy account; it contrasts with the predictable invective which made out Vespasian's grandfather as a contractor for migrant labourers from Umbria – Suetonius could find no shred of evidence for this (1.4).

The evident admiration the author has for Augustus and Vespasian as rulers, and the care with which he rebuts the invective against them, gives the possible impression that he felt more instinctive sympathy for the municipal aristocracy of Italy than for the degenerate and arrogant republican nobility. If so, it was not an equestrian prejudice. The same impression comes from Pliny's pride in his local Comum or from Tacitus' support of the men from the municipalities who still kept to the straight old ways and felt uncomfortable before the histrionics of Nero. By Suetonius' day the old aristocracy had almost disappeared from the senate, and the vanity of ancient nobility was a safe subject for Juvenal's scathing pen: *Stemmata quid faciunt?* What's the use of a family tree?[9]

Otho and Vitellius also came from relatively new families, and the detailed accounts given of them contrast with the poverty of the rest of these two lives, which offer little more than potted history. Both belonged to old Italian families which rose to distinction at Rome under Augustus. Otho's grandfather came from a prominent Etruscan family and rose to the praetorship through intimacy with Livia. The family remained in high favour with the Julio-Claudians (1). The origins of the Vitellii are obscured by flattery on one side that made them out as old patricians, and on the other by the invective of Cassius Severus who spoke of a freedman who repaired shoes. What is beyond doubt is the success of the Publius Vitellius who was a procurator of Augustus (1-2). The slanders of him by the sharp-tongued Cassius Severus may have been one of those attacks on distinguished people that provoked Augustus to legislate against libel. The high favour he enjoyed emerges from the promotion of all four of his sons to the senate; but they were all to go their different ways, Quintus though a quaestor of Augustus and recipient of a panegyric to be stripped of his rank by Tiberius, and Lucius to be the prime courtier of Claudius' reign (2.2-3.1).

Family background was in fact a traditional concern of the biographer, and precision about the status of the subjects of the life was pioneered by Alexandrian biographers. The lives of Euripides contain the (false) information derived from Aristophanes that his mother was a vegetable seller. Not all scholars were so incautious. Apollonius quoted Aeschines' invective against Demosthenes for the allegation that the latter's father was a cutler; but he also quoted Demosthenes' counter-attack to show that he was a substantial owner of a knife factory. 'What's your family? Who are your parents?' is the question the Cyclops asked Odysseus, and which biographers continued to ask: Suetonius' interest and method are

---

9. See Tacitus *Ann.* 16.5 on municipal morality, and Juvenal *Sat.* 8 on degenerate aristocracy. It should not be imagined, however, that S was anti-aristocratic. For his respectful vocabulary, see Alföldy (forthcoming).

again the result of his scholarly background. Nevertheless, it is also clear that he is interested in questions of social standing for their own sake.[10]

This is borne out by his treatment of the early careers of the Caesars. He sees the early life primarily as a pursuit of honours and dignity not (as Plutarch tends to do) as a preliminary insight into the man's character, let alone (as we tend to) as a 'formative' period. One great merit of his account of Julius' rise is that he sees it as an aristocrat's ruthless struggle to vindicate his *dignitas*. Julius constantly takes his stand on his honours: indignant at humiliating treatment by pirates (4.1), vindictive at a slight to his magisterial standing by an informer (17.2), driven by offence to his pact with Pompey (19.2) and finally committing himself to civil war in defence of his dignity (29-30). Plutarch by comparison is too concerned with Caesar's ambition as a moral failing to perceive its social context.

Enumeration of *honores* was a standard feature of Roman tradition, as witnessed by funeral orations and honorific inscriptions. But such sources only advertised successes, not failures. Suetonius' interest in fluctuations of dignity comes over most clearly where dignity meets rebuffs. Tiberius' early career mounts to a peak of distinction at the point of his retirement to Rhodes (10.1); it then declines to a nadir of degradation when he abandons Roman dress (13.1); finally and unexpectedly it rises a second time to glory. Claudius' youth is a story of indignities: he is assigned a brutal barbarian as a pedagogue (2.2), fails to achieve respect through his publications (3.1), is underrated and kept from all public life by Augustus (4), and is driven to despair of dignity by Tiberius (5). If the equestrian order managed to honour him, that was an exception, and hardly an impressive one (6). At last Caligula found it convenient to dig him out and award him a consulship, but he still was made a fool of over the dinner table (8).[11]

Another standard topic of biography was marriage. In Roman society marriages had implications for status, and Suetonius is careful to be specific. Titus might have been thought to be marrying

10. For status as a traditional topic of biography, see J.A. Fairweather, 'Fiction in the biographies of ancient writers', *Ancient Society* 5 (1974) 268ff.; on different accounts of Demosthenes' parents, 237.

11. S's interest in a career seen as a series of 'Rangstufen' is brought out by Steidle (1951) 114f. (also 24f. on Julius). The debt of Suetonian biography to the tradition of *elogia* and *laudatio funebris* was pointed out by Stuart (1928) 189ff. The republican traditions are fully discussed by Lewis (forthcoming).

below his station in taking the hand of the daughter of an *eques*: but the father was praetorian prefect, which made things different. After her death, Titus' second wife was from a better stable, *splendidi generis* (4.2). Vespasian's wife (the mother of two emperors, an unparalleled distinction) was from a very different drawer: once the mistress of an *eques* from Sabratha in Africa, and not even of full Roman status, she latterly had her citizenship vindicated in court by her father; but even he was no more than a quaestor's scribe (3). The writer relishes the particularity of the detail, which is only one of many signs of Vespasian's extraordinarily modest beginnings. This is the man whom Caligula punished for failing to keep the streets clean while aedile by filling his lap with mud (*Vesp.* 5.3) and whose tenure of the province of Africa was blotted by a pelting with turnips at Hadrumetum (4.3).

The detail could be extended almost indefinitely; but enough has been said to demonstrate that Suetonius not only took for granted the traditional social hierarchy but attached great significance to a man's precise place within it, and the fluctuations in his standing. His account shows a world in which standing was by no means static or predictable. Men might rise to heights unhoped for by changes in fashion (the rise of education), the chances of civil war, or the sheer luck of knowing the right people. One corollary of such social unpredictability is a phenomenon to which Suetonius constantly draws attention: the attempt to divine the future. The goddess Fortuna held sway. Twice Galba dreamed that she visited him: on his coming of age he gave house-room to the tired goddess in a dream, and thereafter kept a statuette of her at his house at Tusculum (4.3). Shortly before his fall, she left him in a huff (18.2). Titus took the precaution of consulting the oracle of Venus on Paphos when his father declared his hand in the civil war; she gave the right answer (5.1). Tiberius approached the oracle of Geryon at the beginning of his first German campaign: the golden dice he was instructed to throw still glittered in Suetonius' day under the water of the fountain near Padua (14.3). Dreams, portents, prophecies, coincidences, chance sayings of emperors were all seized on anxiously as signs of the future. But above all astrology was in vogue, with its offer of a scientific certainty in prediction: a horoscope could cost a man his head (*Dom.* 10.3). Titus could lecture two overambitious patricians, suspected of aiming at the throne, that their attempts were in vain 'for the principate was given by fate' (9.1). Presumably he based his own confidence on the horoscope which allowed Vespasian to affirm before the senate that either his sons would succeed him or nobody (25). It is by no means incredible that such remarks should have been made in public, or even that they should have been believed; certainly Suetonius took them seriously.[12]

The official on the principate

How does such a social outlook fit in with Suetonius' political views? How does he regard the principate as a form of government? What does he consider the proper role of the emperor in relation to the different ranks of society?

The 'senatorial' view of the principate was ambivalent. Tacitus regarded it at best as a necessary evil. The preservation of peace demanded that power should be concentrated in one man's hands; but he has no enthusiasm for this state of affairs. His emotional commitment is to the ideal of liberty. The erosion of the powers of the senate and of the freedom of its members form the bitter leitmotif of his history. Trajan was welcomed by him and by Pliny because he was supposed to have achieved the impossible: principate and liberty were reconciled.[13]

Suetonius has no place in a history of the political ideal of liberty. He avoids politics as a subject. Without the dynamic element of narrative he cannot like Tacitus describe the tensions between emperor and senate, the conflict of principate and liberty. It seems that this corresponds to his inclinations. His rare uses of the word *libertas* are neutral, without emotional resonance. He reports various attempts at restoring liberty, but without betraying where his own feelings lie. He seems to approve vaguely of the 'sort of show of *libertas*' which Tiberius allowed the senate (30); but there is no trace of the bitterness with which Tacitus attacks the falsity of this sham. Indeed it is not Suetonius' way to parade his sentiments. Yet he appears happy to accede to the official picture of Augustus as the champion of liberty. He describes a touching incident at the end of Augustus' life when he was cheered by the crew of a passing boat from Alexandria: 'to him they owed their life, their trade, their

---

12. This theme is discussed at greater length in ch.8, below.
13. The classic account of the tensions between principate and liberty is Chr. Wirszubski, *Libertas as a Political Idea at Rome* (1950). On Tacitus' view, ibid. 160ff. The views of S are nowhere discussed in this book.

enjoyment of liberty and fortune' (98.2). This is closer to the 'Peace and Liberty' which Augustus' coins proclaim as restored.[14]

Perhaps the undemonstrative tone of the *Caesars* conceals his real feelings for a republican ideal. Yet there are signs that he felt a warmth towards the principate which Tacitus never betrays. The most telling passage is his account of Augustus' constitutional settlement (28.1-2). Twice, he reports, Augustus considered restoring the republic (after Actium and in 23 BC), but he thought better of it in view of the risk both to himself and the state. Instead he retained control, 'and it is hard to say whether his results or his intentions were better'. That is to say, Suetonius approved both of what he did, and of the reasons for which he did it. As evidence of his intentions he cites Augustus' own words, his hopes of 'laying the lasting foundations of political stability, and of winning the reputation of *optimi status auctor*, "the author of the best settlement" '. And, Suetonius concludes, he ensured that nobody regretted this new settlement, which is described in detail in the chapters that follow.

The tone here verges on the panegyrical: it is far removed from the critical accounts of Tacitus or Dio. The charade of the return of power asserted in the *Res Gestae* and described by Dio has been warped into an unfulfilled intention. Suetonius' Augustus can get credit for the idea of resigning, and escapes criticism for the falsity of his pretence. In Tacitus the ruthless pursuit of self-advantage casts a heavy shadow over any merit in the establishment of peace and security. Suetonius by hiving off Octavian's conduct in the civil wars under a separate rubric (9-18) effectively divorces the 'new settlement' from its historical background.[15]

The signs, then, are that he frankly approved of the Augustan system and shed few tears over the fall of liberty. Do we here see

14. *Libertas* is used with reference to freedom from autocracy at *Tib.* 50.1, *Cal.* 60, *Cl.* 10.3, *Oth.* 12.2; but S shows no sympathy with attempts to restore it. It refers to freedom of speech at *Aug.* 54 and *Vesp.* 13, but in both cases it is associated with words for insulting behaviour, and credit only goes to the emperor for enduring it. At *Aug.* 12 he records the harsh treatment of the Nursines for commemorating their martyrs *pro libertate*: this is simply factual reporting. After Tacitus the evidence for *libertas* as an ideal seems to fall away. On the imperial coinage LIBERTAS AUGUSTA arguably comes in the course of the second century to mean the same as LIBERALITAS, according to the thesis of A.U. Stylow, *Libertas und Liberalitas. Untersuchungen zur innenpolitischen Propaganda der Römer*, Diss. Munich 1972.

15. Cizek (1977) 180 misinterprets this passage. He understands Augustus' 'intentions' (*voluntas*) to be the initial intention to restore the republic. This is

the viewpoint of the loyal civil servant, impatient with the illusions of the senatorial élite and its talk of senatorial rule and liberty? There surely is a palpable contrast between the stance of the *ab epistulis* and the consular historian. But to exalt it into a difference in political opinion is to fall again into the trap of making Suetonius a Whig. His warmth of admiration for Augustus is by no means incompatible with republican traditionalism.

Emperors and social rank

When the consuls forgot to make an announcement about Caligula's birthday, he dismissed them from office, 'and for three days the state was without supreme power' (26.3). Of course the emperor was supreme, and his action demonstrated it, but technically the consuls remained heads of state: they gave their names to the year, and dating by regnal years of the emperor was confined to Egypt. There is not the slightest sign of impatience in Suetonius with traditional claims of the supremacy of the senate and its magistrates. Nero was supposed to have dropped hints of a plan to abolish the senate and entrust provincial and military commands to *equites* and freedmen. Does the equestrian official approve? On the contrary, he classifies it with the emperor's desire to feed people alive to an omnivorous Egyptian, as an indication of indiscriminate savagery (37.2). Caligula announced on his return from the expedition to Germany that he was 'only coming to those who wanted him, the equestrian order and the people; he would no longer play citizen and princeps to the senate'. He was murdered within months before he could carry out even more monstrous ideas (49.1-2).

As Suetonius was aware, different emperors appealed to different sections of society. Reactions after their death are usually the clearest indication. Domitian's death was taken indifferently by the people (i.e. the urban masses); but the army was very upset, while the

---

confuted by the next sentence, which cites Augustus' *novus status* edict as evidence for his *voluntas*. The contrast between *eventus* and *voluntas* underlies Tacitus' famous arguments for and against Augustus at *Ann.* 1.9-10. There the supporters of Augustus lay emphasis on his achievement, peace (9), while his critics point to his motives, selfish pursuit of power (10). It is possible that S intended here to rebut Tacitus, just as his citation of Augustus' letters to Tiberius at *Tib.* 21 refutes a view mentioned by Tacitus (*Ann.* 1.10), and as the inspection of an autograph of Nero (52) refutes Tacitus' allegation that Nero was a plagiarist (*Ann.* 14.16); cf. Townend (1967) 88.

senate was beside itself with joy (23.1). The people rejoiced at
Tiberius' death, shouting 'into the Tiber with him' (75.1); there
was dancing in the streets at Nero's passing, though some put
flowers on his grave, and the Parthians missed him (57); Galba was
honoured in death by the senate alone (23). But there is no sense
that an emperor meets particular approval for appealing to one
section of society rather than another. Domitian may be thought to
have favoured the equestrian order by extending previously freedman
posts to it (7.2). But Suetonius gives no hint of equestrian support
for the emperor, and no hint that either it or he did not share the
senate's joy at his murder. His account of reactions to Nero's death
is less than adequate. Tacitus records that the 'sordid plebs', the
theatre- and circus-going masses, were upset, and that only the
dependants of the great houses rejoiced. That is wholly convincing
– Nero's showmanship had its purpose. Suetonius' picture of the
plebs rejoicing and only the exceptional mourner seems to be a
deliberate distortion. It is as if he did not care to admit Nero's
popular appeal.[16]

   In fact, what Suetonius likes is a sort of consensus. He is almost
overanxious to show that hated rulers were hated by all ranks
(*omnes ordines* is a recurrent expression).[17] Nero in his salad days
had delighted all from senators to populace by his generosity and
geniality (10). By the end he provoked the hatred of all (45.2). Not
only did he plot to poison the whole senate, but to let loose fire and
wild beasts among the populace (43.1). His war-taxes afflicted
all ranks (44.2). The Great Fire is confidently ascribed to his
machinations. It is treated as a sign of his cruelty to the people to
balance the executions of senators (38). Caligula is represented as
equally indiscriminate. He was brutal and arrogant in his treatment
of the senate; and no less so to 'other ranks'. Twenty *equites* were
killed in a violent expulsion from the theatre, and he deliberately
set the equestrian order at odds with the plebs by letting the rabble
into the reserved seats. But he tormented the people too by taking

---

16. S. Gsell, *Essai sur le règne de l'empereur Domitien* (1894) 343f. thought
that S favoured Domitian because of his good turns to equestrians. But Gascou
(1976) 272ff. shows that S's approval is for good administration, not for backing
the equestrians. For Tacitus on reactions to Nero see *Hist.* 1.4.

17. *Omnes ordines*: Aug. is liberal to all (41.1) and loved by all (57.1);
Claudius makes adjustments to the privileges of all (22); Nero is genial to all
(10.2) but subsequently antagonises all by taxes (44.2); Galba earns the hatred
of all (16.1, here *universi ordines*). Tacitus never uses this expression.

down the sun awnings at midday, and by shutting the granaries and declaring famine (26). He vilified senators; but he also attacked the equestrian order for its dedication to the arena, and voiced the wish that the Roman people had a single neck (30.2). On a less dramatic scale, Galba too offended all ranks by refusing requests to all, high and low (14.3-16.1); and Domitian, whatever the reactions to his murder, was feared and hated by all (14.1).

The other side of the coin is that good emperors are universally loved. Titus was the darling of mankind (1). He never deprived a citizen of a penny (7.3), his benevolence shone on all who made requests and to the universal people (8.1-2); he never harmed a soul (9.1) and when he died the whole people mourned, and the senate loaded him with honours (11). But this is fairy-tale stuff, the ruler who never lived to show his true grit.[18] Vespasian is more down to earth. The only criticism levelled against him was of stinginess: yet his generosity benefited every type of man – the list descends hierarchically from consulars to lyre-players (17-19). Above all, the model is Augustus. If his intention was that nobody should regret his rule, it was also his achievement, and Suetonius undertakes to document it (57-60). Honorific decrees of the senate he passes over, for they might be suspect. But the *equites* spontaneously celebrated his birthday each year for two days; while 'all ranks' threw an annual tip into the pool of Curtius for his safety; and when his house burnt down there was a spontaneous whip-round among the tribes and individuals (57). Then there are formal indications of universal love: the title 'Father of his Country' was conferred by a spontaneous move of the people subsequently formalised in the senate (58). Individuals in their wills, the cities of Italy, the provinces and the kings of allied peoples all demonstrated their loyalty and affection (59-60). It is an impressive catalogue, not only of how people felt about Augustus but of the sort of universality of response which Suetonius looked for.

The search for consensus is neither peculiar to Suetonius nor indicative of a special political stance. It is the traditional Roman view, from which few would have dissented. Cicero in his essay *de Officiis* invoked the authority of Plato: it was vital that the statesman should 'care for the whole body of the republic, and not neglect one

18. On the panegyrical form of the *Titus*, see Luck (1964). Cizek (1977) 133ff., who attempts to establish S's judgments of emperors by a point-scoring system, is led to infer S's extreme admiration for Titus. This is too simple.

section in supporting the other'. Those who failed to obey this rule were responsible for unrest and discord. The very notion of party politics was abhorrent to Cicero. Similarly, the emperor by common consent existed for the benefit of all citizens, not to secure the advantage of any section or party.[19]

By what kind of conduct did Suetonius expect an emperor to keep 'all ranks' on his side in this way? One possible model for an ideal is that offered by Titus. But universal benevolence is not a practical ideal: no government can be nice to all its subjects all of the time. Titus is best set aside as a nine-day wonder. It is Augustus, for whom the biographer's admiration is unconcealed, who embodies the Suetonian ideal; and this is to accept, respect, support and reinforce the social hierarchy itself.

To our eyes Roman society may appear solid and static. The same families held office and prestige from generation to generation. Mobility is the exception, and the chances of social betterment for the peasant labourer seem slim indeed. Yet to their own perceptions it was rather different. Fortune, a cruel, whimsical and inexorable goddess prevailed. The footsteps of the fortunate were dogged by the threat of calamity, loss of property, public disgrace, sudden death. The Romans lacked the buffers against misfortune that Western civilisation enjoys: the advance of medical science that has thrust back the arbitrary incidence of death; insurance schemes that protect property from sudden loss; and above all the political stability that regularises and minimises the impact on the individual of a change of government. In the times of which Suetonius writes there were two periods of catastrophic civil war, one lasting for some twenty years. All but two of the Caesars (Gaius and Claudius) lived to experience one or other of these periods of disruption. Nor was there a great measure of stability for the political classes in the intervening periods. Loss of life, property or standing was a recurrent threat through most of the reigns of Tiberius, Gaius, Claudius, Nero and Domitian. Only Augustus and Vespasian are credited with achieving any real sense of security, and in both cases the peace was only relative, after civil disruption had reached a peak of intensity.

Against this background emperors could be seen as using their

19. So Cicero *de Officiis* 1.85. On Cicero's social outlook, see J. Béranger, 'Ordres et classes d'après Cicéron', in C. Nicolet (ed.), *Recherches sur les structures sociales dans l'Antiquité classique* (1970) 225ff.

powers in one of two directions: to counter the arbitrary effects of
fortune, or to intensify them. The most precious gift the good
emperor could offer was order. Vespasian regarded it as his first
priority to give the shaken state 'stability and adornment' (8.1). He
brought the armies under control, disciplined the provinces, cleaned
up the city and 'purged the highest ranks, depleted by slaughter and
contaminated by neglect' (9.2). On a larger scale Augustus did the
same. He purged the senate, overflowing with an 'unsightly and
unsettled rabble' and restored it to its old splendour (35.1). He
'thought it important to keep the people pure and untainted by any
infiltration of foreign and servile blood' and so was most sparing in
his awards of citizenship (40.3). He 'corrected the extreme confusion
and laxity of practice in watching spectacles and imposed order'
assigning senators the front row, banning embassies from the best
seats because freedmen had been caught among them, separating
soldiers from civilians, the bachelors from the married (44).
Throughout the metaphors indicate the author's strength of feeling:
social disorder is confusion, unsightly, pollution, contamination,
filth; order is purity and 'splendour'.

The autocrat had power to 'raise men of the basest birth to the
fullest honours' (*Jul.* 72). Julius' profession to 'reward foot-pads
and cut-throats if they helped him defend his dignity' was shocking
to a Roman. He was considered justly murdered because 'he took
and distributed honours as he liked', *ad libidinem*, raising newly
enfranchised citizens and semi-barbarous Gauls to the senate, setting
a freedman's son in command of three legions (76). Promotions like
this were as arbitrary as the operation of Fortuna, and did nothing
to promote the order and arrangement that Roman society aspired
to achieve. It was arbitrary for Tiberius to give high office to men
simply for lasting out a drinking bout (42.1), for Claudius to allow
the personal inclinations or venality of his freedmen to affect
the distribution of honours, advantages and punishment (29.1). It
showed outright contempt of the whole desire to achieve social order
to plan, as is incredibly alleged against Caligula, to appoint a horse
consul (55.3). Social promotion was not regarded as wrong in itself;
but it should be linked with merit. *Honor* should go to the *honesti*.
When Vespasian found the senatorial and equestrian ranks depleted
and contaminated, he turned to the towns of Italy and the provinces
and adlected the most respectable, *honestissimo quoque* (9.2). Augustus too had turned to the towns of Italy for a 'supply of respectable
men', acting on affidavits from their local communities in assigning

equestrian ranks in the army (46). It was not by favouritism towards a particular order that an emperor earned affection, but by scrupulously maintaining its dignity through promotion of the suitable, and demotion of the unsuitable.

A tyrannical emperor could wreak worse havoc on the social order. The upper classes stood in danger of their lives (under Claudius thirty-five senators and three hundred *equites* are stated to have been executed through the machinations of his freedmen (29.2), and his was a relatively blood-free reign). Their property was under constant threat from the avarice of emperors in fiscal straits. To these subjects I shall return. But it is worth glancing forward to one in particular among the groups of virtues and vices by which Suetonius judges his Caesars.[20]

The 'civility' which was one of Augustus' most prominent virtues is above all the behaviour of the emperor who respects the social hierarchy. Caligula, who lost patience with the role of citizen and princeps in the senate (49.1) showed no respect to men of social standing: he allowed ex-magistrates to run in attendance on his sedan, and let the rabble sit in the equestrian reserved seats (26). He regarded himself as a god, above interest in the traditional human order (22). Augustus on the contrary emphasised his mortality (52), treated the upper classes as his social peers and the senate with deference (53-5). The arrogance which allowed Julius to distribute honours to anyone he cared, reflected a contempt for social order. He thought the *respublica* was an empty name (77); in political terms it may have been so, but to Suetonius it also spelt the traditional social order.[21]

The ideal emperor for Suetonius, then, is by no means one who offers a challenge to the high standing of the senate or to the traditional social structure of the republic. Far from being the enemy of the senate, he must be the friend of all ranks, *omnes ordines*. But this does not involve a sort of indiscriminate egalitarianism. The emperor must act as protector and champion of the hierarchy itself: maintaining the respective levels of dignity of each of the ranks by 'purifying' their membership, and by himself showing each its due of respect, acting the fellow-citizen, not the remote god. 'Nothing

20. For cruelty, avarice and arrogance as the prime vices of emperors, see below, ch.7.

21. Contrast the way in which Augustus (28.2) and Vespasian (8.1) preserve the *respublica*, not of course in a constitutional sense. See further Alföldy (forthcoming).

more unequal than equality' was an old Roman dictum. Suetonius' passion for order and distinction of rank represents a characteristically Roman attitude. One cannot here establish a contrast in outlook between the equestrian and any senatorial historian.

Only in one area can a real contrast in outlook be drawn between Suetonius and Tacitus. Suetonius is not interested in politics. He underestimates the drive that motivated each of his Caesars to increase and secure his power, to master the wills of other men, even by deceit and violence. He has little conception of the preciousness of freedom; to him it is dignity which the good ruler protects and the bad takes away. In this there are several factors at work, and it is hard to know how much weight to give to each. Perhaps it is the outlook of an equestrian official, loyal and unpolitical. Perhaps it is a matter of genre, analytical biography not narrative history. Perhaps it is a sign of the times, of the reconciliation of the upper classes with autocracy which marks the period following the death of Domitian. But perhaps most important is the character of the author himself, a scholar, not a man of action, bookish, diffident, conscious and proud of his own standing, but without ambition for glamour or power.

Chapter Six

THE EMPEROR'S JOB

Roman narrative historians have disappointed modern scholars by their accounts of imperial administration. Too Rome-centred, obsessed with the activities of the senate, they have been felt to make too little of the basic task of the emperor in administering a vast empire. An imperial secretary like Suetonius, it might be hoped, should know better. But does he?[1]

Administration in the *Caesars*

To his credit, Suetonius understands that emperors were administrators. He asks himself 'What sort of a man did he prove in positions of power and in running the state in peace and war? (*Aug.* 61.1), or 'What was his record in the administration of the empire?' (*Dom.* 3.2). His rubric system offers a promising framework within which to answer these questions. Partly his assessment is in terms of virtues and vices. More will be said of these moral categories in the next chapter. But an equal weight is given to the analysis of imperial activities under morally neutral categories.[2]

With the grammarian's tidiness of mind, he breaks up the subject into its component parts. He subdivides geographically: there is the running of the City, of Italy, and of the provinces and dependent kingdoms. He subdivides socially: treatment of the senate, the

---

1. On the emperor's administrative role, see Millar, *Emperor passim*, developing at length his argument from 'Emperors at work', *JRS* 57 (1967) 9ff.

2. 'Administration of the empire' is a Suetonian category of thought, though it covers more than the chapters here under discussion. *Administrare* or *administratio* are used in rubrics at *Aug.* 46, *Cl.* 25.5, *Vit.* 12 and *Dom.* 3.2. Alternatively S speaks of 'ruling' the empire: thus *Aug.* 61.1, *qualis in . . .regenda . . .republica fuerit exposui.* Note also the use of expressions like 'setting the state in order': *Jul.* 40.1 *conversus hinc ad ordinandum reipublicae statum.*

equestrian order, the Roman citizen body, foreigners and slaves. He distinguishes areas of public life: religious affairs, military life and civilian life. Then within these divisions, there are further subdivisions. 'The City', for instance, covers several topics which are rarely absent from a life: building, games, distributions, corn-supply and utilities. Now, there is a fair amount of fluidity in his deployment of all these topics and subdivisions from life to life. He does not exactly stereotype. Yet the pattern is regular enough to allow us to say with some confidence that he has an underlying notion of what administering the empire ought to involve. His scheme would be equally applicable to the second dozen Caesars as to the first.[3]

Good administration earns his warm approval. The long account of Augustus' reorganisation of the state (28-50), though set out in neutral language, plays at least as large a part in creating a good impression as the description of his virtues (51-6). In the cases of both Caligula and Nero he draws a sharp line between the acceptable and unacceptable aspects of their reigns. 'So far I have described a *princeps* of sorts, but the rest is about a monster' (*Cal.* 22.1). 'I have brought together the preceding items which are partly unobjectionable, and partly merit more than lukewarm praise to separate them from his outrages and vices which follow' (*Ner.* 19.3). In each case what precedes the break is a neutral analysis of activities; what follows is a loaded catalogue of vices. The implication is that a *princeps* has a busy job to get on with, and will perform numerous actions that cannot usefully be attributed to any particular 'virtue'. Simply to be active was something. Nero not only let correspondence build up unanswered at the height of the Vindex crisis, but even on the eve of his overthrow was more interested in a new type of water-organ than in military developments (40.4-41). Domitian's long hours of seclusion gave rise to the joke that he was busy killing flies with his pen (3.1). However, activity in itself is not necessarily beneficial. The good impression created by Claudius' activities is undermined by the revelation of corruption at his court (25.5). Galba's administration was venal, arbitrary and odious (14-15).

---

3. The relevant passages are as follows: *Jul.* 38-44, *Aug.* 28-50, *Tib.* 33-7, *Cal.* 15.4-21, *Cl.* 14-25, *Ner.* 11-19, *Galb.* 14.3-15, *Vesp.* 8-11, *Dom.* 4-8. These have never been subjected to a thorough analysis; for a start, see Steidle (1951) 112.

Does it follow that Suetonius gives a good and useful analysis of imperial administration? Before false hopes are raised, it should immediately be made plain that he neither offers nor attempts to offer a full and systematic analysis of imperial administration. He constantly frustrates us by using unexpected categories or handling them in a slightly unexpected way. In the examination of any reign, discussion might be expected of topics like foreign policy and handling of the military forces; finances; legislation and administration of justice; relations with the senate; use of the imperial administrative service; provincial government. Is this what Suetonius gives us?

At first sight, it does seem that these are among his categories. There are chapters on wars and troops, senate, provinces. The lively account of Claudius' jurisdiction (14-15) shows his concern with the administration of justice. Richly informative chapters on imperial shows and buildings illuminate an important part of the imperial budget. Yet this impression is misleading, and can only bring disappointment. He is not out to dissect the reign.

Take the senate. There is a long and valuable chapter on Augustus' handling of the senate (35-38.2), including, as we have seen, details of the new offices he established. But this is nothing approaching all he has to say on Augustus' relations with that body. For his encouragement of freedom of speech in the House, and the courtesy he paid to senators both in session and in social life, we must turn to the chapters on his virtue of civility (53-4). For his grants to senators in need, the section on liberality is relevant (41). Handling of political opponents appears under *clementia* (51), information on conspiracies by senators is found along with other conspiracies (19). As for the division of control over the provinces which laid the basis of the relationship of *princeps* to senate, this appears only in a muted form under consideration of provinces (47). In fact, in this and each other life, information on relations with the senate is scattered throughout. He has not taken a pigeon-hole marked 'senate' and thrown into it every conceivable senatorial item; far less has he used the material to analyse the emperor's relations with the senate as a whole. On the contrary, the senate is so important that it pervades the lives, casting light on numerous different questions.

The same objections apply to all the other topics the modern reader expects: they dissolve on inspection. Details of shows and building, together with distributions of money and corn to troops and urban populace, must indeed have represented one of the largest drains on the imperial exchequer. But Suetonius is simply not concerned to estimate the cost of these liberalities overall, nor to set them against the sources of revenue. Taxation is only considered in the case of those rulers held to be rapacious. Again, details of wars are indeed gathered together. But he does here little more than list the major extensions of conquest. Nero's handling of the Armenian question is not considered germane (18). Even among conquests, he only lists those in which the emperor had a personal hand. Agricola's British victories are absent from the scoresheet of Domitian's wars (6.1).

The gaps are so substantial that it cannot be a matter of either ignorance or carelessness. Suetonius glosses over major items which even the most superficial reading of the historians would draw attention to. Then we must recall the near complete silence on the question where his expertise might have been relied upon, the emergence and growth of an administrative service under the emperor's direct control. We are forced to the conclusion that our categories are not his. It will not help to blame his ineptitude. The challenge is to see the subject through his eyes and to discern what the focus of his interests really is.

The biographer's angle

Biography is not, after all, history. Suetonius' rubrics are intended to make a life less, not more, like history, and we have no right to demand of a series of lives that they present a systematic analysis of the principate. The author's focus is in the first place on the Caesar as an individual. One sign of the single-mindedness with which Suetonius pursues a biographical theme is in a point of style: that in sentence after sentence, quite without regard for stylistic variation, the grammatical subject is the Caesar who is subject of the life. It is a notable (and probably significant) exception when he records a list of measures taken 'under' Nero (16.2-17). It is not his normal practice to list everything that happened to occur in the reign, and lay it at the door of the emperor. In making an exception for Nero, he will not be trying to give him credit for the actions of others but to deprive him of credit for purportedly imperial actions that were not his own. Tradition assigned Nero's best actions to his advisers, Seneca and Burrus.[4]

Any action that bears the stamp of the Caesars' own touch especially attracts his attention. In war he knew that the emperor was supreme commander and acted indirectly through his legates, as did Augustus (20). But his main interest is in the 'expeditions' in which the emperor took part in person. He notes (with disappointment, one suspects) that Tiberius acted through his legates and 'undertook no expedition thereafter [after his accession]' (37.4). The one passage which does approach extended military narrative is the description of Caligula's German expedition: that bizarre episode which showed up an emperor in so odd and unimperial a light, instructing his troops to gather sea-shells on the shore (43-9). Next to expeditions, he values 'peregrinations', peaceful tours by the emperor of his provinces. He wrote, indeed, under an emperor with a quite exceptional taste for peregrination. Augustus might be used as a sort of a precedent. 'Nor is there, to my knowledge, any province other than Africa and Sardinia, which he did not visit', and this he thinks more due to persistent bad weather than to lack of inclination (47).

The same tilt marks the picture of the administration of justice in the *Caesars*. His reports of the major legislation of the Caesars is thin and perfunctory (below). Laws after all, even when on imperial initiative, remained the product of public debate. But the personal jurisdiction of an emperor is another matter. He is not interested in the content of their decisions, vital though these were for the developing corpus of Roman law: this was the province of the jurists. But he does comment in detail on the style of their jurisdiction. He thinks highly of those who were energetic and conscientious in giving judgment, Julius (43.1), Augustus (33), Claudius (14) and Domitian (8.1). He comments on their severity (like Julius) or lenience (outstanding in Augustus). In a sense

4. The significance of the passive voice at *Ner.* 16-17 was pointed out by Steidle (1951) 89 and taken up by Croisille (1969/70) 82. Its validity is denied by Bradley in his commentary on the passage (102) on the grounds that this may simply be stylistic variation. Such variation is unparalleled: for the constant use of the perfect active, see Dihle (1954) 50. Blame for administrative abuses is assigned explicitly to subordinates at *Cl.* 25.5 and *Galb.* 14.2. Here S does not directly assign credit to Seneca and Burrus as do the historians (Tac. *Ann.* 13.2, Dio 61.4) but his use of the passive admits that interpretation. On S's concentration on the subject of each life to the exclusion of other personalities, cf. Townend (1967) 84.

Claudius hit the ideal, in following the principle of equity, both fiercer and more pliable than the laws as circumstances demanded; but he spoilt his jurisdiction by the extraordinary inconsistency and frivolity that made him the laughing-stock of the bar. This is illustrated by an unusually rich and illuminating series of anecdotes (15). It is a good point for Nero that there is anything to say about his jurisdiction at all, even if he is not credited with diligence (15.1). He is responsible for two interesting changes in style of judgment: he considered cases point by point, and took the verdicts of his assessors privately in writing. Suetonius does not comment, but the first was probably regarded as laudable, the second not.

By Suetonius' day the emperor's heavy burden of jurisdiction was a familiar facet of his existence. It is interesting to note that a collection of cases heard by Hadrian is preserved under the title *Sentences of the Divine Hadrian*. It is used by the grammarian Dositheus as a convenient example for schoolchildren of a piece of Latin with a parallel text in Greek. This was hardly its original purpose; but neither was it a specialist text for lawyers. With its odd choice of cases, it was presumably meant simply as a specimen to show the emperor at work in judgment. Suetonius' chapters on earlier Caesars in session cater for a similar interest.[5]

The emperor and the games is a third area where the biographer is alert for signs of personal involvement. Emperors frequently attended their games in person, and consequently such shows constituted the most important regular occasion on which the ruler manifested himself to the Roman people as a whole. Suetonius notes that Augustus sometimes watched in private, or excused himself attendance, but that when he did appear publicly, he avoided the tactless error of Julius, who continued to deal with business during the performance. Augustus actually enjoyed the sport (45.1-2). So did Titus, who made known his preference for Thracian light-armed gladiators and joined in the fan-rivalry with the people (8.2). Claudius similarly joined the audience in chanting out the count of gold pieces with which victors were rewarded, and cracked clumsy jokes (21.5). Suetonius has no sympathy for the distant coldness of Tiberius, whose rarity of appearance at games he attributes to unwillingness to grant popular requests (47), or of Domitian, whose

5. The *Sentences of Hadrian* is to be found in the collection *Corpus Glossariorum Latinorum*, ed. Goetz, vol.3, 31-7. On imperial jurisdiction, Millar, *Emperor* 528ff.

refusal of a popular request by a peremptory demand for silence ranks as high arrogance (13.1).

But it was also possible to take imperial participation and partisanship too far, and it is significant when Suetonius categorises such behaviour under other rubrics than the 'administrative' one of games-giving. Caligula's shows may have been laudable, but his behaviour at them was not. He took everything to excess, including a passion for the popular mime Mnester, whom he kissed in public (55). He was more carried away at the races: he lost his temper with the crowd for backing the wrong team and wished they had a single neck (30.2). His racing-team was the Greens: he dined in their stables, squandered money on the driver Eutychus, and lavished signs of favour on the horse Incitatus ('Galloper'). At gladiatorial games he backed the Thracians against the heavy-armed *murmillones*, and forced the latter to lighten their armour (55). Domitian, unlike Caligula and Titus, backed the *murmillones*: it was going too far, however, to throw a spectator to the dogs for criticising his favouritism (10.1). Claudius, again, carried enthusiasm for games too far: it did not become an emperor to relish slaughter and the expressions on the faces of the dying (34).[6]

Only a biographer could report simply as an item of interest that once when Augustus was watching celebrations of a newly-built theatre, his throne broke and he fell on his back (43.5). Suetonius' criterion is never historical significance. His purpose is not even to analyse the main tendencies of the reign with a view to discovering the impact of the Caesar's personality. Perhaps we may give him credit, as imperial secretary, for seeing through the naive view that the public events of a reign are simply a product of the will or imagined policies of the autocrat. Instead he looks for little indications of the individuality of his human subjects carried like flotsam on the great tide of public history.

But there are limitations to how much biography will explain. The genre did not offer ready-made categories for the analysis of a Caesar's life: and though there is much interest in the personal and private aspects of a Caesar, we should not underestimate the attention devoted to public aspects. Biography could be written in many ways. To explain Suetonius' way, it is necessary to consider the antiquarian tradition.

6. On *spectacula* in S, cf. now Bradley (1981).

The antiquarian's view

The problem is one of distribution of emphasis. Why are certain topics illustrated with a profusion of detail, others skimmed over so briefly? As an example we may take his chapters on shows (*spectacula*) given by Caesars. The prominence of this topic in his accounts of administration emerges from the sheer amount of space afforded to it, especially in the lives of Augustus, Caligula, Claudius, Nero and the Flavians. We should also note the precision and density of information which marks the author at his best. Contrast his brief summary of Augustus' legislative programme, vague on all points except his reaction to a demonstration in the theatre (34) with the wealth of detail on his games-giving, down to his punishments for unruly actors, a flogging for the tragedian Stephanio and the mime Hylas, and expulsion from Italy for the cheeky Pylades, who pointed at a hissing spectator (45.4).

The problem is whether Suetonius' distribution of detail reflects his view of the importance of a topic. Did he really believe that more light was cast on Augustus as a ruler by his handling of petty theatrical incidents than by his fundamental recasting of public law? Again, does he regard the precise varieties of performers at Domitian's new quinquennial games (4.4) as more significant than the Rhine and Danube campaigns so curtly summarised (6.1)? One passage could be invoked to support the idea that he did so. A generation later, the orator Fronto was writing the preface to a laudatory history of the Parthian campaigns of his imperial pupil, Lucius Verus. Here in the course of a comparison of Lucius with Trajan, he comes up against a charge that both sent for actors from Rome to amuse their troops on the front. Fronto undertakes a defence of the imperial use of *spectacula* arguing that it is justified by high state reason. The arts of peace are as important, if not more so, than the arts of war; the Roman people is held loyal by the corn-dole and games above all. Government is judged on entertainments as much as serious matters; and whereas the dole reaches a limited public, games reach the whole people. Moreover, games are religious festivals, and such serve to placate the gods.[7]

Certainly this passage rebuts the critics who held that an emperor should have no truck with actors and such frippery, and it is likely enough that Suetonius shared Fronto's sentiments. But it will not

7. Fronto, *Principia Historiae* 2.17 (Loeb ed. vol. 2, 214f.). On the circumstances of composition of the passage, see Champlin, *Fronto and Antonine*

convince us that games mattered more than war, or that Suetonius believed so. The explanation must surely lie in his previous scholarly work *On games*. We have seen that he deliberately plays down the great 'historical' topics like war and legislation; on the other hand, he draws extensively on his scholarly expertise. In the chapters on games in the *Caesars* this expertise shines through again and again.

As a result, there is a profusion of detail that bears little relation to what we regard as imperial administration. If in the *Caesars* he names the artists Augustus disciplined, or the actors Apelles, Terpnus and Diodorus whom Vespasian rewarded (19.1), it was surely because his scholarly studies led him to discover them or to relish such information. An ancient commentary on Horace cites Suetonius to explain the names Bithus and Bacchius: they were a pair of gladiators famous under Augustus who fell simultaneously at each other's swords. Similarly, throughout, his chapters on games show a strong antiquarian warp.[8]

Though the monograph *On games* does not survive, a very fair idea of its scope can be formed from the essay on the same subject by Tertullian. The Christian apologist laid the antiquarian under contribution for the purposes of his attack on pagan rituals. He reports that Suetonius had enumerated which festivals were established by which kings on which days to which gods. He draws on his distinction of the different types of spectacle: circus, theatrical, athletic, gladiatorial. He follows the division of the various aspects of a festival which ought to be considered: origins, titles, apparatus (i.e. ceremonial), place, and type of performance. All these sorts of topic shine through in the *Caesars*. Nero 'was the first of all Romans to institute a quinquennial competition in Greek fashion with three parts, musical, athletic and equestrian, which he called the Neronia' (12.3). Here, and equally in the similar item on Domitian (4.4), the antiquarian's concern for institution and typology is manifest.

Rome 112f. The same theme is employed to devastating effect in a famous passage by S's contemporary Juvenal: the people now only cares for two things, *panem et circenses* (*Sat.* 10.78-81). Della Corte (1967) 100ff. neatly contrasts the Fronto passage with Pliny *Ep.* 9.6 expressing Pliny's contempt for the circuses; but the inferences he draws of political differences of opinion between S and Pliny are illegitimate. Pliny was well aware of the importance of games: cf. *Pan.* 33.

8. For Bithus and Bacchius, see Reifferscheid fr. 196 = Roth 280. For recent interest in the phenomenon of imperial shows, see A. Cameron, *Circus Factions* (1976) 157ff., P. Veyne, *Le pain et le cirque* (1976) 701ff. On the republican period, C. Nicolet, *The World of the Citizen in Republican Rome* 361ff.

He observes – and documents at length – not only that Claudius' games were unusually lavish, but that as well as the usual ones at the usual venues, there were specially designed ones (*commenticia*) and revivals of old-fashioned ones, and ones held where nobody previously had held them.   Only an expert could be quite so interested in recherché details of ceremonial.[9]

Games are a convenient example because, thanks to Tertullian, we have a reasonable notion of what Suetonius' work in this area might have been like. Elsewhere we are not so well served, but the pattern is the same. Antiquarianism is the key, not only to his chapters on games, but to his whole picture of Caesars as administrators. This is the Ariadne's thread to which we must hold if his chapters are not to appear (as they have to many) an ill-assorted jumble of quirkishly selected trivia. The ancient historian was interested in great and memorable deeds, significant individual events, together with their causes and later consequences. The focus of the antiquarian's interest was something quite different. It was not the individual event but the general pattern: *mos*, the practices and customs that formed the texture of daily life. The antiquarian was interested in continuities and changes: the shoes people wore, the games they played, the gods they worshipped; and also the individual actions which originated or altered the customary patterns.[10]

As an antiquarian Suetonius had a prior interest in such patterns. But what is special about the *Caesars* is that he grasped the crucial role that emperors played in sustaining or destroying the traditional pattern of Roman life. He is not concerned with 'administration' by our understanding of the term, that is the government's choice of options in various spheres, military, political, social and economic and the like. He is concerned with the impact which each Caesar as an individual made on the customary pattern of public life.

His main areas of concern are neatly summarised in the rubric

9. Tertullian's relevant chapters are conveniently printed alongside parallel evidence by Reifferscheid (frr. 184-98). The latest edition of the *de Spectaculis* is by E. Castorina (1961), who rightly argues against positing S as the sole source for Tertullian (97-104).

10. It is unfortunate that we lack a modern guide to the Roman antiquarian tradition. For recent on Varro, see H. Dahlmann, 'Varroniana', in H. Temporini (ed.), *Aufstieg und Niedergang der römischen Welt* I vol.3 (1973) 3ff. Varro's work *de Vita populi Romani* would perhaps have cast much light on S: for its fragments, see the edition of B. Riposati (1939). The fragments of his fundamental *Antiquities* are not even properly collected. Briefly, see N. Horsfall in the *Cambridge History of Classical Literature. II Latin Lit.* (1982) 286ff.

with which he introduces the core of his account of Claudius' 'administration' (22). 'In religion, civil and military practice (*mos*) and also in the status of the orders at home and abroad, he made certain corrections, revived some obsolete practices and instituted some new ones'. It is of course very appropriate that he should speak in such terms of an emperor himself notorious for his antiquarian interests, but the rubric may be extended to cover most of the others too. Correction, revival and innovation are the trio of methods; practice (religious, civil and military) and status (descending through the social and geographical hierarchy) are the spheres of activity.[11]

Emperors and custom

Military practice is a sphere where, as we have seen, the distance of the *Caesars* from historiography is at its most marked. The author will give little more than the most summary list of campaigns of the reign; and even here the focus is on expeditions in which the emperor participated in person. So it comes about that no more than a passing allusion is made to the Armenian wars of Corbulo that bulk so large in Tacitus' narrative of the reign of Nero (39.1). But when he comes to the antiquarian question of military practice, especially of discipline, Suetonius shows a characteristic sign of interest – precision of detail. The fullest example is a long section on Augustus' 'changes, institutions and revivals of ancient practice in military affairs' (24-5). In fact this is not all he has to say on the topic: he restricts himself here to a whole list of examples of Augustus' strict discipline, and to a brief discussion of his practice in awarding decorations. More changes come later: the appointment of the new temple of Mars Ultor as the venue for senatorial meetings and ceremonial to do with war (29.2) and more important, the new disposition of troops round the empire, and the establishment of new terms of pay and service, and the new tax this necessitated (49.1-2). He also notices an interesting quasi-military institution, the establishment of the official postal system (49.3).

11. A particularly instructive parallel is Valerius Maximus' collection of anecdotes *On ancient institutions* (2.1-6). Here the topics in succession are (i) senate and equestrians (2.1-2); (ii) military institutions of the people (2.3); (iii) urban institutions: the games (2.4); (iv) civil (2.5.1-3) and religious (2.5.4-6) institutions. Valerius' work is highly derivative, and this may reflect the categories of Varro or another antiquarian. On Valerius and Varro, see R. Helm, s.v. Valerius Maximus *RE* VIII A (1955) 110f. The *Exempla* of Cornelius Nepos may have been another important model.

Later Caesars are not credited with so many changes to military practice, but there are sporadic notices. He attributed to Claudius great facility in distributing military decorations, and some minor changes, notably the reorganisation of the equestrian military career and the institution of 'supernumerary' titular rank (24.3-25.1). Vespasian restored discipline to the army after civil war, though the detail is thin and anecdotal (8.2-3). One item here shows the antiquarian's interest clearly: he tells how Vespasian responded to a request by the despatch runners to be paid boot-money by ordering them to go bootless, 'and so they have run from that day on'. Explanation of the origin of odd current practices is the antiquarian's forte, and there is a good scattering of such passages in the *Caesars*.[12] Finally, Domitian is credited with a whole list of innovations, the last of which are military: after Antonius' rebellion he forbade double legionary camps and the banking of large savings in camp; and he raised the pay (7.3).

We are thus presented with a strange and unexpected view of emperors as military commanders. We lose sight of the crises of disruption and invasion which caused anxiety at the moment in each reign and which were the making of narrative history. There is no picture of emperors facing problems, deploying and redeploying their legions, facing (as did Tiberius) the threat of mutiny, struggling to secure their loyalty and to neutralise the threat of over-successful commanders. Instead the army is seen as an institution stretching through the centuries, as a piece of machinery which the emperor is appointed to superintend, keeping it smoothly functioning by discipline, sometimes changing the odd cog, and in the special case of Augustus overhauling and restructuring radically. As it happens, it is a very Hadrianic point of view. Suetonius' master was one who devoted special effort to inspecting and reviewing his troops, and

12. Other examples of surviving institutions noted by S are: Augustus' signet ring, still in use (50); Claudius' benefits for corn-traders, still kept today (19). The expression 'he was the first to' often points to still current practices: Claudius made leave-of-absence for senators an imperial grant (23.2); precautions against testamentary forgery were designed under Nero (17); Vespasian started salaries for professors (18); Titus started the automatic confirmation of the benefits of previous rulers (8.1). S also notes curiosities that still survived: Augustus' place of rearing (6), and his palace furniture (73); Tiberius' golden dice (14.3); Livia's villa *ad Gallinas* (*Galb.* 1); Vespasian's father's honorific inscriptions (1.2); Titus' statues in the provinces (4.1); also Horace's villa (above, ch.3). Instances could be multiplied. See also della Corte (1967) 153ff. for an interesting discussion of S's antiquarianism.

imposing the cult of Disciplina. He was not, in contrast to his predecessor, bellicose. He preferred to keep his machine well-oiled than to put it into action.[13]

The account of religious matters follows the same antiquarian pattern. Suetonius notices 'corrections', that is to say attempts to keep the state religion in the traditional pattern, uncorrupted by foreign superstitions: Tiberius punished the Jews, Egyptians and astrologers (but relented when the latter threatened to go on strike) (36); Claudius disciplined the Jews and abolished the Druids, but encouraged the Eleusinian mysteries and the cult of Venus at Eryx in Sicily (24.4-5); Nero punished the Christians, that 'new and pernicious superstition' (16.2). The occasional abuse in state religion is also corrected: Augustus purged the Sibylline oracles and stopped boys running naked at the Lupercalia before puberty (31.3 & 4) and Domitian disciplined errant Vestals (8.4). Then there are revivals: by Augustus of a number of old rituals (31.4) and by Claudius of several quaint ceremonies (22), including that of striking treaties with kings by the sacrifice of a pig (25.5). Innovations in religion were not the usual Roman way; but Augustus did institute the offerings of spring and summer flowers to the crossroad gods, *Compitales* (31.4).

Again, the modern reader has a sense of surprise. The topics he might expect are simply missing. Nobody indeed would anticipate more from a pagan author on the rise of Christianity. Suetonius reflects the standard Roman view in seeing it as but one of many disruptive and distasteful alien superstitions, like Druidism. The really striking absentee is the cult of the emperors themselves. The explanation is a matter of categories. For Suetonius imperial encouragement of cult could only be a manifestation of the moral failing of *superbia*. The civil Augustus cannot have suffered this failing; and the whole complex and ambivalent question of his attitude to worship of himself is dismissed in the bland and oversimplified assertion that in the provinces he only accepted the common cult of Rome and himself, and that in the city he refused this honour most consistently (52).[14]

13. On Hadrian's treatment of the legions and the cult of Disciplina, see A. von Domaszewski, *Die Religion des römischen Heeres* (1895, repr. 1975) 44f. and R.W. Davies, *Latomus* 28 (1968) 75ff.

14. Contrast the criticism of Tacitus (*Ann.* 1.10) that Augustus devalued the cult of the gods by allowing cult of himself: also a one-sided point of view. On the cult of Augustus and his religious reforms, see J.H.W.G. Liebeschuetz, *Continuity and Change in Roman Religion* (1979) 55ff.

The religion Suetonius is concerned with is the traditional religion of Rome, described by Varro on monumental scale in the *Antiquities*. Whatever else cult of the living emperor was, it was no part of Roman religion, and it disappears from the antiquarian's purview. There is another example here of the way Suetonius drew on his scholarly background to fill out what could be culled from the standard histories. He describes in some detail the important reform of the calendar by Julius (40) and its re-establishment by Augustus (31.2). There can be no doubt that he drew here on his earlier essay *On the Roman Year*, as can be seen from the later works on the topic by the scholars Censorinus and Macrobius who drew heavily on him.[15]

When we turn to civil life, the detail becomes abundant, and one gets the impression that the scholar is more at home. But even here the coverage is uneven, and it is illuminating to chart the areas in which Suetonius' strengths lie. He is perhaps at his best in matters of civil law. Indeed, he has no pretensions to giving a proper account of the prolific legislation instigated by successive rulers: that could be left to the historians. So we have seen the inadequacies of his summary of Augustus' laws; and even when he attributes two laws to Vespasian (11) he is quite probably confusing Vespasian with Claudius. His interest is in more humdrum matters. He has a good deal to say about imperial control of the civil courts; of extensions of the legal year, and the placing of vacations; of increases and variations in the number of panels of judges, and supervision of their membership. It is not at all clear that this material was to be found in the history books. A sign of expertise is his use of technical terms which were not in common usage – he is the only source to mention the panel of judges called *ducenarii* (*Aug.* 32.3) because its members only needed the low capital qualification of 200,000 sesterces.[16]

Two factors are relevant to this interest in courts. The first is that the author himself may have served as a *iudex* and been honoured with appointment to the senior panel by Trajan, and

15. For the *de Anno Romanorum* see Reifferscheid frr.113-23, printing the parallel texts of Censorinus and Macrobius.

16. The details of S's legal interests are collected and discussed by Tomulescu (1977). He argues convincingly (135-9) that the legislation ascribed to Vespasian is misattributed. For imperial legislation see *Jul.* 42.2-3, *Aug.* 34, *Cl.* 23.1-2, *Ner.* 17, *Vesp.* 11, *Dom.* 7.1. For supervision of the courts, *Jul.* 41.2, *Aug.* 32.3, *Cal.* 16.2, *Cl.* 23, *Ner.* 17, *Galb.* 14.3.

knew court life at first hand. The second is antiquarian interest in legal matters. There is no direct evidence that Suetonius wrote a monograph on this topic, though it would have fitted well into his books *On Rome and its customs*. But lively interest in legal life is amply evidenced in the *Attic nights* of Aulus Gellius, who served, like Suetonius, as a *iudex*, and who scatters numerous discussions of legal topics among his medley of antiquarian and philological subjects. From Gellius we can see that legal antiquities were a favourite stamping ground of scholars like Varro, Verrius Flaccus and Fenestella, as well as of professional lawyers like Ateius Capito. Links between lawyers and scholars remained strong, and the Hadrianic jurist Pomponius, writing a little after Suetonius, is a notable example of a lawyer deeply infected with the methods and interests of the grammarian.[17]

Other areas of civil life are not so thoroughly dealt with, though here too he catches matters that often slipped through the historian's net. The control of public order is a topic on which he has a fair amount to say. He describes the suppression of brigandage in Italy and the control of rioting in Rome both by abolition of new guilds (*collegia*) and above all by the development of the Praetorian Guard. It is worth contrasting Suetonius' implied explanation for the concentration of the Guard in a single barracks (*Tib.* 37.1), with Tacitus' explanation, that Sejanus wanted to build himself a power base (*Ann.* 4.2). Suetonius is surely right to stress Tiberius' concern for public order in the troubled period after Augustus' death. One might reasonably guess that this question was discussed in the essay *On offices*. The games emerge as another potent source of disorder, especially because of the factious rioting of supporters' cliques. Again, it is the author *On games* who speaks with authority; the focus on public order in general seems to owe much to antiquarian expertise.[18]

17. The stylistic links between S and the *Enchiridion* of Pomponius were observed by Schulz, *History of Roman Legal Science* (1946) 169. On the antiquarian interests of Pomponius and other Antonine lawyers, see D. Nörr, 'Pomponius', *Aufstieg und Niedergang der römischen Welt* (ed. Temporini and Haase) II vol.15 (1976) 497ff.

18. On control of public order, *Jul.* 42.3, *Aug.* 32, *Tib.* 37.1. On rioting at the games, *Aug.* 45.4, *Tib.* 37.2, *Ner.* 16.2, *Dom.* 7.1. Theatre riots are thoroughly examined by T. Bollinger, *Theatralis Licentia* (1969) 24ff. On the functions and development of the praetorian guard, A. Passerini, *Le coorti pretorie* (1939) 49ff.

The final area of importance is the control of public morals. This involved not only the disciplining of individuals, especially in the upper orders, who behave improperly (sexually or financially), but more general regulations and innovations to stop 'immoral' behaviour. Some topics are recurrent: the control of cook-shops, with their unsavoury reputations; the limitation of prices and extravagant spending; the ban of certain luxury items from the market.[19] In addition to these 'sumptuary' matters there are sexual ones: Tiberius (35) and Domitian (8.3) both campaigned against prostitution by women of high standing. Domitian legislated against castration (7.1) and directed his campaign of moral rearmament against sodomy (8.3). Vespasian is said to have campaigned against both luxury and lust (11): historically that is plausible and it is frustrating that the two measures Suetonius attributes to him apparently belong to Claudius (above). Finally it is worth observing that some questions we would regard as economic are for Suetonius essentially moral. The control of prices is a sumptuary matter not an economic one; legislation against loans to minors (*Vesp.* 11) was aimed to stop luxury. It is perhaps not unreasonable to guess that when Suetonius reports Domitian's edict to control viticulture and encourage cereal production (7.2) he sees the measure as moral not as economic: wine was a luxury which seduced men from necessities like corn.

Most of the information on public morals will have come directly from the historians. However, the viewpoint from which Suetonius presents the information is characteristic of the scholar. Sumptuary and moral measures were the traditional business of the republican censors. Censors, with their vital responsibilities for *mores* – morals, customs, practices – were a topic of fascination for the antiquarian, as is borne out by the frequency with which Aulus Gellius discusses them in the *Attic nights.* Even if Suetonius could bring no expertise to bear in this area, as an antiquarian he saw clearly the role of emperors as successors to the censors of the republic.[20]

19. On the control of luxuries, *Jul.* 43.2, *Tib.* 34, *Ner.* 16.2.
20. There is no satisfactory study of the censorial activities of emperors. For the censors of the republic, cf. E. Schmähling, *Die Sittenaufsicht der Censoren* (1938), G. Pieri, *L'Histoire du Cens* (1968) 99ff. On the empire, M. Hammond, *The Antonine Monarchy* (1959) 128ff.; S. Gsell, *Essai sur Domitien* (1894) 75ff. on Domitian's censorship. Examples of Gellius' fascination for the censors are *Noctes Atticae* 1.6 (a quotation of a censorial speech), 4.12 (censorial punishments), 4.20 (more examples).

The ranks of society

A hierarchic division of Roman society – senate, *equites, populus* – or of the empire – Rome, Italy, provinces – is so easy and convenient that many historians still use it as a framework for discussion of imperial administration. Suetonius' usage is rather different. He does not, as we have seen, take the opportunity to discuss the relations of emperors with the senate. Nor does he discuss their relations with the plebs nor their provincial administration under these headings. The antiquarian's interests in these areas are limited and formal: in their functioning as institutions and in the maintenance of their status. The two hierarchies may be looked at in turn.

The formal functioning of the senate is an obvious enough topic. There is a full section on Augustus' changes to the way it was run: how he tightened up procedure at meetings, stopped the publication of the senatorial record, changed the functions of various magistrates, and as we have seen, created new 'offices' (35.3-37). Later emperors could not equal Augustus as a reformer, and only sporadic items of this sort are recorded.[21]

The formal functions of the equestrian order are rather less obvious. It supplied the courts with juries, and changes in that field are detailed with some care. It also supplied offices for the army, and Claudius' attempt to change the succession of ranks is noted (25.1). The order met periodically for review, and for the ceremony of the ride-past (*transvectio*) which Augustus revived. But the holding of procuratorial office and the great praefectures, which one might imagine was the most interesting and significant new function of equestrians under the empire, disappears behind a wall of silence, except for the single observation that Domitian shared the high offices between freedmen and equestrians (7.2).[22]

Possibly Suetonius did not regard imperial office as a formal function of the order to which he belonged. Certainly it was not a traditional one. But this is not the only odd omission. The formal

21. Other changes recorded are Caligula's ban on appeals to the emperor against judgments by magistrates (16.2), Claudius' changes of the functions of quaestors (24.2), Nero's appointment of unsuccessful candidates to legionary commands and his use of consuls for reading imperial letters to the senate (15.2).

22. On Claudius' (ineffective) reform of the equestrian career, see H. Devijver, 'Suétone, Claude 25 et les milices équestres', *Ancient Society* 1 (1970) 69ff. On the much debated grant of jurisdiction to procurators, P.A. Brunt, 'Procuratorial ·jurisdiction', *Latomus* 25 (1966) 460ff. Above, ch.4, for S's omissions.

functions of the *populus* were to meet and be counted for the census and the vote, and to collect corn. Suetonius gives a couple of valuable details about the functioning of the corn-dole under Julius (41.3) and Augustus (40.2): one could wish for more. But the remarkable omission here involves the elections. He knows that Augustus revived old-style elections (40.2) and that Gaius again made an attempt at revival (16.2). Yet he says nothing of the most significant change under Tiberius, when in AD 14 elections in practice passed from the people to the senate, and the people was deprived of its most important republican function. There was much too that could have been said of Augustus' changes to election procedure in the years leading up to AD 14, including the creation of privileged voting-centuries named after his dead grandsons. Suetonius holds his peace.[23]

One cannot avoid the feeling that Suetonius plays down what is not traditional. The same feeling is provoked by his description of the maintenance of the status and dignity of the orders. Augustus by his purges of the senate 'restored it from an ugly rabble to its old glory' (35.1). Vespasian found both senate and *equites* 'depleted and contaminated by the civil wars' and restored them 'by removing the most unworthy and by adlecting all the most respectable Italians and provincials' (9.2). Similarly the ideal is to keep the citizen body respectable, and this results in surprising angle on imperial grants of citizenship. Augustus is credited with a desire to keep the people 'pure and uncorrupted by any contamination from foreign and servile blood' and Suetonius therefore, in remarkable defiance of the historical facts, attributes to him extreme sparingness in grants of citizenship (40.3-4). Similarly Claudius, who figures in other sources as one who sold the citizenship for glass beads, appears in Suetonius as executing foreigners who laid false claim to citizenship (25.3).[24] The focus of his attention here is on what sort of distinctions the emperor awarded to what sort of people. Claudius undertook to appoint nobody to the senate who was not a third-generation Roman; but went back on his word by appointing a freedman's son, citing the censor Appius the Blind as precedent. Here the philologist comes

23. On the corn distributions, see G. Rickman, *The Corn Supply of Ancient Rome* (1980) 55ff. The elections under Augustus and his successors is an important but controversial subject: see A.H.M. Jones, *Studies in Roman Government and Law* (1968) 29ff., and more recently (with references to intervening discussion) A.J. Holladay, 'The election of magistrates in the early principate', *Latomus* 37 (1978) 874ff.

24. Augustus and Claudius are central in other accounts of the extension of citizenship under the early principate: A.N. Sherwin-White, *The Roman*

into his own, and convicts Claudius of error, since *libertinus* in the days of Appius indicated servile stock not servile birth (24.1).[25] The award of honorific rank and military decorations is another issue: Claudius gave consular decorations even to procurators (24.1), while Nero awarded triumphal decorations to men of equestrian rank and not even for military achievements (15.2). In both these cases concern for the proprieties of social order overrides any sense of *amour propre* in the equestrian official.

Rome, Italy and the provinces are treated in no less formal and hierarchical a fashion than the social orders. Suetonius is interested in what Caesars did to improve the functioning of Rome as a city and to enhance her dignity. He gives some details of the reorganisation of the city into districts with local officials (*vicomagistri*); of measures taken to protect the city from fire, flood, famine and rioting, though as has been seen, he says nothing of the important new offices that emerged with these measures. He also sees building works as lending Rome her proper dignity, very much as purges of the senate restored dignity to that order. Until Augustus, Rome's architectural adornment did not measure up to the 'majesty of an imperial power': he 'found it brick and left it marble' (28.3). By Vespasian the city was again 'deformed by burnt or ruinous buildings': the emperor gave a personal lead in the work of restoration by shouldering rubble (8.5).[26]

Rome enjoys relatively spacious treatment. But the material on Italy and the provinces is thin indeed. Any idea that the equestrian bureaucrat might regard 'provincial administration' as the emperor's real job, and more important than his treatment of the senate or the metropolis, must dissolve on a reading of these chapters. Suetonius' only interest in the provinces appears to be in changes in their status, between imperial and 'senatorial' government, or from client kingdoms to provinces, and in fluctuations in their dignity. Italy's

---

Citizenship[2] 225ff. Contrast S's account of Claudius with that of Dio 60.17.4-8, let alone the satire of Seneca *Apocolocynthosis* 3. That Augustus claimed to be sparing in granting citizenship is now confirmed by an inscription, J.M. Reynolds, *Aphrodisias and Rome* (1982) no. 13. S is therefore here, as elsewhere, taking the 'official' line.

25. S's quibble over the meaning of *libertinus* has been challenged and remains unclear: S. Treggiari, *Roman Freedmen during the late Republic* (1969) 52f.

26. The fullest chapters are on Augustus' improvements in Rome (30.1) and on Claudius' aid for victims of fire and improvements to the corn supply (18-19). Nero introduced new fire regulations (16.1). Julius had various plans for the enhancement of the city including a public library (44.1-3).

dignity was enhanced by the numerous colonies with which Augustus provided it. Just as Suetonius is conscious of the emperor's ability to grant marks of dignity to persons, so he shows them dignifying provincial cities with rights of Roman citizenship or the more restricted Latinity, or, like Vespasian, depriving them of their technically autonomous status (*libertas*) for ill-discipline.[27]

Yet it is the merest hint he gives of this vast subject. One might imagine that he is hampered by his Rome-centred historiographical sources. But he does not even make use of Augustus' own list in the *Res gestae* of provinces in which he planted colonies or of the geographical lists of *municipia* and colonies which were available to the elder Pliny. Suetonius' ideals are quite as Rome-centred as those of any senatorial historian: witness his assumption that the imperial city ought to enjoy corresponding architectural glory. He attributes no 'policies' of provincial government to Caesars (if indeed they had any worthy of the name). Nor does he reveal any conception of process, of a progressive Romanisation of the provinces by the spread of Roman institutions and status. Individual Caesars granted benefactions as they saw fit, and it may be that neither they nor their officials saw their actions as part of a process.[28]

One item shows him ignoring the potential political dimensions of a subject, on which his historical sources laid great stress. In mentioning how Augustus took over those provinces 'which were neither suitable nor safe for rule by annual magistrates' (47), he blandly accepts the official view of the settlement of 27 BC by which Augustus secured his power-base. The antiquarian represents this corner-stone of the principate as a piece of reorganisation demanded by administrative efficiency.[29]

27. On the division of senatorial and imperial provinces and client kingdoms, see *Aug.* 47-8 (only in most general terms), with changes under Claudius (25.3), Nero (18) and Vespasian (8.4): S's list is by no means complete. On Italy there is very little; see *Aug.* 46, *Tib.* 37.3, *Cl.* 25.2.

28. Grants (or cancellations) of privileges for cities are mentioned at *Aug.* 47, *Tib.* 37.3, *Cl.* 25.3, *Vesp.* 8.4. Millar, *Emperor* 394ff. shows how important such activity was. In stressing the personal nature of these grants and in playing down the idea of process implicit in (e.g.) Sherwin-White's *The Roman Citizenship*, Millar makes S's viewpoint more plausible.

29. Contrast with S the account of Dio 53.12, where what S offers as fact is represented as a pretext. If however Millar is right to argue that the distinction between senatorial and imperial provinces lay largely in the method of appointment of governors (*JRS* 56 (1966) 156ff.), there is some plausibility in the official view given by S. Exactly the same view is found in Strabo's account of the division: 17.840.

Traditionalism and principate

In place of the categories of analysis that might seem natural to a present-day historian, there has emerged a rather different set of Suetonius' own. Together they constitute a clear and self-consistent conception of the emperor's role. The main themes are perhaps most neatly summed up in his characterisation of the achievement of Vespasian, who 'made it his priority to give the battered and tottering state stability, and then to adorn it' (8.1). Order and dignity are the two great ideals: by his corrections, revivals and new institutions, and by his distribution of the marks of dignity, the emperor could promote order and dignity in the three spheres of life (military, civil, and religious), in the social orders (senate, *equites*, and people) and in the different geographical circles of Rome, Italy and the provinces.

The vision is of the ideal emperor as a sort of overseer of a vast and complex mechanism, which he must service, keep in efficient working order, improve, adapt and polish until he can hand it over gleaming and resplendent to his successor. This vision may at one level be characterised as an antiquarian one. The mechanism is a complex of institutions and practices, the object of the antiquarian's study. 'Institute', a favourite antiquarian's word, is recurrent. Not every new institution is necessarily to the good: what a Caesar institutes may be very revealing of his character.[30]

Suetonius does not approve of innovation for its own sake: Domitian is the only Caesar whose 'innovations' are listed as such (7), and given Roman hostility to words expressive of novelty, that must tell against him. 'Institution' is a much more respectable activity. Correction and discipline are necessary parts of the emperor's calling; but Suetonius does not like an emperor to relish severity, and the fact that the core of Tiberius' reign is presented as a series of disciplinary measures (33-7) creates a poor impression against him. Restoration of the traditional is what most warms the antiquarian's heart. Augustus and Vespasian are great restorers.

---

30. The use of the word *instituo* is extremely frequent in the *Caesars* (see Howard-Jackson Index s.v.); I gave only some notable examples of imperial 'institutions': *Jul.* 20.1, 41.3, 43.1; *Aug.* 24.1, 30.1, 31.4, 35.3; *Tib.* 42.2; *Cal.* 15.1, 22.3; *Cl.*22, 25.1; *Ner.* 16.2, 32.2; *Tit.* 8.1; *Dom.* 4.4, 13.2. *Constituo* is almost synonymous, though not so frequent: *Jul.* 40.2; *Aug.* 18.2, 49.2; *Tib.* 37.1; *Cl.* 18.2, 21.3; *Ner.* 10.1; *Vesp.* 18. For the exercise of ingenuity, see the use of *excogito* and *comminiscor*: *Aug.* 30.1, 37, 46; *Tib.* 43.1, 62.2; *Cal.* 19.1, 32.1; *Cl.* 41.3; *Ner.* 29, 34.2; *Vesp.* 23.3.

Augustus particularly is constantly bringing things back to their 'pristine' state: the calendar (31.2), the senate (35.1), the assemblies (40.2), and the wearing of togas (40.5). It was a pity that Claudius, who so nearly approaches the role of a true administrator, could not pick on more valuable customs to revive than quaint and obsolete ceremonies (22).

Suspicion of novelty, enthusiasm for the traditional, and the conception of the Roman state as a great agglomeration of practices to which each new generation makes its own contribution: these are by no means exclusively antiquarian viewpoints. On the contrary, they represent a fundamental Roman habit of mind, recognisable from Cicero's *Republic* or Livy's history. Roman antiquarianism was the product, not the origin, of such attitudes of mind. Emperors themselves publicly voiced similar attitudes. Claudius justified his extension of membership of the senate to Gauls in terms of traditional practices; and a series of imperial pronouncements from the second century AD reveals strong suspicion of any innovation. Suetonius' picture of the good emperor's role, and the assumptions implicit therein, were calculated to strike a sympathetic chord in the reader's heart.[31]

It is precisely here that the author's *Tendenz* may be suspected, and that the loyal official emerges from behind the mask of the antiquarian. We have noted in passing some remarkable cases of omission, *suppressio veri* and tendentious interpretation. Augustus' 'restoration of the republic' is muffled with all its hypocrisy. The division of provinces between autocrat and senate is simply a matter of administrative convenience. The emergence of the praetorian guard as an instrument of power is veiled behind a series of convenient measures against rioting. The muzzling of the power game by the abolition of the reality of elections is quietly forgotten – though specious restorations are mentioned. Above all, there is the nagging suspicion that silence about the growth of the equestrian imperial service is no accident. Augustus' creation of four mighty prefectures fades from view, while the practical administrative

31. For Roman traditionalism compare Claudius' Lyons speech (Tac. *Ann* 11.24; Smallwood, *Documents . . . of Gaius, Claudius and Nero* no.369) with its model in Livy, the speech of the tribune Canuleius (4.3-5) and Cicero's account of the growth of Rome, *de Republica* 2.2ff. The suspicious attitude of the Antonines towards innovations is observed by W. Williams, *JRS* 66 (1976) 77 and 82. For a recently discovered example, see the letter of Pius to Barca, published by J.M. Reynolds, *JRS* 68 (1978) 114, lines 82-3: 'You are not unaware that such innovations cause rivalries between the cities.'

purposes they served are highlighted. Claudius' grant of powers of jurisdiction to procurators, which provoked Tacitus to an indignant reference to the conflict of senate and *equites* in the republic, is converted into an instance of respect for the senate: Claudius actually asked permission for the step, *precario* (12.1). And the secretariat is taken for granted, glimpsed periodically in action, but never formally 'instituted'.

The overall effect is a very un-Tacitean picture of the principate as an institution. The theme of its innate hypocrisy and incompatibility with *libertas* disappears. We forget the unrepublican essence of the autocracy, its relentless aggrandisement of its own power. Naturally there is abuse and corruption, but it lies in the moral failings of the Caesars themselves. The root conception of the principate is optimistic, of a potential bulwark and support of the great Roman tradition.

The courtier understood well how to please his sovereign. Suetonius once presented Hadrian with an old statuette of Augustus that bore his childhood name of Thurinus (*Aug.* 7.1.). It was a nice gesture between antiquarian courtier and antiquarian emperor. Hadrian would also surely appreciate the underlying conceptions of the *Caesars*: like Augustus, he saw that the best way to present the principate was under a veil of traditionality.

Chapter Seven

VIRTUES AND VICES

Suetonius' sympathy goes to the emperor who performs his administrative functions properly; who accepts the hierarchy and traditions
of Roman society, strengthens and enhances them; who maintains
public order and morals; and who passes on to his successor the *res
publica* of his ancestors, purged of its faults and improved by new
institutions.

But this is only half the story. There is another, ethical dimension
to his portrayal of a Caesar in his public capacity. Was he virtuous
or vicious? It is only after minute examination of his record in
certain areas of moral behaviour that a Caesar is finally assessed.
Was he clement, or cruel? Liberal, or mean and grasping? Civil,
or arrogant? Continent, or self-indulgent, luxurious and lustful?
These are the polarities in terms of which emperor after emperor
is judged. Some – Augustus and Titus – rate highly on all counts.
Others – Caligula, Galba and Vitellius – are all black. But the
majority lie in between with mixed records, either virtuous in some
respects and vicious in others, or less virtuous at the start, only to
degenerate to vice.[1]

1. Suetonian virtues and vices are analysed by Mouchova (1968) 42-51, more
briefly by Steidle (1951) 112. Since the observation that his categories are
limited in number is important for the argument, the breakdown of the
individual lives is worth recording. Julius: 54, avarice; 73-5, clemency and
moderation; 76-9, arrogance. Augustus: 41-3, liberality; 51-6, clemency and
civility. Tiberius: 26-32, civility; 42-5, luxury and lust; 46-9, avarice; 50-62,
cruelty. Caligula: 22-35, pride and cruelty; 36-7, luxury, 38-42, rapacity. Nero:
10, initially liberal, clement and genial; 26-31, luxury and lust; 32, avarice:
33-8, cruelty. Galba: 12 and 14.2-15, cruelty and avarice. Vitellius: 10-11,
greed, cruelty, insolence. Vespasian: 12-15, civility and clemency; 16-19, liberal
or rapacious? Domitian: 9, initial clemency and liberality; 10-11, cruelty;
12.1-2, rapacity; 12.3-13, incivility. The structure of the life of Titus is
apparently chiastic: 6-7.1, suspected cruelty, incivility, luxury, rapacity; 7.2-9,
in fact proves modest (7.2), liberal (7.3-8.1), genial (8.2), clement (8.3-9). Otho
and Claudius are the only absentees (see below).

A biographer can reasonably be expected to interest himself in the cháracter and moral qualities of his subject. Plutarch, as moral philosopher, could regard the examination of the ethical make-up of the great men of the past as a central aim for his biographies. Historians too, because they were often concerned with the role of individuals in history, often assessed (and still do) the moral qualities of the characters involved. Cicero took it for granted that character sketches should be a standard component of a historical work. It was common to include an assessment of major historical figures in the form of an obituary notice; and even apart from the moral judgments which these entailed, the narrative frequently carried judgments, explicit or implicit, of the behaviour of the characters involved.[2]

But Suetonius goes way beyond anything met in ancient historians, or even in ancient biographers. The contrast with the historians is sharp, and, as has been seen, essential to his approach. Like a historian, he may note various moral qualities in passing. Thus Augustus is credited with gravity and constancy in stopping abuse of the dole (42.2) and with severity in punishing the amanuensis who betrayed the contents of a letter (67.2); and in a discussion of his intentions in making Tiberius his successor he is characterised as 'a most circumspect and prudent prince' (*Tib.* 21.3). There is nothing remarkable or abnormal about such off-the-cuff judgments. What is at issue is Suetonius' habit of devoting long chapters to the documentation of given qualities and defects. Actions, which for the historian formed the thread of the narrative, are dispersed under virtue and vice headings, reduced to the status of items of evidence.

Such an approach was normal no more for the biographer than the historian. Ancient, like modern, biographies often tried to hit off a man's character. Just as physical features could be evoked in a pen sketch, so could the special features of character that made a man distinctive and individual. Suetonius himself provides an example in his memorable sketch of the idiosyncrasies of Claudius (30-9). Yet two points set this portrait on its own. The first is that it is concerned with peculiar characteristics. Suetonius' virtue and

---

2. Cicero *de Oratore* 2.63 in a list of the conventional topics of historiography includes 'not only the record of men's actions, but the life and character of anyone particularly famous and renowned'. On such sketches in the historians, see Leo (1901) 234ff. The link between Plutarchan lives and the biographical element in Greek historians is stressed by A. Wardman, *Plutarch's Lives* (1974) 2ff.

vice chapters are not to be understood primarily as a means of distinguishing character. The restricted range of categories he employs makes that almost impossible. It is very rare to find a quality documented that is not also possessed (or by contrast lacked) by most other Caesars. Petty jealousy (*livor* and *malignitas*) was special in Caligula: he resented the fame of heroes of the past and of great authors, and even tripped down the steps in a fit of pique when a charioteer won louder applause than himself (35.3). Nero was unusual in his 'petulance': he roamed the streets at night with the young bloods and assaulted unsuspecting passers-by (26). Supreme benevolence is the mark of that fairy prince Titus: he fretted to have wasted the day in which he had done nobody a favour (8.1). Such rare cases apart, Suetonius' concern is different. What he does is to measure each Caesar against a set scale of criteria. Each virtue/vice category applies as it were a litmus test. A good emperor will show up positively on the tests of clemency, civility, liberality and continence, a tyrant negatively on the same tests.[3]

The second point is that the moral qualities Suetonius analyses are not of merely private significance. There is generally a perceptible division between the public and private aspects of the lives. Topics like personal appearance, literary interests and religious beliefs are treated apart from the reign. But while Claudius' eccentricities appear among such personal topics, the virtues and vices of other Caesars form a central part of the discussion of their reigns. They are tests of their qualities as emperors, not as private men.

Suetonius' approach, therefore, is not (as Leo believed) the product of any biographical tradition . He uses these categories because he wishes to assess each Caesar's performance in his public role. In fact the closest analogy to his method lies in the tradition of regal and imperial panegyric. The literary parentage of this aspect of the *Caesars* is a tradition going back to Xenophon's encomium of the Spartan king Agesilaus. But it is not so much the literary pedigree that matters. It is more interesting to explain how it was that Suetonius found this a natural way of viewing a Caesar. To the modern reader there is something strange and unsatisfactory about discussing a reign in terms of moral categories. Yet there should be no question that for Suetonius and his contemporaries his method was self-evident.

---

3. Plutarch's character sketches are discussed with reference to his portrayal of physical appearance by Wardman (1967). Wardman shows the contrast in portrayals of moral character in *Plutarch's Lives* 144ff. Further, above, ch.3.

Virtues in the language of public life

Virtues made a praiseworthy emperor, vices a tyrant. This assumption was daily reinforced in any Roman (including the emperor himself) by the norms of the language of public life. In the first place, it was the language of panegyric. Only one imperial panegyric survives from the early empire – Pliny's of Trajan – and this may lull us into supposing that such speeches were reserved for special emperors and special occasions. But the formal thanks to the emperor by the senior consul before the senate was a regular ritual. Pliny's performance survives because it was a masterpiece of its type, and because the rhetoricians of the fourth century copied it as a model. Consular thanks will only have been one of many occasions in the year when the senate listened to panegyric. Any notable occasion, successes at home and abroad, or even failures, triggered off a torrent of rhetoric. Pliny reports that Trajan put a ban on speeches of thanks, except those formally permitted: the problem was too much, not too little. Fronto, the leading orator of the next generation, was to deliver frequent panegyrics of Hadrian and Pius: a letter to him from Pius admits how predictable such occasions could become.[4]

The court was an even better venue for panegyric than the senate house, and as a courtier Suetonius must often have listened to the catalogue of the virtues of Trajan or Hadrian. Formal congratulations were sent from all over the empire on red-letter days – imperial birthdays, New Year's day, the anniversary of accession. Suetonius served a peripatetic emperor: on tour there was no more escape from panegyric than at Rome. Each arrival at a new city will have been marked by speechifying, and then each departure. Perhaps the most vivid indication of the part played by panegyric in the life of the empire is in the contemporary handbooks of rhetoric. Every young gentleman, whether Latin- or Greek-speaking, learnt the techniques of encomium. It was a necessary accomplishment for public life. He came away from the rhetoricians with a ready recipe for the Basilikos Logos, the imperial panegyric. Every now and

---

4. The practice of panegyric, especially in the late empire, is discussed by J. Straub, *Vom Herrscherideal in der Spätantike* (1939) 146ff., and by S. MacCormack, 'Latin prose panegyrics', in T.A. Dorey (ed.), *Empire and Aftermath* (1975) 154ff. For the practice of speeches of thanks behind Pliny's *Panegyric*, see the commentary of M. Durry (1938) 3ff. On Fronto's panegyrics, see Champlin, *Fronto and Antonine Rome* 83ff. The emperor Pius refers frankly to panegyric as a hackneyed theme: Fronto, *ad Ant. Pium* 2 (Loeb ed. vol. 1.126).

again we catch sight of these rituals in Suetonius. When an embassy from Troy offered Tiberius tardy condolences on the death of his son Drusus, Tiberius responded with condolences on their loss of Hector (52.2). When the consuls forgot to publish an edict on his birthday, Caligula stripped them of office (26.3). Claudius was exceptional in allowing the engagement of his daughter and birthdays of his family to pass 'in silence' – that is, one takes it, without speeches (12.1).[5]

On one point the rhetorical handbooks, from hellenistic times to the late empire, are agreed: that to praise a man adequately one must praise him for virtues. Good birth, fortune, wealth and the like offer material for congratulations; but only virtue merits true praise, 'and the rest is cheating'. A man should be praised for his achievements; but for laudatory purposes it was strongly recommended that they be arranged under virtues. Thus the recipe for the Basilikos Logos recommends that the emperor's military achievements must be placed first; but 'courage marks an emperor more than do other virtues ... If your encomium is of warlike actions you should speak of them under the head of courage'.[6]

On this point the schools of rhetoric were in close accord with the schools of philosophy. Since Plato, philosophers had repeatedly emphasised that virtue was the vital qualification for kingship. Monarchy could be justified because the ruler was the 'best man', the superior of his subjects, not in birth, wealth or military strength, but in moral excellence. A deluge of philosophical tracts *Peri Basileias*, forerunners of the mediaeval 'Mirrors of Princes', urged rulers to virtue. Kingship was a 'godlike thing', but only in virtue could the king imitate the gods. A brief essay survives by Musonius Rufus, a Roman *eques* under the Flavians who was a practising Stoic: the argument is that the emperor must be a philosopher, since the four virtues recommended by the philosophers were the essence of kingship.[7]

5. The most interesting and specific example of rhetorical instructions to the panegyrist are the two treatises ascribed to Menander; these are now edited and translated by D.A. Russell and N.G. Wilson, *Menander Rhetor* (1981).

6. On the encomiastic tradition see Russell and Wilson xviiiff.; also T. Payr, 'Enkomion', *Reallexikon für Antike und Christentum* 5, 332ff. The insistence on disposition under virtues goes back to Anaximenes *Rhetorica ad Alexandrum* 35 (dating from the fourth century BC).

7. Hellenistic kingship literature is a wide but elusive theme. P. Hadot, 'Fürstenspiegel', *Reallexikon für Ant. und Christ.* 8 (1972) 555ff. offers the

Practice reflected the recommendations of rhetoricians and philosophers. A formal panegyric like Pliny's on Trajan is a *tour de force* in demonstrating imperial virtue: twenty separate virtues are here mentioned within three introductory chapters alone, and the rest of the speech repeats them and at least fifteen more as a leitmotif. But there were other contexts where imperial virtues could be exalted on a less massive scale. The erection of honorific inscriptions and dedications to commemorate regal benefits had been a widespread custom since the hellenistic kingdoms. Imperial inscriptions strain to represent the favours which they celebrate in terms of the virtues of the emperor: his liberality, providence, indulgence, munificence. The most memorable of such dedications was offered by the senate to Augustus in return for his 'restoration of the republic': a golden shield awarded in the best hellenistic regal tradition, 'for virtue, clemency, justice, and piety to the gods and his country'. Caligula, Suetonius reports, was awarded another such shield, to be escorted ritually in an annual procession to the accompaniment of hymns of praise of his virtues sung by a choir of noble boys and girls (16.4).

By the second century, the emperor's virtues had become a cliché. Trajan's new title, *Optimus Princeps*, most excellent prince, sums it up. This title was officially conveyed by the senate. But it was perfectly normal in recording the ruler's name to add complimentary epithets *ad lib*. 'Most just prince', 'most provident', 'most pious', 'most indulgent', 'most brave', 'most liberal' and the like are regularly tacked on to the end of the formal titulature of the reigning emperor. From the mid second century such epithets became so clichéd that refuge was sought in blanket superlatives: 'most outstanding in all virtues', 'full of all virtues', 'excelling all previous princes in virtue'.

It is hard here to distinguish what is the product of competitive flattery and what is deliberately engineered by propaganda. Evidently emperors wanted to have virtues attributed to them – the

---

most convenient survey of the literature. The most thorough discussion of the ancient texts is the unpublished thesis of Oswyn Murray, *Peri Basileias: Studies in the Justification of Monarchic Power in the Hellenistic World* (Oxford D. Phil, 1970). The standard English treatment by E.R. Goodenough, 'The political philosophy of hellenistic kingship', *Yale Class. Studies* 1 (1928) 55ff. takes the fragmentary 'neo-Pythagorean' texts perhaps more seriously than they deserve. See also F. Dvornik, *Early Christian and Byzantine Political Philosophy; Origins and Background* (1966) 1, 241ff. (to be treated with caution). Musonius' essay *On the Need of Kings to Philosophise* is preserved in Stobaeus *Anthology* 4.7.67, 279f. Hense.

alternative was to be supposed vicious. How successfully they could manipulate their subjects by use of court poets or official documents and coins is not clear. But at least these official documents, and particularly coins, show that virtue-language was a two-sided game. The subjects claimed that their rulers ought to be virtuous, and demonstrated their loyalty by praise of virtues; while the emperors proclaimed their own possession of virtues, with the double implication that they were doing their duty and deserved loyalty and affection. On the coinage this was accomplished by representing virtues as goddesses on the reverses, so that one side bore the head of Augustus, and the other the image of LIBERALITAS AUGUSTI or whatever. This practice started under Tiberius, though it did not achieve momentum before the civil wars of AD 68-69, when the rival sides used the coinage to press their claims. It reaches its apogee under Suetonius' emperor, Hadrian: he is the first to mint a series of virtues, just as he mints a series of provinces, to illustrate how many virtues he possesses: Justice, Clemency, Indulgence, Patience, Liberality and Tranquillity mark this Augustus.[8]

This then is the background to the Suetonian assumption that virtues make the good emperor and vices the bad. It was a doctrine promulgated by philosophers, instilled by rhetorical education, turned into routine by the lip-service of panegyrists and beneficiaries, and exploited by the emperors themselves. Even had the biographer himself rejected the doctrine (he clearly did not), the fact that people in general did judge their rulers in terms of virtue and vice was itself a justification for analysing which virtues and vices each Caesar possessed, or was believed to possess. It is appropriate enough that the closest analogy to Suetonius' method of documenting individual virtues in turn by adducing a series of instances is the method prescribed by the rhetoricians for encomium. If Suetonius gives as much – or more – space to vices than to virtues, we may recall that the handbooks recommend exactly the same approach for invective,

8. Virtue-language on inscriptions and coins is the subject of the paper by Martin Charlesworth, 'The virtues of a Roman emperor: propaganda and the creation of belief', *Proceedings of the British Academy* 23 (1937) 105ff. I have argued for modification of his views, particularly about the Golden Shield, in 'The Emperor and his virtues', *Historia* 30 (1981) 298ff. on which the present account depends. On complimentary epithets, see R. Frei-Stolba, 'Inoffizielle Kaisertitulaturen im 1. und 2. Jahrhundert n.Chr.', *Museum Helveticum* 26 (1969) 18ff. I have stressed the role of the civil wars in stimulating 'virtue' propaganda on coinage in 'Galba's *Aequitas'*, *Numismatic Chronicle* 141 (1981) 20ff. See also Bradley (1976) on virtues on S and on the coinage.

with the substitution of vice for virtue; and that in practice the panegyrist, like Pliny, set off the virtues of the reigning emperor by contrasting them with the vices of his predecessors.[9]

The function of virtues

In that he documents both virtues and vices with characteristic scholarly impartiality, Suetonius differs from both panegyrist and writer of invective. But one point he does hold in common with them is that the function of virtues is to generate popularity, of vices to induce hatred. For all but two of the Caesars, he gives an estimate of the degree of popularity they enjoyed, whether this manifested itself in their lifetime or immediately after their death. There is a close correlation in all cases between the virtues or vices documented and the degree of popularity reported. Augustus was adored by all ranks and conditions of men (57-60); that follows naturally after the record of his liberality to all ranks (41) and of the innumerable proofs of clemency and civility (51-6). Tiberius lived feared and fearing (63-7); that is the result of the vices which broke out after being so long ill-disguised (42-62). Galba made himself unpopular by the report of his vices even before he arrived (12-13) and rapidly earned universal hatred (16). Titus, the darling of mankind (1), only won his popularity after the vices he was supposed to possess turned out false fears, and the greatest virtues emerged (7.1). If the reactions after Domitian's death were mixed (23.1), that is appropriate enough in a ruler whose virtues and vices were for long equally balanced (3.2).

Virtues and vices are not the sole factor behind such reactions. The whole record of the reign counts. But that they are the most sensitive test is confirmed by the two exceptions. Claudius and Otho are the only Caesars for whom Suetonius vouchsafes no estimate of

---

9. On the formal debt of S to encomium, and particularly Xenophon's *Agesilaus*, see above, ch.3. It is instructive to compare S's statement of purpose in adopting his analytic method of treatment, 'so that the aspects of the life may be demonstrated and assessed more easily' (*Aug*.9) with Aristotle's justification for organising encomium by topic and not chronologically: when the argument is concerned not merely to report an action but to demonstrate something about it, its truth, quality or quantity, chronological narrative is inappropriate because hard to follow; it is simpler and more comprehensible to state which actions demonstrate which qualities (*Rhetoric* 3.16.1416B16ff., paraphrased).

popularity, for good or ill. They are also the only ones for whose reigns he documents neither virtues nor vices. Claudius' vices are treated as part of the characterisation of his personality. The emphasis is on what an odd sort of man he was, not on the unpopularity of his rule. Otho is the one Caesar of whose reign Suetonius says nothing at all. He passes straight from his rise to power to his fall. For once, there are no rubrics. Neither is there assessment of popularity.

To this degree, then, Suetonius' Caesars are what Max Weber termed 'charismatic' rulers. That is to say, they depend for their legitimation on the personal qualities that set them apart from other men, and not simply on 'bureaucratic' criteria, the effectiveness with which they performed their functions.[10] It is an integral part of this outlook that qualities or defects should be regarded as an essential part of the ruler's nature, not mere accidents of the circumstances of the reign. It was not enough for an emperor to be clement because he never had the opportunity to shed blood. Mildness ought to be in his physiological make-up. Seneca stated quite categorically that no emperor could be clement unless he was so by nature. Yet there was an old debate, already raised by Polybius in his account of Philip V of Macedon, and repeatedly aired in Plutarch's *Lives*, occasioned by the variation in the actual performances of rulers. Many who started their reigns mild degenerated later to cruelty. Did power actually warp an autocratic character? Did it reveal hidden weaknesses? Or did circumstances and the advisers he followed at a given moment dictate uncharacteristic behaviour? Greek moral philosophers were loth to concede that human nature might be susceptible to change. *Physis* was determined by birth and remained a constant. At the same time, the charismatic function of royal virtues created a strong disinclination to attribute a ruler's behaviour to anything but nature. If his 'virtues' won him the adoration and the support of his subjects, it would be very unfortunate to have to admit that those virtues were adventitious and not genuine.[11]

10. For Weber's views on bureaucracy and charisma, see *Economy and Society*, ed. G. Roth and C. Wittich (1968) 3, 1111ff. For a recent discussion of the principate along Weberian lines see P. Veyne, *Le pain et le cirque* (1976) 560ff. The term charisma is also invoked by H. Kloft, *Liberalitas Principis* (1970) 181; see also the same author's introduction to the volume *Ideologie und Herrschaft in der Antike* (Wege der Forschung 528, 1979) 14ff.

11. Seneca *de Clementia* 1.1.6 for the statement that clemency must be natural. For Polybius on Philip, see esp. *Histories* 7.11ff., but also 9.22.7-26.11

If as a biographer Suetonius was likely to take an interest in human nature, his inclination coincided with the contemporary concerns of men living under rulers who sought support by advertisement of their virtues. He is anxious to demonstrate that virtues or vices were 'natural' inborn characteristics. Tiberius' cruelty was early detected by his teacher of rhetoric, Theodorus of Gadara, who called him 'mud mixed with blood' (57.1).[12] Domitian was sadly lacking in civil disposition from his youth up: when his father's mistress Caenis offered him the usual kiss on return from abroad, he coldly preferred his hand (12.3).

Yet everyone knew that autocrats might be forced to act out of character. Suetonius is aware of the difficulty and airs the question occasionally. The classic dilemma was Vespasian's handling of finances. Some said he was naturally stingy: what better evidence than that of the old retainer who, refused his freedom, muttered, 'the old fox has changed his fur, not his ways'. Yet there was no doubt that civil wars had imposed an intolerable strain on the treasury (16.3). Suetonius gives Vespasian the benefit of the doubt on the grounds of his liberal support of the arts (17-19.1), but he does not deny that the emperor kept his bad reputation on this score (19.2). His verdict on Domitian also gives weight to both nature and circumstances. Initially he gave several signs of natural inclination towards clemency and liberality (9). If he later proved cruel and extortionate, 'as far as one can make out, financial straits made him rapacious, fear made him cruel over and above his natural inclination'.[13]

The choice of virtues

The prominence Suetonius gives to moral categories makes sense not simply in terms of literary conventions but also, and more

---

on Hannibal. The prime discussions of character change in Plutarch are *Aratus* 51.3 (on Philip), *Sulla* 30.4., *Sertorius* 10 and 25.

12. It may be noted that the anecdote about Tiberius and Theodorus is referred elsewhere to another emperor and another teacher: *Suda* s.v. Alexander Aegeus tells it of Alexander and Nero.

13. For other passages where S attributes behaviour to character (*natura* or *ingenium*), see below n.26. The meaning of *super naturam* at *Dom.* 3.2 is disputed: see Steidle (1951) 95. The normal sense would be 'in addition to his nature', but some have taken it as 'against his nature' in order to reconcile the passage with *Dom.* 9. I render 'over and above' in order to preserve possible ambiguity.

illuminatingly, in terms of the mental attitudes of contemporaries living under an autocracy which relied heavily on the language of virtue for its legitimation. For the same reason it ought to be enlightening to ask which the imperial qualities are to which Suetonius gives prominence. No earlier author known to us applied this method to the Caesars and was thereby compelled to formulate the moral criteria which distinguished a good emperor from a bad one. Nevertheless, Suetonius is not out to write a 'Mirror of Princes' and convince his readers of what the ideal *ought* to be. His method is based upon assumptions. He can tacitly take for granted which the vital virtues are because he expects his readers to be of one mind with himself.

But the matter is not so simple as it might seem. The range of conceivable imperial virtues was enormous. On the most conservative estimate there were at least fifty virtues celebrated by panegyrists or honorific inscriptions. In truth the scope was limitless, for any imaginable human quality might be attributed to the emperor, and it was the natural impulse of the panegyrist to do so.[14] Suetonius, by contrast, is highly selective. As we have seen, his virtue-and-vice chapters are reducible to four recurrent areas: clemency, civility, liberality and the restraint of luxury and lust. It is not just a matter of terminology (in fact the names he gives to virtues and vices differ slightly). More impressive is the consistency with which he documents the same patterns of behaviour in emperor after emperor. Individual records vary, between mildness and bestial cruelty, between open-handedness and unscrupulous extortion. But the spheres of activity within which performances vary themselves remain constant. Was there a widely acknowledged set of essential imperial virtues, or is this a set of his own?

There was indeed one school of thought which held that there was a given set of imperial virtues, and precisely four in number. This was the doctrine the rhetoricians taught their pupils: 'Always divide the actions of those you are going to praise into the virtues. There are four virtues: courage, justice, temperance and wisdom.' The same prescription is found in handbook after handbook. It derives ultimately from Plato who identified these four as the sum of all virtues. The Stoics accepted the Platonic canon, and argued that all other virtues were sub-categories of the four. The rhetoricians

14. Various virtues attributed to various emperors are listed by L. Wickert, 'Princeps' *RE* XXII (1954) 2231ff.

took their cue from the philosophers, and by the imperial period the primacy of the four virtues was taken for granted. It is likely enough that the philosophical tracts on kingship emphasised the need for these virtues; they are certainly the ones Musonius demanded in an emperor. They are in practice acclaimed in emperors by a series of orators: by Aelius Aristides a generation later than Suetonius, and frequently in the numerous panegyrics surviving from the fourth century AD.[15]

But Plato's canon is not Suetonius'. Temperance (*sōphrosynē*) they have in common, but in other respects they part widely. Courage, which the rhetoricians claimed was the appropriate heading for military achievements, hardly enters Suetonius' account: he is more interested in discipline, military institutions and the like. Wisdom could cover the ability 'to legislate well and dispose and arrange the affairs of subjects to advantage', but Suetonius, who thought Augustus very prudent and recorded Claudius' reputation for stupidity, never uses wisdom as a heading. Justice was an obvious heading for an author so interested in imperial jurisdiction; yet the only people to whom he attributes this quality are provincial governors, Augustus' father (3.2), Galba in Spain before his proclamation (7.1), and the governors under Domitian whose strict supervision ensured that they were never more restrained or just (8.2).[16]

It is not wholly surprising that Suetonius parts company with Greek rhetoricians and philosophers. Though the Romans paid lip-service to the Platonic canon, they had strong ideas of their own about *virtus*, and were little inclined to acknowledge that a Roman might learn much from a Greek about morality. Their own ancestors

15. For a sketch of the history of the Platonic canon, H. North, 'Canons and hierarchies of the cardinal virtues in Greek and Latin literature', in L. Wallach (ed.), *The Classical Tradition* (1966) 165ff. The instructions cited are from Menander Rhetor's *Basilikos Logos*, Russell and Wilson 85f. They are fairly closely followed by Aelius Aristides' panegyric. S.A. Stertz, *CQ* 29 (1979) 172ff. argues, I believe rightly, that this is a model panegyric not aimed at a specific emperor; but the view is controversial, see C.J. Jones, *CQ* 31 (1981) 224ff. In fact very few surviving panegyrics, and none of the Latin ones, do follow the scholastic rules.

16. It should be stressed that though S does not use these Platonic qualities as categories, he did not necessarily think them unimportant. He sees courage in Otho's death (12.1), prudence in Augustus (*Tib.* 21.3), folly in Claudius (38.3). Justice was a central category in kingship literature and takes pride of place in Marcus' *Meditations*: P.A. Brunt, *JRS* 64 (1974) 7. Doubtless much of what S records under headings like clemency, liberality could be regarded in Greek terms as illustrating justice.

set a better example. The two panegyrics that survive by outstanding Roman orators, Cicero and Pliny, pay no attention to the Greek canon. Cicero praised Pompey for the qualities that made a great general: understanding of warfare, manliness (*virtus*), authority and good luck. Pliny in his *Panegyric* uses no fixed set of virtues at all. He abandons the method of disposition by virtue headings. Far from confining Trajan to a handful of qualities, he is at pains to give the impression of the boundless profusion of his talents which leaves the orator at a loss where to begin or end.[17]

Pliny is much more representative of Roman opinion than are Musonius or Menander Rhetor. The Romans were not fond of systematic theoretical structures, and there is no sign that they ever attempted to define the cardinal virtues of an emperor. Nothing could be more misleading than to see (as has been fashionable) a Roman canon in the Golden Shield of Augustus. The 'Virtue, Clemency, Justice and Piety to gods and country' for which Augustus was honoured correspond neither to the panegyrists nor to the coins, nor to Suetonius. Of course these virtues are acclaimed in other emperors, but they have no status as a set. Of what use would such a set be? Only the theoretician and the instructor needed rigid rules. For practical purposes flexibility was best.[18]

The most we can hope for, therefore, is partial correspondence between the virtues met in Suetonius and any group elsewhere. Only one of the Augustan shield virtues, clemency, is important in Suetonius. Justice, as we have seen, he does not mention. The only piety in which he is interested is that show of loyalty to their predecessors and family which each of the Julio-Claudians put on at the beginning of his reign in order to win popularity and to establish a dynastic claim. More of the Suetonian virtues can be paralleled on the coinage of Hadrian's reign. CLEMENTIA and LIBERALITAS are there; and the goddess of chastity, PUDIC-ITIA, is depicted for the first time under Hadrian, though it is almost certainly the chastity of the ladies of the imperial household which he is advertising. However, there are far more coin virtues

---

17. On the native Roman tradition of *virtus*, see D.C. Earl, *The Political Thought of Sallust* (1961) 18ff. The use of *virtus* in Latin texts is discussed exhaustively by W. Eisenhut, *Virtus Romana* (1973). Cicero's encomium of Pompey occurs in his speech *pro Lege Manilia* 27-48. This contrasts with passages in the rhetorical treatises where he largely transcribes hellenistic sources: see Russell and Wilson xxii.

18. Against assertions to the contrary, see *Historia* (1981) 300ff.

which Suetonius does not notice; and there is one of his central imperial virtues, civility, which is depicted neither in this nor in any other reign.[19]

Perhaps the closest we can get to Suetonius is in Pliny's *Panegyric*. In one passage in the introduction (3.4) Pliny reels off a series of contrasting pairs of virtues and vices which cover very much the same ground as do Suetonius' pairs. He is congratulating himself on his fortune in having Trajan to praise: his virtues are so outstanding that there is no danger the emperor will take him to be hinting at his possession of the opposite vice: 'that he will mistake talk of humanity for criticism of his pride; praise of frugality for luxury; of clemency for cruelty; of liberality for avarice; of benignity for jealousy; of continence for lust; of hard work for laziness; of fortitude for timidity.' All the main Suetonian polarities are here: humanity (equivalent to civility) and pride, clemency and cruelty, liberality and avarice, luxury and lust with their opposites, frugality and continence. Hard work and laziness are closely associated with luxury and lust: how emperors slept or played are topics Suetonius often discusses together with their eating and drinking habits, their taste for jewelry and furniture. In addition Pliny has thrown in two pairs which only surface exceptionally in Suetonius: malignity and jealousy were special to Caligula, and though Suetonius says nothing of fortitude, timidity marks the tyrants Tiberius (63-7) and Domitian (14-16), and is among the fatal weaknesses of Claudius (35-7).

The closeness of the links between Suetonius and his old *contubernalis* Pliny makes good sense. They saw eye to eye on questions of ideology. Pliny meant his *Panegyric* as a model against which future princes could measure themselves. It could also be used as the measure for past princes, and it is difficult to imagine that Suetonius did not know this popular masterpiece, and did not owe at least something to it. But even if this is right, it is not good enough to stop here having identified a new Plinian 'canon' of imperial virtues and vices, an instant recipe for a 'perfect prince'. What we need to explain is the significance of this particular selection of virtues and

19. S describes the show of piety towards predecessors with which Caligula (15.1-3), Claudius (11.2-3) and Nero (9) opened their reigns. These items all belong to the accession narrative, not to the analysis of virtues and vices. On the Hadrianic coinage, see *Historia* (1981) 307ff.

vices, and why Suetonius found it convenient to return to them again and again.[20]

To grasp what Suetonius is doing, it is better to focus on the vices than the virtues. In his list of pride, cruelty, avarice, luxury and lust we see not merely a group of imperial vices, but aspects of abuse by the powerful of those in their power which had been long since denounced by writers of the republic. These are the abuses that marked the misgovernment of Sicily by Verres. The Sicilians could have put up with Verres, inveighs Cicero, had he had no more than the occasional failing. What made him intolerable was the simultaneous occurrence of every possible vice – luxury, cruelty, avarice and pride. This catalogue must have been familiar to the jury in the extortion courts. The tax-collectors of Syria complained that they were ruined by the avarice, pride and cruelty of the governor Gabinius. Historians spoke the same language. 'Avarice and luxury,' says the elder Cato in a speech in Livy, 'are the two plagues which have proved the destruction of every great empire.' Lust, cruelty and inhuman pride are unleashed when Hannibal sacks a city; pride, cruelty and avarice are equally the fault of a Roman commander or a Numidian king.[21]

From republican historians the vices passed to imperial historians. Roman emperors abused their subjects in much the same ways as republican governors had abused their provincials. Cruelty, avarice, pride, luxury and lust are constantly met throughout Tacitus' *Annals* and *Histories*. They also colour the account of Alexander written by Curtius Rufus at an unknown point in the early empire. There the hot-blooded young conspirator Hermolaus inveighs against Alexander very much as a Roman conspirator might accuse an emperor. The vices which for Hermolaus prove him a tyrant are cruelty, lack of liberality and pride; Alexander is careful to refute each charge in order (8.7-8).[22]

20. Pliny makes explicit the role of his *Panegyric* as a yardstick in *Ep.* 3.18.1-3. The links between S and the *Panegyric* are discussed by della Corte (1967) 77ff.; see also Lewis (forthcoming).

21. On these vices and their place in the political vocabulary of the late republic see J. Hellegouarc'h, *Le Vocabulaire latin des relations et des partis politiques sous la République* (1963) 439f., though he underestimates the role of vices in political language in general. R. Combès, *Imperator* (1966) 329ff. is valuable on virtues and vices attributed to republican governors. For lists of vices see respectively Cicero *in Verr.* 2.2.9, *de Prov. Cons.* 11, Livy 34.4.2, 21.57.14, 43.7.8, 32.21.21.

22. It is frustrating that there is no agreement about the date of composition of the Alexander History: estimates range from the mid first to the fourth

Against this background, Suetonius' vice-and-virtue pairs make better sense. Vices were what antagonised the emperor's subjects, and the vices that antagonised them were naturally the forms of abuse that affected them directly. Suetonius is not compiling a list of all the qualities desirable in a ruler, nor attempting to catalogue all the qualities each Caesar brought to his work. He is analysing the way the Caesars treated their people, and the way the people reacted to them. The areas of vice or virtue are thus natural ones of conflict of interest between ruler and ruled, and especially the propertied classes among the ruled. As Aristotle puts it in the *Nicomachean Ethics* (1130b1 f.), injustice is motivated by the pursuit of honour, wealth and personal safety, together with the pleasure that derives from them. Wherever the upper classes valued their status, property and personal safety they were likely to resent an autocrat who threatened their possession of these advantages in order to secure his own. The cruel emperor shed blood to secure his own protection; the avaricious one seized property to fill his exchequer; the proud one exalted his own status and diminished that of his subjects; the luxurious one dissipated the tax-payer's money on his own pleasures, and showed that he had his own, not his people's, welfare at heart.

Suetonius writes from the point of view of the subject anxious about his neck, his pocket, his standing, and his comfort. It follows that it is the presence or absence of vice that most concerns him. The virtues are largely negative ones. Clemency is to refrain from punishing subjects, or to punish them less severely than the law and the emperor's absolute powers might allow. Liberality partly involves generosity with money; but Suetonius is as much concerned that spending should not lead to extortion. Civility is a matter of not acting like a god and autocrat, but rather refusing distinctions and prerogatives. The weight of the emphasis is even clearer in his treatment of self-indulgence. Luxury and lust feature as tyrannical vices alongside cruelty and the rest. But chastity, modesty or restraint are never listed among the positive virtues in the way the rhetoricians recommend; Suetonius follows biographical tradition in simply

---

centuries A.D. See now J.E. Atkinson, *A Commentary on Q. Curtius Rufus' Historiae Alexandri Magni Books 3 and 4* (1980) 19-57 making a Julio-Claudian date highly plausible. For the way this work reflects contemporary conditions, see A. Heuss, 'Alexander der Grosse und die politische Ideologie des Altertums', *Antike und Abendland* 4 (1954) 65ff.

describing the private life of moderate emperors along with other personal details.[23]

It is intrinsically likely that Suetonius' criteria reflect those generally taken for granted by the propertied classes. Nor is there reason to suppose that an emperor would have been inclined to challenge them. It is a prime advantage of Suetonius' method that it projects in such sharp focus assumptions which elsewhere remain blurred. The approach has other advantages too. The author is able to discuss the emperor's record in certain important areas, the exercise of punishment, the handling of finances, the pitching of status, and the use and abuse of imperial power for gratification of private pleasures. Such topics can be seen as a whole; in the chronological narrative of the annalist they must remain dispersed.

But does the approach in fact come off? The answer should be carefully nuanced. There are both advantages and disadvantages in abandoning chronology. Where the topic is such that numerous small items contribute to establishing a real pattern, and the pattern genuinely varied from Caesar to Caesar and did reflect their personal inclinations, Suetonius can give insights which the historians missed or blurred. But the more the political and historical background to a particular event matters, the more dangerous it is to tear it from its context in order to build up a generalisation.

Punishment[24]

Suetonius is least happy in his treatment of clemency and cruelty. *Clementia* was perhaps the most widely publicised of all imperial virtues: at the same time the one most insistently demanded and the most sinister in its abuse. In the pages of Tacitus there is one context above all where *clementia* is relevant. Trials and executions, mostly of senators and their families, but also of other members of the upper classes and of the imperial family itself, mar the record of reign after reign. Such trials and deaths may reasonably be termed

23. Luxury and lust feature among other tyrannical vices at *Tib.* 42-5, *Cal.* 36-7, *Ner.* 26-31, *Vit.* 10.2. But Augustus' *continentia* (68-78) is part of his private life, and similarly *Cl.* 33; *Vesp.* 21. Domitian's private life is also treated as something private, though the tone is critical (22).

24. The relevant chapters are as follows. On *clementia, Jul.* 73-5, *Aug.* 51, *Ner.* 10.1-2, *Vesp.* 14-15, *Tit.* 8.3-9, *Dom.* 9. On *saevitia, Tib.* 50-62, *Cal.* 23-33 (pride and cruelty taken together), *Cl.* 34, *Ner.* 33-8, *Galb.* 12.1-2 and 14.3-15, *Vit.* 14, *Dom.* 10-11.

'political' – not indeed in the sense that any dispute over policies or forms of government lay behind them, but because they were the product of the emperor's determination to secure his own power. The emperor's power was always threatened by the potential disaffection of his subjects. A sense of insecurity might lead him to condemn (or allow to be condemned in the senate) anyone whose loyalty could be called into question however trivial the grounds. Insecurity also lent itself to rich exploitation whether by interested parties in the palace or by rival factions in the senate.[25]

The ideal response was to grant the opponent free pardon in return for future loyalty. Such *clementia* was pioneered by Julius (75) and imitated by Augustus (51) in order to disarm their opponents in times of civil war. It could also be an effective technique of disarming supposed opponents in times of peace. Vespasian is said to have reacted to suspicions against Mettius Pompusianus, whose astrological forecast was only too promising, by appointing him consul (14). Titus, more romantically, is shown forgiving two alleged patrician conspirators, seating them next to himself at the games, and offering them the gladiators' swords to try (9). The publicity value of such gestures lent itself to exploitation. A milder penalty than deserved might be represented as clemency, and certain emperors tried to have their cake and eat it. Domitian had no hesitation in executing dissidents, but prefaced their condemnation by loud advertisement of his clemency (11.2).

The Romans sometimes asserted, or wrote on the assumption that, only a man naturally predisposed to mildness could genuinely exercise *clementia* and that emperors who resorted to repressive tactics, executions and tortures did so because innately cruel and bloodthirsty. Possibly there is truth in this view: but it cannot be the whole truth.[26] Inevitably there was an element of political

25. The literature on *clementia* is extensive. See M. Griffin, *Seneca: a Philosopher in Politics* (1976) 133ff. for an introduction to the subject and discussion of Seneca's vital essay; T. Adam, *Clementia Principis* (1970) for further discussion and bibliography. The sinister overtones of *clementia* are stressed by Charlesworth, *Proc. Brit. Acad.* 23 (1937) 113. On Tacitean *clementia*, cf. B. Levick, *Tiberius the Politician* (1976) 87ff. The evidence on the theme of *maiestas* trials under the principate is collected by R.A. Bauman, *Impietas in Principem* (1974).

26. Suetonius seeks the root of clemency or cruelty in the subject's nature at *Jul.* 74.1, *Tib.* 57.1 and 59.1, *Cal.* 11 and 29.1, *Cl.* 34, *Ner.* 7.1 and 26.1, *Vit.* 10.1, *Dom.* 3.2. For the statement that true clemency could only be natural, Seneca *de Clem.* 1.1.6 (cited above). The same assumption lies behind the

calculation in any exercise of clemency. Moreover the situation might not be in the emperor's control. His fears and suspicions could be exploited by rival factions or by interested subordinates. Suetonius makes out a good case for the natural bloodthirstiness of Claudius by invoking his conduct in two of his characteristic activities, watching the games and giving judgment (34). A man who waited all day to watch an execution by cudgelling, and who had two commemorative paper-knives made from the swords of a pair of gladiators who hacked each other to death, was evidently not over-squeamish. But Suetonius himself indicates that this had little to do with Claudius' numerous political executions which resulted from the uncontrolled intrigues of his family and palace staff (29) who skilfully exploited his timidity (37). Here the handling of the relationship between character and politics is laudable. As a courtier, perhaps, Suetonius had a feeling for the nature of palace intrigue.

But elsewhere his account is marred by the desire to attribute everything to character. Tacitus too believed Tiberius a cruel and bloody tyrant. But his narrative shows fairly that most of the political trials and executions of the reign were associated with the rivalry between Sejanus' faction and its opponents, and the bloody aftermath of Sejanus' overthrow. Suetonius, because he is only concerned to demonstrate Tiberius' character, suppresses this narrative context and gives a gravely distorted picture. It may well be that Tiberius executed a guardsman for filching a peacock from his aviary (60). The anecdote chimes with what is said elsewhere of his disciplinarian severity and his taste for delicatessen. But it cannot help explain his execution of members of his family and shift some of the responsibility from Sejanus' shoulders (61).[27]

Suetonius' aim is not to explain the political crisis of Tiberius' reign but to compile a dossier of his inhumanity. His cruel deeds are too many to enumerate and Suetonius therefore proposes to exemplify the various forms his savagery took (61.2). On this excuse he reduces the vast question of the political and treason trials of the reign, which occupies most of the first six books of Tacitus' *Annals*, to a paragraph of unreliable generalisations (61.2-5). 'Some defendants stabbed themselves ... others took poison actually in the senate;

debate over Caesar's clemency, on which see S. Weinstock, *Divus Julius* (1971) 237ff.

27. Tacitus states his view that Tiberius was naturally cruel at *Ann*. 6.51. But so bald a statement does not do justice to the complexity of his portrayal.

even so their wounds were bound up and they were dragged off, still quivering, to execution.' He refers to two episodes involving the *eques* Vibullius Agrippa in AD 36 and Albucilla in 37. 'Because tradition forbade the strangulation of virgins, immature girls were raped by the executioner before strangulation.' He refers to the luckless daughter of Sejanus. 'There was none of the condemned who was not thrown on the Wailing Steps and dragged off with a hook.' At most this form of extreme punishment can only have been common in the first flush of the backlash against Sejanus and his supporters.[28]

In a word, if we had to rely on Suetonius for an understanding of the catastrophe of the end of Tiberius' reign, we would remain largely in the dark. Our ignorance about the similar crisis at the end of Domitian's reign is not dispelled by his list of senators executed on the most trivial of grounds (10.2-4). Often, elsewhere, all cases of cruelty are lumped together as flowing from the same cause and arranged conveniently in hierarchic order. Thus with Nero: first murders within his own family (33-4); then of his wives (35.1-3); then of more distant relatives, friends and members of the household (35.4-5); so to outsiders, and above all the great conspiracies (36-7); and finally the Roman people itself, which he deliberately attacked by starting the Great Fire (38). Suetonius is out to prove Nero a monster, not to understand the problems involved, and so conjures up this image of universal destruction. He suppresses the severe doubts as to Nero's responsibility for the fire. He deliberately trivialises Nero's motives to underline his monstrosity. He thereby plays down the political element: Britannicus was murdered because he had a better voice as well as constituting a threat (33.2); his mother because she nagged (34.1); and the prefect of Egypt, Caecina Tuscus, because he took a dip in the baths especially built for Nero's projected visit (35.5).[29]

It is in such cases that the loss of narrative is most dismaying. But that said, we should not belabour Suetonius too far. First, he

---

28. The inadequacies of S's picture of Tiberius are stressed by Bringmann (1971), who joins the chorus of abuse of the rubric system. For Vibulenus (or Vibullius) Agrippa, Tacitus *Ann.* 6.40; Albucilla, 6.48; Sejanus' daughter, 5.9. Note however that the detail of twenty executed at *Tib.* 61.4 is more precise than the 'immense carnage' of *Ann.* 6.19.

29. The triviality of the grounds on which tyrants executed their victims is repeatedly underlined by S: see *Tib.* 58 and 61.3, *Cal.* 27.3, *Ner.* 37.1, *Galb.* 14.3, *Vit.* 14.1, *Dom.* 10.2-4. He tends therefore to exaggerate the trivial in order to blacken their characters.

was probably giving his readership what they wanted and expected. They felt that natural disposition played a crucial role in affecting the way a ruler behaved. They were not necessarily wrong. Secondly, his chapters on cruelty and clemency have the great advantage of broadening the focus from too narrow attention to the senatorial aristocracy. The biographer's special calling was to discern character in small things as well as great. Suetonius' anecdotal material has the effect of conjuring up a vivid picture of the wide social range affected by the emperor's powers. He prefers to illustrate Augustus' clemency not by the famous senatorial cases (easily accessible in any history book) but by two plebeians: Augustus merely fined Junius Novatus for a highly scurrilous letter of abuse, and exiled Cassius of Padua for declaring at a dinner that he would happily run the emperor through (51.1). Others were less mild. Tiberius, when a fisherman offered him a mullet and a lobster, had him scarified in the face with his own catch (60). Caligula callously fed up beasts for the amphitheatre on condemned criminals when the price of meat rose too high (27.1). One is constantly reminded that the autocrat wielded unlimited power *de facto* if not *de iure* over all who happened to incur his displeasure. The games offered the best chance for the populace to see and applaud its ruler; but he could be no less vicious then. Caligula burnt alive the poet of a farce who made a *double entendre* at his expense (27.4). Vitellius supposedly had some plebeians killed for insulting his favourite team, the Blues (14.3). Domitian, no better, had a man thrown to the dogs for criticising the emperor's bias against 'Thracian' gladiators (10.1).

Suetonius' chapters are not, then, primarily concerned with the emperor's treatment of political opponents, actual, potential or alleged. They do not offer an analysis of the exercise of formal judicial powers. They look at Caesars as men possessed of power, arbitrary and absolute, and show the terrifying consequences when power is not kept in check by moral restraint.

Imperial style[30]

When it is a matter of describing the conduct and bearing of the Caesars towards their subjects, Suetonius' analytical system comes

30. The relevant chapters are as follows. On *civilitas*: *Aug.* 52-6, *Tib.* 26-32, *Cl.* 12.1-2 (contrasting 35.1), *Ner.* 10.1, *Vesp.* 12-13, *Tit.* 8.2 (contrasting 6.1); note also *Tib.* 11.1-3 on Tiberius in Rhodes before his accession, *Cal.* 3.2 on Caligula's father Germanicus, *Cl.* 1.4 on Claudius' father Drusus. On pride: *Jul.* 76-9, *Cal.* 22-6 (pride and cruelty), *Dom.* 12.3-13.

into its own, for he is able to pull together disparate items that do indeed reveal coherent patterns. Roman emperors found themselves in a deeply ambivalent position. It is characteristic for monarchs to use devices of pomp and ceremonial in order to set an unbridgeable gap between themselves and their subjects, to enhance their majesty and thus to secure their power. But Roman society was deeply penetrated by the ethos of the republic which demanded that no single citizen should excel all others. This sentiment proved the downfall of Julius; so that while he was the model for later Caesars in both clemency and liberality, the model of 'citizenly' behaviour was set by Augustus, in deliberate reaction to his adoptive father. Even so, the conduct of individual Caesars fluctuated greatly in this respect. The further they allowed their standing and prerogatives to deviate from the citizenly norm, the more they were held to suffer from Julius' moral failing of pride.[31]

Suetonius documents with some care these fluctuations from the ideal which he terms *civilitas*. From historical accounts he could derive information on the two most important features of the style, the pose of refusal of any mark of abnormal status, and the elaborate show of respect towards the senate. The familiar narrative of Julius' last months, largely revolving round his supposed desire to become king, is readily compressed into documentation of his pride (76-9). The no less familiar accounts of Augustus' long string of 'refusals' (52-3) and Tiberius' initial encouragement of senatorial freedom (30-1) could likewise be pressed into service. The attitudes of Caesars to their own worship also attracted much attention, ranging from approval of Augustus' refusals (52) to horror at Caligula's enforcement of cult, including exotic sacrifices of flamingoes, peacocks, pheasants and the like (22), paralleled in the narratives of the Jewish writers Philo and Josephus.[32]

Suetonius' method allows him swiftly to evoke a coherent pattern by drawing such items together. He can also supplement this

31. The discussion draws on 'Civilis Princeps: between citizen and king', *JRS* 72 (1982) 32ff. For the monarchical ceremonial elements of the principate, see A. Alföldi, *Die monarchische Repräsentation im römischen Kaiserreiche* (1970). The ambiguity of the monarch's standing in mediaeval and early modern Europe is the subject of the study of E. Kantorowicz, *The King's Two Bodies* (1957).

32. On the ideology of refusal, see J. Béranger, *Recherches sur l'aspect idéologique du principat* (1953) esp. 137ff. On the refusal of divine honours, M.P. Charlesworth, 'The refusal of divine honours: an Augustan formula', *Papers of the British School at Rome* 15 (1939) 1ff.

information by anecdotal material, not all of it necessarily drawn from the histories, depicting the social etiquette of the behaviour of emperors in contact with the upper classes. Augustus and Tiberius are nicely described exchanging courtesies with the aristocracy. Augustus walked round the senate house greeting individual senators by name, accepted invitations to people's celebrations until he grew old and found the press of guests at an engagement party tiresome, and sat at the bedside of a junior senator he hardly knew to dissuade him from suicide (53.3). Tiberius would step aside to make way for the consuls, and followed the funerals of distinguished men as far as the pyre (31.2-32.1). Claudius made a great issue of his own civility, yet spoilt the show by attending dinner parties with a bodyguard and searching the beds of the sick men he visited for concealed weapons (35.1). On the other hand there is the ceremonial that grew up round the person of the ruler. Caligula caused shock by allowing ex-magistrates to run in attendance on his chariot (26.2) whereas Augustus quietly entered the city at night to avoid troubling people, and travelled round the city in a closed litter (53.2). Tiberius would allow no senator the trouble of attending his sedan (27). To pay respects to the emperor at his morning salutation was a privilege, and Augustus won credit by his ease of admission (53.2). But Claudius had callers frisked (35.2), a habit which Vespasian creditably abandoned (12).[33]

Mostly it is the upper classes who are involved in such social rituals. But a civil emperor was also affable to the *plebs*. Augustus admitted the humble to his salutations and exchanged relaxed banter with petitioners (53.2). Similarly Nero admitted the general public to watch his physical and rhetorical exercises (10.2), while Titus admitted them to public bathing sessions (8.2). Augustus delighted the public by canvassing the electorate for his candidates and placing his own ballot in the box (56.1). The emperor's conduct at the games belongs to the same pattern. It was part of Titus' affability that he humoured the crowd by cheering for his favourite teams (8.2). Domitian's arrogance led him to turn down a request from the crowd with a peremptory command for silence (13.1).[34]

33. Imperial etiquette and ceremonial are described fully in Friedländer, *Sittengeschichte* 1, 90ff. (*Life and Manners* 1, 86ff.). The evidence is used by Alföldi, *Monarchische Repräsentation* 27ff. to emphasise the ceremonial elements.
34. The significance of imperial civility at the games is discussed by A. Cameron, *Circus Factions* 175ff., tracing a line of continuity from the early principate to Byzantium. That the games were a prime venue for exalting the

Such items do much to bring alive a picture of the emperor in his everyday surroundings. We owe them to the biographer's eye for small detail, and perhaps also to the courtier's appreciation of the texture of court life. The author's enthusiasm for the ideal of civility fits in with the enthusiasm for traditional social values manifest elsewhere in the *Caesars*. It is valuable evidence that there was nothing exclusively senatorial about this ideal. Even if there were courtiers in some reigns who pressed on the emperor the desirability of maintaining his distance, Suetonius was not one of them. He wholeheartedly embraces the ideal set out at length in Pliny's *Panegyric*, welcoming Trajan as a ruler who conducted himself as 'one of us', a fellow-citizen, modest and sociable.[35]

It is his rubric method which allows him to isolate patterns of conduct which in historians and even in the *Panegyric* are interwoven with numerous other themes. But the novel method of presentation also brings with it a subtle shift of emphasis. What he documents is a moral quality, *civilitas*. He appears indeed to have coined the term; previous authors speak of emperors acting 'civilly', in various respects, but this is the first time that 'civility' emerges as a moral quality. The underlying assumption is that there was a fixed social etiquette to which the good emperor would conform, and which the bad one would reject.

What disappears from sight in the process is the awareness that any particular act of 'civility' might be a carefully thought-out move in a game. Asinius Gallus proposed in the senate that Tiberius should have the power of nominating a number of magistrates five years in advance. On Tacitus' showing it was a shrewd move that thrust at the secrets of power. Tiberius felt challenged, and made an elaborate refusal on the grounds that his power ought not to be amplified; and so, by a speciously laudable speech, he held on to the realities of power (*Ann.* 2.36). The episode is characteristic of Tacitus' treatment of Tiberius' 'moderation'. He sees his civil words and gestures as smoke thrown in the eyes of the senate while he reinforced his actual domination. Tacitus thus subtly penetrates the nature of civility. No emperor by his gestures actually diminished

---

imperial image is argued by P. Veyne, *Le pain et le cirque* 682ff. See also Bradley (1981).

35. On the ideal in the *Panegyric*, see F. Trisoglio, *La personalità di Plinio il Giovane* (1972) 85ff. The most important passages are *Pan.* 2.3-8; 20-4; 71. For the idea that courtiers might resist civility, cf. *SHA Hadrian* 20.1, *Pius* 6.4, *Sev. Alex.* 20.3.

the reality of his power; on the contrary, by posing as refusing autocratic distinctions, emperors actually consolidated their position and won the approval of the upper orders. The behaviour of Caligula and Domitian was merely counterproductive.[36]

Suetonius too thinks that Tiberius' behaviour was, in general terms, hypocritical (42.1), and states that Claudius' civility was a show (35.1). But his method (unlike Tacitus') does not allow him to expose the element of sham. The more civil gestures he assembles, the more apparent it is that the emperor is civil not arrogant, good not bad. His method thus presupposes the genuineness of the act: to conform to the etiquette is enough.

But herein Suetonius probably reflects the sentiments of his contemporaries more nearly than Tacitus. The principate had long since been indispensable and therefore acceptable. They did not need to see through the hypocrisy of autocratic devices. The vital thing was that the émperor should behave with restraint and with respect for the established order. If the civility which that involved was in a sense fraudulent, they preferred to be deceived.

Finances[37]

Financial dealings lend themselves a great deal more readily to treatment by rubric than to chronological narrative. Every emperor, no matter whether 'good' or 'bad', must be involved in the dual process of expenditure and raising sufficient revenue. It is a positive help here to have the evidence 'gathered into titles and bundles'. So

36. On Tacitus' treatment of the 'moderation' of Tiberius, see R.S. Rogers, *Studies in the Reign of Tiberius* (1943) 60ff., with B. Levick, *Tiberius the Politician* (1976) 89. It has been noted that Tacitus only uses the word *civilitas* in the *Annals* with reference to Tiberius' reign, by I. Lana, 'Civilis, civiliter, civilitas in Tacito e Svetonio', *Atti Ac. Sc. Torino* 106 (1972) 469ff. He explains this by the state of preservation of the text, underestimating Tacitus' motive in unmasking hypocrisy. At almost every occurrence of the term Tacitus seeks by one means or another to deprive Tiberius of real credit: see *Ann.* 1.33, 1.54, 1.72, 2.34 with 4.21, 2.82, 3.22, 6.13. Only once does Tiberius appear to get away with it: 3.76.

37. The relevant sections are as follows. *Liberalitas: Aug.* 41-3, *Ner.* 10.1, *Tit.* 7.3-8.1, *Dom.* 9. *Avaritia: Jul.* 54, *Tib.* 46-9, *Cal.* 38-42, *Ner.* 32, *Galb.* 12, *Dom.* 12.1-2. Undecided: *Vesp.* 16-19. Also relevant are chapters where expenditure is *not* rated as liberality. Buildings, doles and games: *Jul.* 38-9, *Aug.* 29, *Cal.* 17.2-21, *Cl.* 20-1, *Ner.* 11-13, *Vesp.* 8.5-9.1, *Dom.* 4-5. Wasteful extravagance (*nepotatus*): *Cal.* 37, *Ner.* 30-1, *Vit.* 13. S's views on the financial conduct of the Caesars are examined at length by Reekmans (1977), who pays, however, too little attention to S's own system of categorisation.

presented, the material can demonstrate a pattern of behaviour. Thus the author of a recent study of imperial liberality appreciated Suetonius' neat categorisation of different aspects of liberality and used it as the basis for his own presentation. The same types of liberality recur from reign to reign: building, games-giving, donatives and other bounties; grants to impoverished senators; aid to cities in time of disaster; and support of poets. One could similarly use Suetonius as a guide to the standard methods of revenue-raising: taxation; the levying of 'voluntary' contributions (*collationes*) on special occasions; inheritance; confiscation of the property of the condemned; in dire straits the auctioning of imperial property; and for the unscrupulous the execution of the rich, the sale of office and judgment and other forms of corruption.[38]

The breakdown of imperial spending and revenue-raising is so conveniently set out that it is tempting to look here for a balanced analysis of the imperial budget. But a budget is not what Suetonius offers. He gives figures quite frequently, whether for the 800,000 sesterces which Nero daily granted Tiridates during his visit (30.2) or the five denarii which Galba tipped a musician (12.3). But there are no overall figures. The information on taxation is frustratingly vague. We are told that Vespasian revived some old taxes, introduced others and raised provincial tribute in some cases to double the old level (16.1). But there are no details or figures for these significant changes, apart from the colourful detail that he introduced a tax on urinals and silenced the protesting Titus by demonstrating that the money smelt good enough (23.3). Again, it would have been possible for Suetonius to give precise figures for the totals spent by Augustus on largess to the troops and the city *plebs*, land-settlements for veterans, hand-outs of corn, subventions to the public treasury, games and building. But though he almost certainly knew the *Res Gestae* which preserved these figures, he is vague, if not positively inadequate, on the subject, and only used figures to show that the level of Augustus' largesses varied (41).[39]

The biographer is simply not interested in analysing the budget. His concern is primarily moral. The question for him is not 'how much?' but 'how good or bad?'. Even behind the apparent neutrality

38. The value of S's breakdown of liberality is appreciated by H. Kloft, *Liberalitas Principis* esp. 77ff. For the main types of both benefaction and revenue-raising, see Millar, *Emperor* 133ff.

39. The *Res Gestae* is (almost certainly) cited directly at *Aug.* 43.1. There was once a prolonged debate on the extent of S's use of the *RG*, but this has long since died away: see Funaioli (1932) 614f.

of his rubrics, strong moral presuppositions are implicit. His handling of building and games-giving is significant. Tiberius is criticised
as mean partly on the grounds of failure to build or put on shows
(47). The implication is that these activities were normally evidence
of liberality. Yet though he provides ample enough details of these
activities for most emperors, he takes most of this evidence of
liberality out of its moral category and treats it with other routine
affairs as part of 'the job'. Moreover, expenditure on palace and
entourage is classified as luxurious and again discounted. Thus
Nero merits only criticism for his expenditure on the Golden Palace
(31); and although Galba is criticised for meanness to his entourage
(12.3), Nero's granting of estates to his favourites rates as extravagance (30.2).

At the root of Suetonius' treatment is a dilemma. It is difficult to
confess that a man is simultaneously good and bad. Yet it was
difficult to be liberal without extortionate revenue-raising, or to
spare the pocket of the tax-payer without also appearing mean. Vice
and virtue, as the ancients knew, were easily confused: extravagance
could be represented as liberality, economy as avarice. Suetonius'
categorisation of financial measures into good or bad depends
on conventional criteria of the acceptable and unacceptable. The
preoccupations of the propertied classes are apparent behind them.[40]

Cicero argued that generosity was only truly virtuous when the
recipient merited the benefaction. Suetonius moves from the same
assumption. He cares more that money should be spent on right
and proper objects than that it should simply be spent. Augustus'
massive liberalities to troops and *plebs* are dealt with, as we have
seen, rather vaguely. Suetonius is at pains to stress that all orders
benefited from his generosity: he specifies interest-free loans (to the
wealthy, presumably) and grants to senators (41.1). He goes on to
stress that Augustus was by no means out to buy popularity
(*salubrem magis quam ambitiosum principem*): he rebuked the
people for an excessive demand for subsidised wine, was strict in
his distribution of bounties, and was only deterred from abolishing

40. On the conventional moral categories, see Kloft, *Liberalitas Principis*
136ff. See also for an interesting attempt to relate imperial monetary policy to
ancient moral categories, D.R. Walker, *The Metrology of the Roman Silver
Coinage* Part III (British Archaeological Reports, Supp.40, 1978) 106ff. On
the confusion of virtue and vice, cf. Tac. *Hist.* 1.30, *luxuria specie liberalitatis*
('luxury in the guise of liberality') and 1.37, *parsimonia pro avaritia* ('avarice
posing as thrift').

the corn-dole by the political dangers implicit in the move (42). The Augustus of the *Res Gestae* is hardly recognisable in this transformation.[41]

The manifest suspicion of the purchase of popular support helps explain Suetonius' treatment of buildings and games. He knew that they could impoverish an emperor and drive him to extortion, as happened with Domitian (12). Nevertheless, he never actually criticises an emperor for either of these activities and Vespasian gets credit for his desire to provide employment by his building programme. 'Let me feed my little people', he rebukes the man with a labour-saving invention (18). Private building, however, was quite another matter from public building (*opera*). Nero was ruinous in nothing so much as his house-building (*aedificando*), that is his erection of palaces (31). The same contrast holds for Pliny's Trajan. He is sparing in house-building; the streets no longer thunder with passing wagonloads of masonry (as they had under Domitian, who rebuilt the Palatine). But in public work he is magnificent (*Pan.* 51.1-3).[42]

Wasteful spending leads directly to extortion, as is demonstrated in the cases of Caligula (38.1) and Nero (32.1). Suetonius is at least as anxious that the emperor should make no unjust exactions as that he should be liberal. Titus, fantastically, is praised for taking not a penny from a single citizen (7.3). This means, of course, not that he remitted taxation, but that he resorted to none of the exactions that typified the tyrant, such as executions of the rich on trumped-up charges. Whereas Caligula extorted contributions on the most spurious grounds, such as for a dowry for his daughter (42), Titus refused even the customary collations. Through procurators emperors controlled much of the tax-gathering. But Nero is said to have appointed them with the encouragement 'Let's make sure no one has a penny left' (32.4) and Vespasian supposedly appointed corrupt ones in order to squeeze them dry later 'like sponges' (16.2). Now taxes might be justified by the circumstances: Vespasian's were perhaps a marginal case but Caligula's 'new and unheard of' taxes on the sale of cooked foods, litigation, porterage and prostitution were unacceptable, as was his failure to publish these innovations

41. Cicero *de Officiis* 1.42-6 lays down the criteria for true liberality. Sallust reflects on the contrast between largess and liberality in his contrast between Cato and Caesar: *Catiline* 54. Tacitus too is realistic about Augustus: 'he seduced the troops with gifts and the people with corn' (*Ann.* 1.2).
42. On attitudes to imperial luxury see below.

except in the minutest script (40-1). An unwritten code of practice also lies behind reactions to the practices of emperors in receiving inheritances. Augustus set the ideal standard in turning down bequests from strangers (66.4). Even so his will revealed that he took fourteen hundred million in twenty years (101.3). Other Caesars exploited this rich source of income by forcing men to make them their heirs.[43]

Suetonius' criteria bear close relation to the ideal depicted by Pliny in Trajan. It was a wonder, remarked Pliny, that the open-handed Trajan could make his books balance. Yet he achieved it by frugality, personal economy in contrast to public liberality (*Pan.* 41). The feat was not such an easy one that the right moral disposition would guarantee success, and Suetonius is not always quite honest in laying out both sides of the ledger. He attacks Tiberius bitterly for meanness (46-8); but suppresses here the evidence of his scrupulous avoidance of extortion. Elsewhere he lets slip that Tiberius told his governors to shear their sheep, not fleece them (32.2), and was himself a model of economical living (34.1). His handling of Augustus also tells less than the whole truth. Not only does he obscure the extent of his liberalities; he says nothing in this context of his introduction of the new 5 per cent inheritance tax that financed bounties to veterans. The first direct tax Romans had been asked to pay in time of peace for nearly two centuries, it aroused, as Dio's narrative shows, bitter opposition and resentment. Suetonius only alludes to it as one of his laudable provisions for the army (49.2).[44]

It is not simply the moral categories that are to blame here, strange though they seem to the modern mind. All ancient authors

43. Executions of the rich are perhaps the commonest and most objectionable of tyrannical abuses S documents: *Tib.* 49, *Cal.* 38.3, *Ner.* 32, *Dom.* 12.1. Note that Vespasian, whom S is disinclined to condemn, was proof against this sort of temptation (13). For the code of practice over inheritances, see R.S. Rogers, *Trans. Am. Phil. Ass.* 78 (1947) 140ff. For bad practice, *Cal.* 38.2, *Ner.* 32.2, *Dom.* 12.2 (abandoning earlier high principles, 9.2). For the ideal, Pliny *Pan.* 43.

44. S's critical treatment of Tiberius is the more notable in contrast with Tacitus' grudging allowance of his high standards, e.g. *Ann.* 3.23. See further Townend (1962). S's favourable treatment of Augustus contrasts with Tacitus' cynical assessment (above n.41). On the new *vicesima hereditatum* tax, Dio 55.25 and 56.28, 4-6; C. Nicolet, *The World of the Citizen in Republican Rome* (1980) 184f. emphasises the importance of the fact that the citizen had no direct tax to pay between 167 and 43 BC when civil wars changed the situation.

use moral categories in discussing imperial finances. Behind the language of vice and virtue lie the anxieties of the interested parties: the men of property who ultimately had to foot the bill for imperial liberality and extravagance. Once sold on the proposition that Augustus was a model ruler, Suetonius could never tell the whole truth.

Pleasures[45]

The antiquarian's analytical approach pays off best in those areas of public life where small items can be used to establish patterns, and are not fraught with political overtones. The fourth main area of tyrannical vice, 'luxury and lust', demands a rather different treatment, and will be reserved for the last chapter. It only half belongs in the context of public life. Indeed some might question whether it belongs to public life at all. The description of Augustus' private life in its massive and minute detail (61-96) is so valuable precisely because it is treated as something private. The facts are offered as simple facts, relished merely for their authenticity: he decorated his house with curiosities, like the bones of prehistoric animals, rather than paintings and statues (72.3), he was fond of figs (76.1) and relaxed by playing 'nuts' with dwarves (83). Even where discussion touches the political arena with the accusations of immorality of triumviral days, Suetonius remains dispassionate, showing up the invective for what it is, but conscientiously documenting from the emperor's own correspondence a weakness for what was regarded as a vice, dicing (68-71).

It is, we may feel, to be regretted that he did not sustain this dispassionate approach for the lives of Tiberius, Caligula and Nero. By including the lurid catalogues of their indulgence or extravagance in the context of their public lives, he abandoned the biographer's schema, and with it his dry informative tone. But what matters here is to see the reason why Suetonius abandons his objective tone in the 'tyrant' lives. He does so because he assumes the extravagance and indulgence of emperors to be a matter of public significance,

45. Luxury, lust and extravagance are treated as of public significance in the following passages: *Tib.* 42-5, *Cal.* 36-7, *Ner.* 27-31, *Vit.* 13, *Tib.* 7.1-2. Other lives sustain a more dispassionate tone: *Aug.* 68-78, *Cl.* 32-3, *Galb.* 22, *Vesp.* 21, *Dom.* 21-2. The account of Julius (45.3-53) is generally critical, and sensitive to the public repercussions of his reputation; but the idea of a 'reign' is of restricted relevance to this life.

and herein he reflects the general assumption of antiquity. Behind this were several, overlapping considerations.[46]

The first was crudely financial. 'Luxury' was a competitive business, a rivalry in displaying wealth and refinement. It could lead to crippling expense. Suetonius states that the extravagance of Caligula, who squandered a reserve of twenty-seven hundred million sesterces accumulated by his predecessor (37), and of Nero, who followed the same pattern (30.1), led directly to fiscal crisis and extortion. We have no notion of the proportion of the imperial budget that might be spent on the palace, entertainment and other 'luxuries' but there is no reason to doubt that it could be substantial. Seneca makes the staggering allegation that Caligula spent the tribute of three provinces on a single dinner. Whether true or not, this shows how Romans felt about imperial luxury. Pliny, as we have seen, proclaimed that it was by personal frugality that the liberal Trajan made the accounts balance; he even auctioned off surplus property and palace furniture. A papyrus has been found in which an anonymous emperor announces a remission of taxes made possible by his own frugality. By the second century economy had become a settled part of imperial style, and men looked back to the prodigality of earlier Caesars with shock.[47]

Combined with the feeling that the emperor had a duty to spare the tax-payer was the expectation that he should set a positive example. The life of the public figure was in the limelight. He could not escape. 'Great fortunes can have no secrets. The imperial house, even its bedroom and secret corners, lie open to view, and everything confidential is exposed to publicity.' Yet the prince's life must be a model to his subjects, a perpetual censorship. Emperors concerned themselves with the moral conduct of their subjects, particularly of

46. That luxury (*tryphē*) was a prime cause of undoing for governments was a commonplace of hellenistic historiography, as can be seen in the book of quotations on the subject collected by Athenaeus, *Deipnosophists* 12. Discussed by A. Passerini, 'La tryphe nella storiografia ellenistica', *Studi Italiani di Filologia Classica* 11 (1934) 35ff. It also became a commonplace of Roman republican moralising thought, in the elder Cato (Livy 34.4.2), the annalist Piso (frr. 34 and 38), Sallust and Livy himself. Thus D. Earl, *The Political Thought of Sallust* (1961) 41ff.

47. Cf. Seneca, *Consolatio ad Helviam* 10.4 for Caligula's banquet; Pliny, *Pan.* 41.1 for frugality; P. Fayum 40, edited by Schubart in *Archiv für Papyrusforschung* 14 (1941) 44ff., for the remission of taxes. Trajan's auction is described by Pliny *Pan.* 50; Millar, *Emperor* 148 assembles evidence of parallel cases. It is interesting to note that Caligula gets no credit for his auctions at *Cal.* 38.4-39.

members of the senate, and they lay wide open to the charge of hypocrisy if their own conduct was anything less than exemplary. Even Tiberius knew this much: his supporter Velleius praised him for setting a model, and Suetonius records that he served reheated dishes at a formal dinner as an example of public economy (34.1). Yet he failed to carry conviction. It was in the middle of a 'moral purge' that he awarded key posts to two senators who had kept him company in an all-night drinking party (42.1).[48]

There was a further, practical, objection to *la dolce vita*. 'How may a king avoid turning to idleness and pleasures?' asks Ptolemy Philadelphus in a fictional dialogue with a group of Jewish savants. 'By remembering that he rules a large and populous realm and should put his mind to nothing other than the care of his people.' The conscientious ruler had a tremendous burden of work which put heavy demands on his physical endurance. Trajan, according to Pliny, set the pace for future princes, to shake off their inertia, delights and sweet slumber. Marcus warns himself in his private *Meditations* against the temptations of the pillow; and we find his tutor Fronto vainly writing to urge him to take a break, catch some sleep and relax. Marcus, at first too busy even to read his master's letter, only replies that he is the slave of duty. Not all Suetonius' Caesars set such high standards for themselves. Augustus worked late into the night, and never slept more than seven hours (78); Vespasian (21) and Claudius were early risers, though the latter sometimes nodded off during business (33.2). Yet the wastrels evidently lacked this sense of dedication to the job. If Caligula slept little, it was only because he suffered from insomnia (50.3).[49]

Economy, image and the demands of duty all conspired to make the emperor's private life less than private. Suetonius had every

48. Pliny *Pan.* 83.1 on the exposure of the emperor's private life. It is a traditional topic, met for example in Cicero *de Officiis* 2.44, Sallust *Catiline* 51.12, Seneca *de Clementia* 1.8.3f., Cassius Dio 52.34.2-3 (Maecenas' speech). For the idea that subjects modelled themselves on the ruler, see below, ch.8, n.3. What S means by Tiberius' moral purge (*correctio morum*) is not quite clear since Tacitus states that he refused to take on any such responsibilities: *Ann.*3.52-5. On the idea of regal hypocrisy, cf. Isocrates, *Nicocles* 38: 'Kings are quite wrong to compel others to behave decently without themselves being any more restrained than their subjects.'

49. For Ptolemy's question, Aristeas, *Letter to Philocrates* 245. Pliny *Pan.* 59.2 and *passim* for Trajan's sleepless energy. Marcus, *Meditations* 5.1 for his warnings to himself, with Fronto *de Feriis Alsiensibus* (Loeb ed. vol.2, 2ff.) for the tutor's warnings.

justification in recording such details, and his treatment of the vices of luxury and lust as public accurately reflects the sense of public outrage provoked by the behaviour of some Caesars. What is to be regretted is that he suspended his critical faculties in the treatment of Tiberius, Caligula and Nero. Had he handled the allegations of vice against them as coolly as those against Augustus, citing original documents, invectives and correspondence, the value of his account would be enormously greater. The failure is not one of the rubric system, but of his sources and his natural sympathies.

Suetonius' moral categories accurately reflect the preoccupations of the class for which he wrote. It was open to emperors to secure their power by executing their critics, by distributing bounties to their supporters at the price of extortions from others and by magnifying their appearance of power through titulature and ceremonial. Citizens with influence, wealth and prestige of their own stood to lose by all these processes. A potential conflict of interest lay at the heart of the problem. Yet they interpreted it as a moral, not a political, problem. A 'good' emperor would naturally exercise restraint in all these areas, so minimising the tension. A 'bad' one would pursue his own advantage alone, and would betray himself in his personal behaviour. Luxury and lust were the signs of a ruler who only used power to his personal advantage and not that of his people. The biographer's interest in character is compounded by the scholar's use of rubrics. The effect, however, is not to distort contemporary perceptions, but to throw them into sharper relief.

Chapter Eight

EMPERORS AND CULTURE

Suetonius' picture of the private lives of the Caesars has attracted by its lively detail the many who have turned to it for entertainment. But to the serious-minded it has long been a stumbling-block. Can we take seriously an author who writes about such subjects, or in such a manner?[1]

It does Suetonius ill justice to cast him as the writer of a *chronique scandaleuse*. Whether as scholar, antiquarian or biographer he was interested in how people live. Private life was no less legitimate a subject for biography than public life. If he reports that Augustus had a taste, pandered to by Livia, for deflowering virgins (71.1), there is no more reason to suppose that he had an eye to a prurient readership than when he reports that the same emperor had a fondness for green figs (76.1), composed epigrams in the bath (85.2), or carried a piece of seal-skin as a protection against lightning (90). Such detail was the traditional stuff of biography in antiquity (nor will it come as a surprise to modern biographers). Habits of eating, drinking and sexual behaviour, cultural interests and religious practices were very much conventional topics.[2]

---

1. Robert Graves' lively translation of the *Caesars* (first published in the Penguin Classics series in 1957, reissued with an introduction by Michael Grant in 1979) has played a large part in spreading S's popularity in the English-speaking world. His novels *I, Claudius* and *Claudius the God* (1934), however, with their numerous dramatisations which draw heavily (but not exclusively) on S have been more influential. The example of professional distaste for gossip in S cited above, ch.1, n.37, is an extreme one, but the point of view remains widespread among scholars: thus Paratore (1959) 341; Syme, *Tacitus* 502; Flach (1972) 288. There have been several opponents of this attitude, but their tone is on the whole apologetic: thus Mooney (1930) 24f. Gugel (1977) 73ff. sets out to analyse the 'Erotica' at length: his search for artistic variations does not seem to me a profitable line of approach. Bradley in his Commentary on the *Nero* 153f. thinks of the market for gossip.

2. See above ch.3. It is interesting to compare the account of Atticus' private life in Nepos' *Life*, 13-18.

Nor should such detail be regarded as beneath the notice of the historian. To enquire into the private life of an emperor is to attempt to see him in the context of the social and cultural life of his day: to see him engaged in the pursuits of the Roman upper classes around him, to see moreover the impact that his presence had upon the life of those around him. The emperor was not a purely political figure, and his significance extended to spheres other than politics. Already we have seen how Suetonius' chapters about the Caesars' 'liberal studies' illuminate their role as men of culture and patrons of learning. Other aspects too of their private lives help to build up a valuable picture of the society and culture of the early empire, and to evoke a vivid image of the lives of Caesars and their courts.[3]

There is, however, a methodological snag. The value of such details must depend upon their authenticity. If what Suetonius purveys is mere gossip and fantasy (as is often assumed), it may indeed be worthless. Nor is there usually any method of controlling the reliability of any particular item. Even if Suetonius sometimes names sources, like Augustus' freedman Julius Marathus who vouched for his physical particulars (79.2), this is the exception. The fabrication of lurid allegations was a traditional feature of Roman invective. The temptation is to suppose that the more lurid an item, the more likely it is to be a product of malicious gossip. But while individual items may justly arouse suspicion, it is a different matter when we consider Suetonius' picture as a whole. It is the coherence of his information that provides the best guarantee of its authenticity. His details contribute to a pattern that is internally consistent and also consistent with our other information on early imperial society. If there is fabrication (as there undoubtedly is) at least it is by contemporaries who knew the limits of the plausible. In this respect the *Caesars* are worlds apart in point of reliability from the numerous ancient lives of authors, or indeed the later imperial lives (*Historia Augusta*) where fabrication flowed into the vacuum left by plain ignorance.[4]

3. The only serious cultural history of imperial Rome is the old but admirable classic of Ludwig Friedländer, *Darstellungen aus der Sittengeschichte Roms*, first published in 1861-71, best consulted in the tenth and last edition of 1922 (4 vols). The English translation, *Roman Life and Manners under the Early Empire*, 4 vols (1908-28) suffers from abridgment.

4. On republican language of invective see R.G.M. Nisbet's commentary on Cicero *In Pisonem* (1961), esp. 192f.; also I. Opelt, *Die lateinischen Schimpf-wörter und verwandte sprachliche Erscheinungen* (1965) 148ff., offering a valuable index of Roman attitudes mirrored in terms of abuse. Such fabrication

As a starting point we may take an example that illustrates a number of points. The life of Titus is one of the weakest, marred by uncritical panegyric. But before on accession Titus becomes the 'darling of mankind' we are treated to a much more revealing account of his early life, spent in the Julio-Claudian court. Titus was brought up at the court of Claudius, as playmate to his son Britannicus. They shared the same teachers; and indeed Titus was still at the young prince's side at the fatal dinner when Nero despatched his rival. Together, Titus and Britannicus experienced another curious episode. A 'face-reader' was summoned by the freedman Narcissus to tell Britannicus' fortune. He also told that of Titus, and was emphatic that it was he, not Britannicus, who was the future emperor (2).

This episode may be partly fabrication (for Titus' benefit); yet the scenario is credible. So is the rest of the picture of Titus' upbringing. He was deemed a model pupil, not only a capable horseman and a fluent orator in both Latin and Greek, but an improvisor of extempore verses and no bad musician, with a gift for singing and dancing (3). If in these respects he resembles Nero, brought up in the same surroundings, he does so too in his less laudable pursuits. As a young man, he kept company with the prodigal, extending drinking-bouts into the the small hours. He surrounded himself with a troupe of deviants and eunuchs. Some of his favourites were accomplished dancers who went on to successful careers on the stage. He also had a notorious *affaire* with the eastern queen Berenice. Small wonder men feared in him a second Nero (7.1).

Court and culture

The first point this case-history exemplifies is the role played by the imperial court in the social and cultural life of the Roman aristocracy. Titus, brought up within the palace as the playmate of Britannicus was hardly an exceptional case. He will have been one of a crowd of sons of favoured courtiers and members of the aristocracy who frequented the palace. He probably owed his place to the influence of the freedman Narcissus who got Vespasian his command in the invasion of Britain (*Vesp.* 4.1) and is glimpsed manoeuvring in support of his protégé Britannicus in the incident of the fortune-teller.

---

is quite different from the fictions in the Historia Augusta documented by Syme, *Ammianus and the Historia Augusta* (1968) or in Greek poets' lives, exposed by M.R. Lefkowitz, *Lives of the Greek Poets* (1981).

Titus' presence in the palace was due to the old Roman social institution of the *contubernium*. A young noble of the republic learned the arts of war and government by joining the 'mess' (*contubernium*) of a magistrate abroad. A young man learned the art of speaking by joining the mess of an orator, as Albucius Silus joined Plancus' *contubernium* (*Gramm.* 30), or Suetonius himself joined Pliny's. Under the emperors it was natural for the ambitious to give their sons the best opportunities by living in the emperor's *contubernium*. Emperors willingly surrounded themselves with young men in conformity to established practice. It was an old custom which Claudius revived to invite not only his own children but the sons and daughters of the nobility to attend his dinners; they sat at the feet of their parents' couches (32). It is a striking statistic that emerges from the *Caesars* that despite civil war and changes of dynasty, nearly every emperor had known the court in his youth. Galba was a favourite of Livia, and had his cheeks pinched by Augustus (*Galb.* 4.1). Otho was the son of a Claudian courtier, certainly known personally to the emperor who publicly expressed the compliment that he himself could hardly hope for better children (*Oth.* 1.3). Vitellius is alleged to have spent his teens on Capri as a sexual favourite of Tiberius (*Vit.* 3.2). Even if we question this allegation, there is no reason to doubt Vitellius' presence in the imperial *contubernium*. It was a situation which easily gave rise to ribald comment; as when the young Julius was at the court of Nicomedes of Bithynia (49.1) or when the young noble Valerius Catullus raised a laugh by declaring that his sides were sore from the *contubernium* of Caligula (36.1).

Emperors did not live in glorious isolation. It was a topic of panegyric that they had no such thing as a private life, since they lived bathed in limelight. The presence of the young aristocracy in the palace reflected the presence of their parents. Perhaps indeed we should imagine many courtiers actually living in the palace; Suetonius applies the same term, *contubernium*, to their relationship with the emperor as to that of imperial mothers, mistresses, and the Greek men of learning who had a regular place in the entourage. Vespasian disgraced himself during Nero's tour of Greece and was dismissed from the *contubernium* (*Vesp.* 4.4). Perhaps, like his son Titus, he lived at court already under Claudius.[5]

5. On the topic of the publicity of imperial private life, above ch.7 at n.48. The institution of *contubernium* seems to have escaped investigation; but see

Whether or not courtiers actually took up lodgings in the palace, they lived on terms of close social intimacy with the emperors. The dinner-table had a central place in social life, and this alone justifies Suetonius' attention to imperial dinners. Emperors habitually dined not with their own nuclear households, let alone their slaves and freedmen, but with courtiers and members of the upper classes. Augustus never dined in the company of a man of servile origins, with one exception. His dinners were frequent and select; he would let his guests assemble and start dining before he joined them (74). Like Domitian, he did not stay on for the drinking afterwards (cf. *Dom.* 21). But others did: when Tiberius told the senate, on appointing men to plum jobs, that they had been excellent company round the clock (42.1), senators will have taken for granted the background of hospitality at the Palace. An invitation to dinner was a highly valued honour: Vespasian as praetor actually thanked Caligula formally before the senate for the honour of a dinner-invitation (*Vesp.* 2.3). In the provinces, a local magnate paid as much as 200,000 sesterces to buy himself an evening in Caligula's company (39.2). Sceptical though we may be of the orgiastic excesses attributed to Caligula or Nero, the background they assume of the presence of the aristocracy at the imperial table is credible. Caligula is supposed to have seduced women of distinction when their husbands were his guests (36.2); and it was when dining between the two consuls that he was tickled by the thought of the ease with which they could be executed (32.3).

Because the Palace was a centre of social life for the favoured and their children, it played a large role in affecting the cultural life of the city. The young Vitellius is almost a paradigm: in his teens with Tiberius on Capri, he later drove chariots with Caligula, diced with Claudius, and presided at the theatrical performance at which Nero first played the lyre in public (*Vit.* 3-4). It is plausible enough that imperial tastes had wider repercussions in society at large. It was a commonplace of ancient thought and of imperial panegyric that the ruler set an example which his subjects almost inevitably followed, and that the proper way to rule was not simply by imposing laws, but by setting the right example. So for Pliny, Trajan's life was a model to which his subjects pliably directed themselves. Of course, there is exaggeration in this view: for imperial

above ch.1 n.5. Note the use of the term in relation to Nero's mother (34.1), Vespasian's mistress (3) and men of learning under Augustus (89.1) or Tiberius (56).

mores were not only a model, but also in part a reflection of the *mores* of high society. But that there was a link is clear enough.[6]

The strength of the *Caesars* is that imperial behaviour is not seen in a vacuum, but set against the background of the conduct of a social class. Caligula (54.1) and Nero (20-5) each took their passion for the races to the point of appearing publicly as charioteers. If we isolate them, we are in danger of seeing their behaviour as either wholly eccentric or else crazed by the thirst for popularity, Nero's greatest weakness (53). Yet Augustus himself put on shows in the circus in which young men of the highest nobility appeared as charioteers and matadors; and in reviving the Troy-game in which the young élite fought mock-battles on horseback he regarded it as traditional and proper for young men to come thus into the public eye (43.2). Nero's grandfather Domitius, whom Augustus selected as husband to his own niece Antonia, had in his youth won fame for his skill as a charioteer (*Ner.* 4). It was not so shocking at the time as it might seem to later generations that Caligula put on races in which none but those of senatorial rank (i.e. senators and their families) took part, and decked the circus in scarlet and gold for the occasion (18.3). Vitellius carried to the end a limp resulting from a fall while charioteering with Caligula (*Vit.* 17.2). It was not necessarily a dishonourable wound: Augustus compensated the son of his favourite Nonius Asprenas with a golden torque for a similar accident (43.2). An episode from Nero's schooldays illustrates vividly the fascination which the glamour of the circus exercised on the young aristocracy: caught discussing with his schoolfellows how the Greens charioteer had been dragged behind his chariot, he lied to the master that it was Hector they were talking of (22.1). His schoolfellows will have been courtiers' sons like Titus who cared no less passionately about the races. Titus' ostentatious support for the 'Thracian' side in the gladiatorial arena (8.2) is the product of his upbringing: Caligula, as it happens, supported the same side (54.1).[7]

6. The importance of the court for social life was squarely grasped and well illustrated by Friedländer, *Sittengeschichte* 1, 33-5 (*Life and Manners* 1, 30-3). The necessity for the ruled to base their conduct on that of the rulers was stated by Plato *Laws* 711. Ovid *Metamorphoses* 15.834 speaks of Augustus as ruling morals by his own example. Velleius Paterculus 2.126.5 similarly praises Tiberius: 'the best of princes teaches his citizens to do right by doing it, and though his power is supreme, his example is superior'. Pliny *Pan.* 45.6 describes Trajan's life as a perpetual censorship by example. For later elaborations, see *SHA Sev. Alex.* 41, *Valer.* 5.4-7; Claudian *Pan IV Cos Hon.* 296ff.

7. Evidence of widespread participation by the upper classes of the early empire in public games and races is collected by Friedländer, *Sittengeschichte*

Emperors and hellenisation

Emperors cannot bear sole responsibility for the morals of their times. The court played its role as disseminator, but in its turn it merely responded to larger historical waves of fashion. The common factor that emerges throughout Suetonius' account is the progressive hellenisation of Roman society. What is involved is far more than familiarity with the Greek language, though indeed facility in Greek is attributed to Caesar after Caesar. Beyond this, Suetonius gives us a vivid illustration of the degree to which the Roman aristocratic lifestyle had become penetrated by the fashions and standards of contemporary hellenistic culture.[8]

Part of the story is the hellenisation of Roman education which has already been traced in an earlier chapter (2). Titus may be taken again to exemplify a change. Praised for his singing and dancing (3.2), he had absorbed what was a standard part of the Greek educational curriculum, *musikē*. It was with considerable reluctance that Romans had admitted music to their culture. When the biographer Cornelius Nepos published his *Lives* in the mid first century BC, he found it necessary to apologise for this cultural difference: 'There will doubtless be several who dismiss biography as trivial and unsuitable reading when they read who taught Epaminondas music, and find that among his talents was the ability to dance well and to sing to the flute with accomplishment.' He assumes that a leader of the Roman establishment, a *princeps*, will find such conduct indecent and inconceivable for himself, and merely asks for understanding of cultural differences. Yet by the time of Titus' boyhood, *musikē* had evidently acquired respectability in court circles.[9]

This is the essential background to Nero's notorious passion for music. The young Nero, like Titus, had learnt to identify himself with hellenistic culture. He acquired his skill with other disciplines as a boy (20.1). Imperial power gave him the opportunity to summon to court the leading Greek maestro, Terpnus. He made his public

2, 19-21 (*Life and Manners* 2, 17f.), together with repeated (and vain) attempts by senate and emperor to control this phenomenon.

8. Two recent works have succeeded in lifting the study of hellenisation out of the rut of viewing the 'arts' in isolation: J. Griffin, 'Augustan poetry and the life of luxury', *JRS* 66 (1976) 87ff. and J.H. D'Arms, *The Romans on the Bay of Naples* (1970) which demonstrates the interdependence of leisure, luxury and the arts in this favourite Roman resort.

9. For Nepos' apologies, see *praef.* 1-3 and *Epam.* 1.1-3. On the fashion for music under the empire, Friedländer, *Sittengeschichte* 2, 186-8 (*Life and Manners* 2, 360f.).

début in Greek Naples, and justified his behaviour by quoting a Greek proverb, 'Hidden music wins no respect' (20.1-2). It was from Alexandria that he imported the novelty of a claque of young nobles who would lead the applause at his performances (20.3). The mixed reception which his wholehearted hellenism met at Rome drove him to his tour of Greece: 'only the Greeks knew how to listen and were worthy of his art' (22.3). Roman society at large may have been too old-fashioned to swallow a musical *princeps*; yet he was not out of step with the young nobles with whom he grew up. Caligula was proud enough of his song and dance to summon three ex-consuls to watch his display at dead of night (54.2). It must be assumed that Britannicus too had some musical talent. Traditionally it was by the singing of a ballad that he signed his own death-warrant. In Suetonius' view, Nero was jealous of Britannicus' voice (33.2). As he had reported, Nero's own voice was feeble and husky and caused him much trouble (20.1).

Nero or Titus could blame their parents' generation for their 'corruption', for it was they who had eagerly filled the court with the Greeks who made inevitable the assimilation of Greek tastes. It is under Tiberius, who had developed marked hellenistic tastes on Rhodes, that the presence of Greeks at court makes itself most insistently felt. They were regular members of his entourage before his accession: they formed the third of three classes into which he divided his *comites* in making a distribution of money (46). It was already on Rhodes that he admitted the astrologer Thrasyllus into his *contubernium* as a man of learning (14.4). Thrasyllus must have lived with him from that moment to the end; certainly he is found in Tiberius' company as a *comes*, just before Augustus' death (*Aug.* 98.4) and just before Tiberius' own (*Tib.* 62.3). But not only was Tiberius persistently mean to his suite of Greeks (46); they too felt the rough edge of his temper, and one Xeno was exiled for a tactless use of the Doric dialect (56). Even if Tiberius took his taste (especially for grammatical learning) to extremes, there was no novelty in a Greek entourage. Augustus had benefited from the company of the rhetorician Apollodorus of Pergamum and the philosopher Areius of Alexandria in his youth, and Areius' sons Dionysius and Nicanor must have joined his *contubernium* during his reign (89.1). There were others too whom Suetonius does not mention.[10]

10. For other Greeks at Augustus' court see Bowersock, *Augustus and the Greek World* 30f.

Another sign of the fashion for Greek ways is the strong pull exercised by the bay of Naples. The 'golden crescent' had been a popular resort since the late republic. Suetonius gives us more than one glimpse of the eagerness with which emperors turned to the bay in order to 'go Greek'. Augustus spent the last days before his death there. He was in sunny mood, and distributed money and clothes to his companions, ruling that they should speak and dress *à la Grècque* if Roman – and vice versa. The money was to be spent on goods from Alexandria alone (98.2-3). Visiting the island off Capri which he dubbed 'Apragopolis' – a Greek city of *dolce far niente* – he improvised over dinner two lines in Greek, and teased Thrasyllus to divine their authorship (98.4). At Naples he watched a quinquennial festival instituted in his honour (98.5). It was to be a Neapolitan festival at which Nero first performed in public (*Ner.* 20.2), and it was surely such festivals that provided the model for Nero's quinquennial festival at Rome, *more Graeco* (12.3).[11]

The bay of Naples, as well as being the centre of Greek culture, was ever a centre of scandal. Augustus reproached the impeccable L. Vinicius for so much as calling on his daughter at Baiae (64.2). For Baiae that was modesty indeed. Caligula's great bridge of boats across the bay was, on the other hand, an eccentricity. Perhaps, as the biographer's grandfather alleged, it was done to controvert a remark by Thrasyllus (19.3). But certainly Baiae, where the rich and fashionable clustered, was the place to stage such an extravaganza. The luxury yachts with their orchestras and choruses in which Caligula cruised the Campanian coast (37.2) were another hellenistic feature familiar at Baiae.

The retreat of Tiberius to Capri took a well-established pattern to extremes. The scandal his retreat provoked strains the modern reader's credulity. Yet sexual conduct too is a cultural phenomenon. Doubtless invention has played a large part, but the credible side of the behaviour attributed to him is its hellenism, plausible enough in a man of hellenistic taste in a hellenistic centre. Grottoes in the woods where young nymphs and Pans disported themselves, Greek pornographic literature (the books of Elephantis) and erotic paintings (43.2), including a favourite picture by the artist Parrasius

11. For the role of the bay of Naples in hellenisation and for its popularity with the Julio-Claudians, see D'Arms, *The Romans and the Bay of Naples*, esp. 73ff.

depicting Atalanta engaged with Meleager (44.2), all chime with contemporary hellenistic taste.[12]

Homosexual tastes derived from the same source, or at least were deliberately dressed up by Romans in Greek fashions. Tiberius called his male favourites *spintriae* after the appropriate Greek anatomical term (43.1). It was a nickname which stuck to the young Vitellius, thanks to his presence in the entourage (*Vit.* 3.2). Caligula had experienced the dangers of the court on Capri (10) and one of his first reactions on Tiberius' death was to have the *spintriae* banned, and almost drowned (*Cal.* 16.1). Homosexuality was certainly widespread in high society. Claudius' complete lack of interest in males (33.2) was the exception. Titus' male favourites and *castrati* (7.1) were *à la mode*. Nero's castrated favourite Sporus achieved notoriety by accompanying the emperor in public in female dress (28). Petronius' contemporary novel, the *Satyricon*, gives a clear enough picture of the services eunuchs offered.

Other diversions were at least in name imports. Domitian used the Greek term *clinopale* to describe his sexual athletics (22). Oral practices were regarded as un-Roman, and it was possible to raise a public laugh by an allusion to the proclivities in this direction of Tiberius, the old goat of Capri (45). One of the surest signs of fashion is when the *parvenu* apes the manners of the aristocracy. The grammarian Remmius Palaemon, born a slave, made a fortune and was able to adopt the luxurious ways of the upper classes. His oral practices were a public scandal, and Tiberius and Claudius thought fit to declare that he was unsuitable to be entrusted with the care of children (*Gramm.* 23). Tiberius' public pronouncements did not necessarily square with his private life.[13]

12. Tiberius' cultural interests are best documented by the paper of A.F. Stewart, 'To entertain an emperor: Sperlonga, Laokoon, and Tiberius at the dinner-table', *JRS* 67 (1977) 76ff.; starting from the archaeological remains at Sperlonga this ranges over Tiberius' cultural interests as a whole. The deficiency in modern 'biographies' of Tiberius which simply omit this dimension of his existence is observed by Syme, 'History or biography: the case of Tiberius Caesar', Historia 23 (1974) 481ff. To make biography out of paraphrase of annalistic historians is precisely what S avoided doing.

13. O. Kiefer, *Sexual Life in Ancient Rome* (Eng. trans. 1934) gives an unsatisfactory account of Roman sexual *mores*. The topic still awaits serious study. For the tendency of court *mores* to affect those lower down the social scale, compare the material on the English restoration period presented by L. Stone, *The Family, Sex and Marriage in England 1500-1800* (1977) 529ff. (Pelican ed., p.349ff.).

One fashion where the Greek manners in sex and in music converged was that of pantomime. Ranging from the tragic to the bawdy this type of semi-operatic performance dominated the stage under the early empire. According to the tradition reported in a lost work by Suetonius, pantomime was imported to Rome from Alexandria by the artists Pylades and Bathyllus. The vogue owed much to Maecenas' passion for Bathyllus, and probably also to support from Augustus, though Suetonius is careful to note that Augustus curbed the excesses of performers by punishing Hylas and Pylades (45.4). Caligula took this fashion, as so much else, to extremes; he embraced the doyen of the stage, Mnester, in public and flogged a spectator who heckled him (55.1). Contemporary evidence reveals that Caligula reflects the behaviour of a class: aristocratic households possessed their own troupes of actors and built private stages for their performances. Nero's operatic appearances may have been a far cry from the bawdier excesses of pantomime (21.3) but are rightly seen against the background of this aristocratic and hellenistic fashion.[14]

A final example of hellenisation may be seen in dicing (*alea*). In the late republic gambling was regarded with extreme disapproval. Suetonius' evidence suggests that by the principate gaming (at least in moderation) had become acceptable. Dicing on festal days was a charge Augustus happily admitted: Suetonius cites three letters at considerable length to show the emperor playing, for fun rather than money, with members of his family and with noble friends (71). There is no reproach either against Claudius' passion for the game, which led him to compose a monograph on the topic, and to fit a travelling board to his carriage (33.2). Even Domitian escapes censure (21). Condemnation is reserved for excess. The spendthrift Nero played for disproportionate stakes, 400,000 sesterces a point (30.3), while Caligula is even supposed to have viewed gambling as a supplementary source of revenue (41.2).[15]

---

14. On pantomime, see Friedländer, *Sittengeschichte* 2, 125f. (*Life and Manners* 2, 100f.). On the introduction of pantomime to Rome, E. J. Jory, 'The literary evidence for the beginnings of Imperial pantomime', *Bull. Inst. Class. Stud.* 28 (1981) 147ff.

15. On dicing, see J.P.V.D. Balsdon, *Life and Leisure in Ancient Rome* (1969) 154-9.

The Flavians and reaction

The hellenisation documented in the *Caesars* is only part of a long process, which was already in full swing in the late republic and went back before that to the first Roman contacts with Greece. The Caesars could use their wealth in taking to the ultimate degree fashions already espoused by the aristocracy of the late republic – only that their feasts were more lavish, their palaces larger and richer, their properties on the bay of Naples more extensive, including whole islands. At the same time, the court acted as a sort of hothouse of luxury and refined taste. Caligula, Nero, Otho, Vitellius, even Titus were products of a court environment. But hellenisation was not a straight-line process, and there are in the *Caesars* unmistakable signs of a reaction.

Titus may again be taken to epitomise the change. The surprise is that so Neronian a figure on his accession renounced his old ways. He changed the company of wastrels for that of sober statesmen; his feasts no longer extended to midnight, and were pleasant but not extravagant; his troupe of favourites and dancers was disbanded; and queen Berenice sadly took her leave (7.2). The implication is that any other course would have ill befitted an emperor. It is hardly an assumption Nero himself would have shared. But after his death, assumptions changed, and the accession of Vespasian marks something of a watershed.

Certainly the tone of Vespasian's own private life is very much more restrained than that of his predecessors. Vespasian was no saint. He had his freedwoman mistress Caenis, and after her numerous concubines (21). He treated such matters light-heartedly: when a woman declared herself dying of love for him and extracted a modest fortune in return for her favours, he had his steward enter in the accounts, 'the price of being loved' (22). But in this earthy realism there was nothing to shock traditional Roman sentiment. In public, Vespasian sought to stem the tide of luxury and lust (11). The principate now offered a new and sterner face.

The new mood continued under Domitian, at least as far as concerned public appearances. His entertainments were frequent but hardly orgiastic: he left the table after sundown, and never stayed for the drinking (21). Pantomimes, which his brother had abstained from watching in public, fell into deeper disfavour, and were banned from all but domestic stages (7.1). A certain senator who was thought too keen on dancing and mime was stripped of his rank (8.3). The ban chimed with the dominant mood, for though Nerva (himself probably a product of the Julio-Claudian court) reversed it, it was reimposed, supposedly at popular request, by Trajan. A vignette by Pliny neatly illustrates the shift of mood in aristocratic households. His protégé Ummidius Quadratus, a budding orator, had a grandmother Quadratilla, rich and aristocratic, whose heyday will have been the reign of Nero. A relic of a past age, she still possessed a troupe of pantomimes, the most famous in the city. But the young Quadratus (to Pliny's approval) made a point of never watching them.[16]

There was a reaction too against the sexual practices of the past generation. Domitian brought the full force of censorial severity to bear against adultery, homosexuality and the breaking of their vows by the Vestal Virgins (8.3-4). Moreover he outlawed the practice of castration (7.1), a ban in which some observers detected a pointed reference to the eunuchs of his brother Titus. Not that Domitian practised what he preached. The numerous epigrams addressed by Martial to his eunuch favourite Earinus lie cheek by jowl with his celebrations of the ban. It was public sentiment that had shifted. Hellenistic fashions in singing, dancing and sex were out.[17]

Biography is a good source for the *mores* of an age. But Suetonius does not see fit to comment on the phenomena he attests: explanation was not the business of the scholar and biographer. For that we must turn to the historian Tacitus. In a notable excursus (*Annals* 3.55) he observes that luxury, having reached a peak in the century between Actium and the fall of Nero, subsequently died away. He points to three factors: first the elimination of the old noble households, partly through their own competitive extravagance; then, linked with the first, the rise of a new class from municipal and colonial backgrounds, accustomed to more austere ways; finally and above all, the accession of an emperor in Vespasian who embodied old-fashioned sobriety and set the tone for the new age.

In conjunction these three factors are convincing. Paradoxically the noble families of the republic were the most forward in hellenisation and the least good custodians of traditional Roman ways, because their wealth gave them opportunity, and their competitive

---

16. On the rescindment and reimposition of the ban on pantomimes, Pliny *Pan.* 46 (a remarkable piece of special pleading). On Quadratilla, *Ep.* 7.24.

17. On Domitian's censorial activity see S. Gsell, *Essai sur Domitien*, 75f. His hypocrisy is criticised by Dio 67.2.3, Juvenal 2.29-33, and by implication and contrast with Trajan by Pliny *Pan.* 45.4-47.

spirit provided the incentive. Of course, new families like the Vitellii from Nuceria might adopt the same ways, but only when access to the centre of power in Rome and particularly at court gave them the opportunity to learn. Vespasian was evidently a different type of man. That was due not only to his relatively modest origins in Reate (1.2) but to the fact that it was late in life that he began to think of a public career (2.2). Only after his quaestorship did he come into contact with court circles, and then perhaps only through the accident that his mistress Caenis was a freedwoman of the imperial household, and presumably a friend of the powerful Narcissus (3-4). It was too late for him to acquire court fashions. It was doubtless with unaffected boredom that he yawned at Nero's *bel canto* and so forfeited his position in the imperial suite (4.4).

But a fourth factor must also be central in explanation of the change: the rising tide of indignation and revulsion generated by the excesses of Nero and his court which is unmistakable in the accounts of the reign. Nero represents the high water mark of hellenistic fashion. It was one thing to 'go Greek' at Naples, another to do so in Rome. Even his dress and hairstyle, in neatly tiered waves, followed Greek fashion to Roman outrage (51). His extravagant gesture in granting the cities of Greece freedom and immunity from taxes (24.2) is the symbol of a genuine and fanatical passion for Greek culture, which, though largely shared by his predecessors, was felt to have passed the bounds of the acceptable. In the backlash it was Vespasian, not his son Titus, who was deemed to offer the proper model.[18]

The reaction was not, however, against Greek culture as a whole, but against those aspects categorised as luxury. Vespasian was emphatic in his patronage of the arts. He not only founded the first chairs of Latin and Greek rhetoric at Rome, but was unusually liberal towards poets, sculptors, actors and musicians (17-19). Domitian was hardly less enthusiastic a patron, though Suetonius is unwilling to give him credit. Despite his alleged neglect of liberal studies, and his choice of the official records of Tiberius for light reading in preference to poetry or history, his care in restoring libraries could not be denied (20). Moreover he instituted art-festivals that outshone even Nero's: a Greek-style quinquennial

---

18. Tacitus' analysis is discussed by B.H. Warmington, *Nero: Reality and Legend* (1969) 169f.; cf. Williams, *Change and Decline* 283f. Nero's hellenism is sympathetically handled by Warmington 108f.

festival of musical, equestrian and athletic events that included a competition in Greek and Latin prose and lyre-playing, both accompanied and solo; and in addition he held at his Alban villa an annual festival of Minerva, patron goddess of the arts, with prizes for orators and poets (4.4). The facts which Suetonius, as connoisseur of festivals and libraries, adduces, seem to refute the slur on Domitian's cultural interests.

The Flavians thus endorsed and promoted one part of hellenistic culture and rejected another. The judgment of what was good ('the arts') and what unacceptable ('luxury') was of course an old one, both at Rome and among the Greeks themselves. But the Flavians by setting an example and giving encouragement played an important part in the process of cultural assimilation at Rome.[19]

Religion, superstition and fatalism

While Titus was being brought up at the court of Claudius his future power was allegedly foretold by a visiting soothsayer. The man's skill was Greek: he was a *metoposcopus*, a 'face-reader' or physiognomist. The incident may serve as a reminder that religious and superstitious belief was another area of culture affected by the process of hellenisation. Here too Suetonius, with his fascination for omens and signs of the future, has invaluable information to supply.[20]

To the modern reader Suetonius may appear disappointing on this subject: he says too little about the religious beliefs of his Caesars, too much about the trivial omens which we regard with contempt. His treatment of the beliefs of Augustus, by far the fullest, sets the pattern. Three paragraphs examine in detail Augustus' superstitions: his fear of thunder, his careful observance of dreams, auspices and portents and his avoidance of unlucky days (90-2). Then comes a paragraph on his attitude to foreign cults: he revered the ancient and approved ones, like the mysteries of Eleusis in

---

19. On Flavian patronage of the arts, see briefly M.S. Woodside, 'Vespasian's patronage of education and the arts', *Trans. Am. Phil. Ass.* 73 (1942) 123ff. For literary circles under Domitian, P. White, 'The friends of Martial, Statius, and Pliny, and the dispersal of patronage', *Harvard Stud. Class. Phil.* 79 (1975) 265ff. is helpful, but does not touch on the role of imperial patronage.

20. S's 'superstition' is handled unsympathetically by Macé (1900) 59ff., much more satisfactorily by della Corte (1967) 55ff. Gugel (1977) 24ff. is mainly concerned with structural problems.

Attica, but despised the rest, taking no notice in Egypt of the bull-cult of Apis, and congratulating his grandson for passing by the temple in Jerusalem (93). To this he finds it 'not irrelevant' to append a list of signs of the future greatness of Augustus, a list of quite unusual length and detail, containing some twenty-six various items (94-7).

Yet for the Roman, religion was not a matter of faith and spiritual searching. Augustus was indeed a remarkable religious reformer and restorer (31), but when the biographer turns to the private life and the inner man, he has no spiritual convictions to document from which these reforms might flow, only a list of what we regard as superstitions. The much scrappier notices of religious beliefs in other lives follow the same pattern. Tiberius neglected religion because of his addiction to astrology, though he was afraid of thunder (69). The neglect referred to is evidently neglect of the other types of sign to which Augustus paid attention. Nero is characterised as a *contemptor* of the gods: after a brief flirtation with a foreign superstition, the cult of Dea Syria, he repudiated the goddess by polluting her shrine with urine. He ignored traditional practices, like inspection of entrails and sacrifice, and only took seriously a good luck charm in the shape of a doll which some plebeian had given him (56). Galba took seriously his cult of Fortune (4.3). Vespasian was passionately convinced of one thing, that it was in their stars that his sons would succeed him (25).

There is little reason to suppose that Suetonius gives an unrepresentative picture of the emperors' attitudes to religion. For the Roman, worship was indeed a matter of ritual practice: it made no demands on the intellect or the emotions. Religions that did make such demands, like Christianity and the Egyptian cult of Isis spreading from the east in this period, were horrific to traditional Roman sentiment. Suetonius makes clear his approval for Augustus' contempt for Jewish and Egyptian cults, and condemns Christianity roundly. On the other hand, Suetonius' documentation puts beyond doubt the seriousness with which superstitious prognostications of the future were regarded. That, for him, is the heart of a man's religion.[21]

21. The strictly ritualistic nature of traditional Roman cults is emphasised by A.D. Nock in *Cambridge Ancient History* 10 (1934) 465. J.H.W.G. Liebeschuetz, *Continuity and Change in Roman Religion* (1979) is an invaluable introduction to Roman religious attitudes. Against underestimating the validity of ritualistic religion, see the warnings of Mary Douglas, *Natural Symbols*[2] (1973).

A famous letter to Suetonius from Pliny provides external evidence of the author's own superstitious convictions (1.18). A bad dream had persuaded him of the advisability of seeking a postponement of a case he was due to plead. The letter has been used to condemn Suetonius, as if to be superstitious were an intellectual failing. This condemnation is an unnecessary intrusion of modern values. Pliny was not shocked by Suetonius' request. Though he tries to cajole him into continuing the case, he never suggests that a dream is no proper ground for seeking deferment. 'A dream comes from Zeus', in Homer's words, and the only question is whether the dreams that come to Suetonius usually turn out true or not. As the biographer records of Augustus, it was possible to have nightmares every springtime which proved fruitless, rarer dreams through the rest of the year that were more reliable (91.1).

Suetonius' signs are better not taken as evidence of his personal failings; it is more revealing to use them to interpret the norms of his society. We may start by observing what types of signs and portents he records in what context. There is here another important contrast with historiography. Roman annalists, influenced by the annual lists of events customarily recorded by the Pontifices, included lists of portents in their narratives. This was a tradition which culminated in Livy, and the interest of a later excerpter, Julius Obsequens, has preserved his portent lists in large part. In religious terms, the significance of portents under the republic was an indication of the temper of the gods; unless the wrath they implied was propitiated, disaster would follow. In dramatic terms this enabled the historian to accelerate the pulse of his narrative: a long list of portents presaged major conflicts and disasters.[22]

Both in religious and artistic terms Suetonius' portents are a very different business. They serve to indicate not the mood of the gods, which can be turned aside, but the inevitable course of the future. And as the biographer has little interest in narrative or drama, they hardly quicken the pulse, but merely demonstrate that what happened was foreseeable. All Suetonius' lists of signs revolve round two issues, and two only: the rise to imperial power and the fall from it. This is clearest in the life of Augustus where all the signs are gathered together in one section: the long list of the signs of his 'future greatness' is arranged chronologically, culminating with the prediction of his victory at Actium (96.2); there is then an abrupt

22. On the contrast in essence between republican and imperial prognostication, Liebeschuetz, *Continuity and Change* esp. 56ff.

jump to signs of his death (97.1-2). The accessions and deaths of Caesars are the subjects of nearly all Suetonius' signs. An exception is the eagle which announced Domitian's victory over the rebel Antonius (6.2), but here too the issue is whether a Caesar will or will not come to the end of his reign. Not only individuals but dynasties have their rise and fall predicted. The life of Galba, the first emperor from outside Augustus' family, opens with the signs of the fall of the Julio-Claudian dynasty (1). Vespasian foresaw the length of the rule of his family in a dream (25). The life of the last Caesar ends with presages of the felicity of the coming Golden Age: the crow that cried that all would be well, and Domitian's dream that a golden hump sprung up on his back (23.2).

Behind Suetonius' signs lies the assumption that the course of future events is predestined, and that destiny can be foreseen if one reads the signs aright. It is an attitude to portents radically different from the republican one. It also involves a vital shift in interest from the fortunes of the state to the fortunes of the individuals upon whom the state depended. The superstitious beliefs that Suetonius documents thus accurately reflect the massive political shift of replacement of republic by autocracy. Correspondingly there is a significant shift in the types of prognostication. There is relatively little in Suetonius of the traditional Roman methods of divination: observation of the flight of birds, inspection of the organs of sacrificial animals, and reports of monstrous and unnatural phenomena (two-headed births, weeping statues, voices in heaven and the like). Instead Suetonius' signs are of the types that best reveal the destinies of individuals. There are occasional oracles: thus Nero is told by Delphi to beware the seventy-third year, an allusion, though he misses it, to the age of Galba (*Ner.* 40.3). Sayings of emperors are regarded as significant; Augustus told Galba that he too would have his nibble of power (*Galb.* 4.1). Odd occurrences may be interpreted: if Vespasian had his lap filled with mud as a punishment for slovenly supervision of street-cleaning, it might be taken to foreshadow the way he received into his bosom the trampled state (5.3). But there are two methods above all that for Suetonius offer a reliable guide to the future: the interpretation of dreams and the reading of the stars by astrology. The range of methods of prognostication Suetonius invokes is wide, and it is difficult to find a word that embraces them all – signs, portents, omens, auspices, dreams, pointers, predictions. He notes that Tiberius' dedication to astrology involved neglect of other methods of prognostication (69). But behind all the types of sign he adduces lies the common premise which provided the foundation of the sciences of dream-interpretation and astrology – that the workings of fate are fixed and can be foreseen.[23]

Suetonius himself clearly took prognostication seriously. But, more important, his evidence shows how seriously it was taken by others at every social level, and how deeply embedded it was in imperial culture. When the physiognomist visited Titus and Britannicus, it was not as an idle amusement like visiting the fortune-teller at the fair. Suetonius specifies that he was brought in by Narcissus. The context can be guessed: the struggle over the prospects for succession between Narcissus and his rival Pallas who supported the young Nero. The physiognomist is summoned as a move in the game of palace politics. There is abundant evidence that all the actors took such moves extremely seriously.[24]

It is conventional to appeal to a rather different mode of explanation. The rationalism of the eighteenth century branded all forms of superstition as the product of 'irrationality'. A 'two-tiered' model of religious belief emerged: on the one hand the upper classes, educated and rational, were (or should be) untouched by superstition; on the other the illiterate masses owed their superstition to their ignorance and 'primitive' condition. On this model, we may argue that the signs reported by Suetonius only represent the calculated manipulation of popular superstition by members of the upper classes who themselves saw through such tricks; and that if indeed any members of the upper classes did themselves believe these signs, that must indicate a 'descent' on their part to vulgar irrationality. The objection to Suetonius' own superstition is that it assimilates him to the vulgar and illiterate.[25]

23. The types of portent to be found in S are analysed by T.B. Krauss, *An Interpretation of the Omens, Portents and Prodigies recorded by Livy, Tacitus and Suetonius* (Diss. Philadelphia 1930). F. Wagner, *De ominibus quae ab Augusti temporibus usque ad Diocletiani aetatem Caesaribus facta traduntur* (Diss. Jena 1888) 7ff. shows that S assumes that portents are in principle veridical.

24. So much is argued and documented in R. MacMullen, *Enemies of the Roman Order* (1966) 128ff. The fullest work on astrology in imperial culture is F.A. Cramer, *Astrology in Roman Law and Politics* (Mem. Amer. Philos. Soc. 37, 1954). See also Liebeschuetz, *Continuity and Change* 119ff.

25. The 'two-tiered' model of explanation in the case of late antique superstition is identified and demolished by Peter Brown, *The Cult of the Saints; its rise and function in Latin Christianity* (1981) esp. 17-22. What he says, drawing on the insights of social anthropology, can be applied with equal justice to all antiquity.

Of the use of superstition to manipulate popular opinion there can be no doubt. Before his accession Vespasian lacked authority and majesty: a miracle-healing staged publicly in Alexandria and the convenient discovery in Arcadia of an image resembling Vespasian did much to enhance his stature (7.2-3). The East had long been in turmoil with predictions of a coming Messiah (4.5); Vespasian took care to identify himself with the promised one, approaching the oracle on mount Carmel and welcoming the predictions of the captive Josephus (5.6-7). Galba was emboldened to declare his hand against Nero by a prophecy conveniently discovered at Clunia in Spain (9.2). Augustus too was surrounded by messianic tales. A halo was observed round his head on his first entry to Rome after the death of Caesar (95). His freedman Julius Marathus was able to allege a slaughter of the innocents on senatorial command in Rome in the year of his birth (94.3). Augustus himself advertised portents, albeit of a less exotic nature. Whether or not he actually met a man called Lucky (Eutychus) riding an ass called Winner (Nicon) on the eve of the battle of Actium, he took care to set up statues of them in his temple of Victory at Actium (96.2).[26]

Calculated manipulation there certainly was; but the thesis cannot be sustained that the manipulators were themselves above superstition. Of Tiberius' addiction to astrological science (69) there can be no question. Nor can one reasonably doubt other emperors' superstitions, like Augustus' seal-skin amulet against lightning (90), Nero's good luck charm (56) or Galba's cult of Fortuna (4.3). Nor can it be maintained that the only function of prognostications was to influence public belief. They could also play an important role in encouraging the actors themselves to undertake dangerous and unpredictable enterprises. Octavian, before embarking from Apollonia on the death of Julius, approached an astrologer in company with his friend Agrippa: the incredible promises of the horoscope cast for Agrippa all but deterred him from taking his turn (94.12). Tiberius' intimacy with the astrologer Thrasyllus in his days of despair on Rhodes (14.4) speaks for itself. Titus, in doubt as to what course to take in the confusion after the murder of Galba,

---

26. On the messianic prophecies surrounding Augustus, see the learned study of W. Déonna, 'La légende d'Octave Auguste Dieu, Sauveur et maître du monde', *Rev. Hist. Rel.* 83 (1921) 32ff. and 163ff., 84 (1921) 77ff. On Vespasian's miracle working at Alexandria and its political value, A. Henrichs, 'Vespasian's visit to Alexandria', *Zeitschrift für Papyrologie und Epigr.* 3 (1968) 51ff.

stopped off to consult the oracle of Venus on Paphos (5.1). Vespasian could allay his sense of insecurity in the suite of Nero by seeing in his emperor's loss of a tooth a fulfilment of a dream promising him future felicity (5.5).

Future emperors were not the only aristocrats anxious about their own fates, and the power of prognostications to give courage was something that cut both ways. The danger to emperors from men who were encouraged by favourable predictions, or who used predictions to strengthen their own followings, was constant. There were repeated expulsions of astrologers from Rome throughout the first century AD. Vitellius, whose own horoscope horrified his parents (3.2), waged war upon the astrologers; when he banned them from Rome, they countered by banning him from the world of the living (14.4). Domitian is vividly depicted on the eve of his murder as thrown into a state of panic by predictions of doom, executing offending astrologers and prophets (14-16). The executions are credible enough, even if we do not believe that he was so frightened of a particular predicted hour that a false announcement that the hour was passed allowed his palace staff to catch him off his guard (16.2). Again, executions of aristocrats for possessing horoscopes foretelling their own rule, like that of Mettius Pompusianus under Domitian (10.3), reflect the widespread practice of consulting astrologers among the aristocracy. To ask to have the emperor's own horoscope cast became a criminal offence. The anxiety of emperors led them to publish their own horoscopes as a countermove; Augustus even minted his birth-sign of Capricorn on a coin (94.12). A sort of confidence-trick was enacted by Titus to disarm potential opposition: in assuring conspirators that 'the principate was given by fate' (9.1) he made the implied assumption not only that he himself was the fated ruler, but that the fact was demonstrable and known.[27]

Widespread belief in and practice of prognostication is a characteristic feature of imperial society. Without attempting a full explanation of this phenomenon, we can point to certain factors. The political shift to autocracy is, as we have seen, one of them: the fortune of the state now depended so much on the chances of the individual who held power. But another factor worth stressing in this context is the compatibility of superstition with the hellenisation

27. For further (abundant) evidence on this topic, see Cramer, *Astrology* 81ff; Liebeschuetz, *Continuity and Change* 122-6.

of culture. The rise in popularity of astrology, and to a lesser extent of dream-interpretation, emerges clearly enough from the *Caesars*. Both these disciplines and most of their practitioners were Greek. Not only that, but they enjoyed high repute in the intellectual world. Tiberius' astrologer friend Thrasyllus was a learned man, and also a commentator on Plato; he stands on an intellectual footing with Tiberius' grammarian friends or the rhetorician Theodorus of Gadara. This fact alone should warn against the interpretation of superstitious beliefs in the imperial period either as representing an advance of 'irrationality' or as a cynical exploitation by the educated upper classes of the vulgar superstitions of the ignorant and uneducated masses.

To a sophisticated and book-learned society there was great attraction in sciences of prediction that were complex in their workings but had an apparent empirical basis: astrology, dream-interpretation and physiognomics all appeared more credible than archaic rituals like the inspection of livers. Their professors were as much in place at court as any other men of high learning. Certainly this is true of the court of Hadrian. The sophist Polemon of Laodicea who wrote an important work on physiognomical interpretation counted himself a friend of Hadrian; he accompanied the emperor on his tour of Asia, and was careful to include in his book a description of the brilliance of Hadrian's eyes, and to comment that this was a sign of excellent character. Astrologers were among the intellectuals at his court. The biographer Marius Maximus claimed that Hadrian was himself an adept astrologer: he predicted each day's events hour by hour. The extremely detailed analysis of Hadrian's horoscope preserved in later astrological handbooks reflects his interest in this discipline. The intellectual vogue for the 'pseudo'-sciences continued after Hadrian. Ptolemy, famous as a geographer, was also the author of the *Tetrabiblos*, one of the most important handbooks of astrology. The same period produced the highly sophisticated *Interpretation of Dreams* by Artemidorus, while the brilliant but neurotic sophist Aelius Aristides published a diary of his own dreams.[28]

28. The academic credentials of astrologers are demonstrated by Cramer 82ff. On Polemon and his friendship with Hadrian, see E.C. Evans, *Physiognomics in the Ancient World* (Trans. Amer. Phil. Soc. 59, 1969) esp. 11-13. Artemidorus is now available in translation by R.J. White, *The Interpretation of Dreams* (1975). On Hadrian's interest in astrology, *SHA Hadr.* 16.7; *Aelius* 3.9; Cramer

The learned scholar Suetonius belongs very much in the company of such men. The dry lists of characteristics in physiognomists such as Polemon offer the closest stylistic parallel to Suetonius' descriptions of physical appearance. Artemidorus' anxiety to raise his art above street-corner quackery is apparent in the care with which he sorts and organises dreams into types within a coherent intellectual framework: he draws on a biographical schema to organise his work. Any feeling of distaste that a highly educated man could be superstitious could not be more misleading. The picture of Suetonius as catering for a vulgar, tasteless, trivial and prurient audience must be abandoned. Here again he emerges as the scholar, at home in a scholarly age and court, of value to us because he understood the ways of previous Caesars and their courts.

162ff. The scientific and rational approach of these authors should not be underestimated; interpretation of the social place of pseudo-sciences must now start from Keith Thomas, *Religion and the Decline of Magic* (1971) esp. 283ff. On the horoscope of Hadrian and two others close to him preserved in Hephaestion *Apotelesmatica* 2.18.22f., see T.D. Barnes, *Phoenix* 30 (1976) 76ff.

Epilogue

PAST AND PRESENT

Any author who looks back to the past is liable to find reflected in it the present he knows. If he looks for lessons or *exempla*, they will be ones with relevance for his contemporaries. This indeed was a justification Romans conventionally offered for the writing of history. The scholarly Suetonius distanced himself from the goals of the historian, and his *Caesars* do not pretend to a didactic purpose. Yet the present might still have its relevance. Contemporary preoccupations might lie behind his choice of material and the questions he sought to answer. There might too be quite irrational echoes, when the past proved to anticipate and foreshadow current events or personalities.

Such echoes have been detected in the *Caesars*. In particular it is tempting to catch fleeting glimpses of Hadrian behind Suetonius' descriptions of his predecessors. There are striking similarities. Suspicion surrounded the circumstances of Hadrian's imperial proclamation. His adoption was only announced as Trajan lay dying: there were those who believed he had died before the announcement, and that his wife Plotina concealed the truth. Similar suspicions surrounded the accession of Tiberius: had he reached the bedside of the dying Augustus in time, or had Livia deceived the public by false bulletins? Tacitus hinted at the worst, and some modern scholars see in this a conscious reminiscence of Hadrian's accession. Suetonius goes out of his way to rebut malicious rumours about Tiberius. He cites, seemingly for the first time, Augustus' own correspondence (*Tib.* 21); and he draws on a source who could describe intimately, and therefore to all appearances authentically, the last moments and words of the old emperor (*Aug.* 98-9). It could be interpreted as a gesture of loyal support by Hadrian's *ab epistulis*.[1]

1. On Hadrianic echoes in the *Caesars* see the judicious discussion of Townend (1959) 290f. Carney (1968) speculates on the basis of hints of personal agreements and disagreements between author and emperor. See also Cizek (1977) 181-92.

This is not the only point at which Tiberius may have reminded Suetonius' contemporaries of their own emperor. Tiberius the cultured dilettante offers numerous possible points of contact. He plagued his grammarian friends with problems as Hadrian tested the professors of Alexandria. Both might be regarded as *Graeculi* in their enthusiasm for hellenistic culture. If Tiberius favoured Parthenius, Hadrian actually restored his tomb. Neither was wholly equable in his relations with intellectuals: while Tiberius turned against the learned Xenon and Seleucus, Hadrian quarrelled jealously with the learned in general, from Favorinus the sophist to Apollodorus the architect. Both were dedicated students of astrological science. Both had reputations as voluptuaries; and by a freak of coincidence the equestrian post *a voluptatibus* which Tiberius instituted is attested under Hadrian.[2]

But Tiberius was not the only Caesar who might foreshadow Hadrian. The philhellene Nero was similarly associated in a love for things Greek. He had an aptitude for some of the arts which Hadrian (but not Tiberius) cultivated: painting and singing (52). Hadrian could not be denied a certain knack for the composition of light verse. Suetonius documents with emphasis, against the sceptics, that Nero's verse was his own (52). They could be linked too in their approach to foreign policy. Hadrian abandoned the conquests of his adoptive father, and Nero was only just deterred from abandoning those of his, so little did he value the glory of expanding the empire (18).[3]

Augustus at times may be seen as a model for Hadrian. Both were anxious to return to traditional ways, *ad priscum morem*. They were scrupulous about traditional Roman religion, and averse to foreign superstitious rites. Both insisted, symbolically, on the wearing of togas on formal occasions. Hadrian the disciplinarian revived military standards that had supposedly lapsed since the disciplinarian Augustus. Hadrian's tours of the provinces were to be the most extensive of any emperor since Augustus: the latter's peregrinations had covered all but two provinces. Both gave close attention to the functioning of the laws and the courts. Each kept his freedmen under tight control. Even if Augustus could be

2. See above ch.4. On Hadrian's literary tastes, *SHA Hadr.* 16; on Alexandrian scholars, 20.2.

3. Townend (1959) 292, following Syme, detects an allusion to Hadrian in S's comment on Nero's attitude to conquest. For Hadrian's painting and music, *SHA Hadr.* 14.8-9.

represented in general as a loyal friend, like Hadrian he was forced
to turn against men who had been instrumental in his rise to power,
and found fault even with the loyal Maecenas and Agrippa. The
links even extend to the coincidental: if Augustus' life was threatened
by a demented camp-follower in Illyria, at loose with a hunting
knife, Hadrian for his part narrowly escaped an onslaught by a
demented slave with a knife in a garden at Tarraco.[4]

From the coincidental to the controversial, any of these points
and more may have struck the Hadrianic reader of the *Caesars*. It
is possible too that the author was aware of them, and even intended
to make his readers aware. But their interpretation is another matter
– whether to see in such parallels signs of loyal support, of malice,
or of a gradual movement from one to another. Intriguing though
such speculations are, the safest course is to abstain. Some coincidences may be the product of life itself, not of the writer's eye. Some
offer evidence of community of cultural interests between Tiberius
or Nero and Hadrian, others of the astonishing extent to which the
founder of the empire grasped the essentials of his role, and acted
as a model to his successors.

To catch the spirit of an age in its reflections on its past one must
penetrate to a subtler and perhaps more elusive level. The concern
of a great part of this study has been to set Suetonius in his
contemporary context, intellectually and socially. It may in retrospect
be worthwhile to delineate some of the broader features of his
outlook.

The death of Domitian marked a turning point of sorts in the
history of Latin literature. Writers could again breathe the air of
liberty and express their feelings without inhibition (or so Tacitus
claimed). Intellectuals congratulated themselves on a minor literary
renaissance. A Golden Age had returned, in which one could look
back in astonishment and relief at the grim era that had preceded.
The empire had paused in its downward progress towards senility,
and recovered a measure of youthful vigour. Suetonius too shares
in this Golden Age euphoria. A crow on the Capitol had predicted
that after Domitian all would be well, and the abstinence and
moderation of succeeding rulers had confirmed their hope (*Dom.*

---

4. On *priscus* in S. *Aug.* see ch.6, p.140; for Hadrian, *SHA Hadr.* 5.1.
Religion, *Aug.* 93; *Hadr.* 22.10. Togas, *Aug.* 40.5; *Hadr.* 22.2-3. Discipline,
Hadr. 10.3, cf. *Aug.* 24. Tours, *Aug.* 47. Jurisdiction *Aug.* 32-3; *Hadr.* 18.
Freedmen, *Aug.* 67; *Hadr.* 21.2-3. Friends punished, *Aug.* 66.1-3; *Hadr.* 15.
Assassination attempt, *Aug.* 19.2; *Hadr.* 12.5.

23.2). The *Caesars* looks back from an age of security to the follies and misfortunes of past generations, and beyond them to the monumental achievement of Augustus.[5]

But even if in this respect Suetonius shares the outlook of a Tacitus or a Pliny, in others he betrays the attitudes of a younger generation. Still probably in his youth at the time of the tyrant's assassination, he had no real experience of the dangers of public life during the reign of terror. If he manifests little of Tacitus' emotional attachment to *libertas*, this may be in part because he had never known what it was to be deprived of it. He reveres the republic as a Roman should: not, however, because it enshrined precious values which tyranny threatened, but because it represented the old, the established order.[6]

One of the overriding concerns which the reign of Hadrian suggests is for systematisation and order. Whether in the tidying up of the frontier system, the rationalisation of the civil law by the publication of the Perpetual Edict, or the formalisation of an equestrian bureaucracy, the reign suggests not a spirit of innovation but of logical extension of well-established traditions. In the work of Suetonius one of the dominant impressions is of a concern for system and order. This may be detected in three different but arguably related ways. Immediately apparent is the unremitting tidiness of the scholar's mind. The categorisation of material, the minute division and subdivision of information pervades all his work, scholarly as well as biographical. This love of analysis and categorisation was doubtless a product of the Alexandrian scholarly tradition. Yet in Suetonius concern for intellectual order is linked to concern for social order. If the reader sometimes has the feeling that imperial lives are forced into a Procrustean schema, it is not so much because literary tradition demanded such treatment (Plutarch demonstrates the contrary) as because the author starts from a clearly formulated mental image of how an emperor ought to behave. His hierarchical arrangement of information reflects a hierarchical

5. The topos of the return of life to literature after Domitian's death is widespread: Tacitus *Agricola* 3; *Hist.* 1.1; Plin. *Ep.* 1.10; 1.13; 3.18.5 (also above ch.2). For the metaphor of rejuvenation, Florus *Epitome* praef. 4-8. The 'renaissance' spirit is discussed by G. Williams, *Change and Decline* 284f. Note also the theme of the return of the Golden Age on the Hadrianic coinage: Mattingly, 'Virgil's Fourth Eclogue', *Journ. Warburg and Courtauld Inst.* 10 (1947) 14ff.

6. On S's lack of emotion towards *libertas*, above ch.5, p.110.

view of the world and particularly of Roman society. Not only does
Suetonius impose order on his facts; he evinces manifest enthusiasm
for the emperor who imposes order on Roman society.[7]

One feature of the *Caesars* that may appear not to square with
so rational and neatly ordered a mentality is the attention given to
seemingly irrational prognostications of the future. Yet this feature
too may paradoxically point in the same direction. While the benefit
of autocracy was to lend stability, unity and order to the potentially
volatile Roman world, its weakness lay in the uncertain transmission
of power from one reign to the next. Not only the threat of violent
usurpation, but the uncertain thread of human life introduced a
constant element of unpredictability and disorder into the ordered
Roman system. Yet if the unpredictable and irrational was the
product of a higher divine rationality and the inscrutable ordinances
of fate, order in the highest sense might remain intact. Suetonius'
care to demonstrate that the rise and fall of both individual rulers
and of dynasties was predictable from empirically observed phenomena may be seen as an attempt to penetrate scientifically a
higher, divine world-order. In this respect Suetonius may have seen
eye-to-eye not only with the astrologically-minded Hadrian, but also
with Marcus Aurelius, whose *Meditations* are a moving testament to
an emperor's self-subjection to a divine world-order, and to his
awareness of the transitoriness of imperial courts.[8]

A second dominant feature of Suetonius' writing is the deep
penetration of hellenistic culture. His methods are those of the
hellenistic scholar. That fact does not set him apart from his
contemporaries. He belonged to a society which set a high value on
a grammatical and rhetorical education of the hellenistic type; one
which had undergone a profound hellenisation in its *mores* and
values as well as its literature and in which patterns of thought
derived from the schools dominated much of intellectual activity in
general.[9] A large part of Suetonius' own writing revolves round
questions related to hellenistic culture, especially the position of
men of learning and literary figures in Roman society. One of the
strengths of the *Caesars* is that he sees his subjects as men of culture,

---

7. See chs.5 and 6.

8. On S and superstition, above ch.8. On the value of Marcus' *Meditations*,
Brunt, *JRS* 64 (1974) 1f.

9. Above ch.2 for the hellenisation of education; ch.4 for the place of learning
at court; ch.8 for the role of the imperial court in the process of hellenisation.

not simply as men of power. His sensitivity on this point is surely not unconnected with Hadrian's passionate (some thought too passionate) espousal of hellenistic culture and his interest in and encouragement of a wide range of intellectual and artistic disciplines, including grammatical scholarship, all of hellenistic origin.

In one respect Suetonius may appear to be out of step with contemporary literary trends. The Latin literature of the mid-second century is held to be characterised by an 'archaising' movement that rejected the classic diction of Cicero or Virgil and turned back to Cato and Ennius and the earliest period of Latin literature in a pursuit of recondite and obsolete language. The orator Fronto is the articulate champion of this movement, while his follower Aulus Gellius amply illustrates it in action, as he depicts his literary circles reading Cato's speeches, Claudius Quadrigarius' histories or Caecilius' comedy. Fronto and Gellius belong to a later generation than Suetonius; yet it is clear that the origin of the archaising movement stretches back. It is hard to dismiss as coincidental the archaic tastes attributed to Hadrian himself. 'He preferred Cato to Cicero, Ennius to Virgil, and Coelius (Antipater) to Sallust,' his biographer reports (16.6). The same tastes can plausibly be traced back to the Rome of the Flavians in the person of the grammarian Valerius Probus. By Suetonius' own account Probus was notable for his interest in archaic literature. 'He had read certain old texts with a teacher of literature in his province (Syria) for the recollection of ancient authors was still alive there, and had not fallen into complete neglect as at Rome.' Probus made a point of collecting any ancient text that he could lay hands on, and concentrated totally on this aspect of research. As a result his most important contribution was a collection of notes on archaic diction (*Gramm.* 24). Probus' memory understandably remained green in the circle of Gellius.[10]

Yet Suetonius himself seems to share no part in this movement. His taste is distinctly for the classical. Both his *Caesars* and his *Illustrious men* show a marked preference for the epoch of Cicero and Augustus. Partly it is a literary preference, as his intimacy with the minor poets of the late republic and early empire suggests; partly it is a matter of sympathy for the social and political ideals of Augustus and even of Cicero (a defence of Cicero's *Republic* is

10. On the archaising movement in general; R. Marache, *La critique littéraire de la langue latine* (1952); G.M.A. Grube, *The Greek and Roman Critics* (1965) 319f.; A.D. Leeman, *Orationis Ratio* (1963) 366f.; G. Williams, *Change and Decline* 306f.

his sole essay of a possibly political nature). But neither the subject-matter, nor his clear, accurate and unfussy style suggest a cult of the archaic.[11]

Suetonius was no archaist. But in drawing up battle-lines between rival movements of 'classicism' and 'archaism' we risk overlooking a more significant common factor that holds them together. That is the triumph of the philologist's craft, *grammaticē*. Fronto's preference for the archaic flowed from an obsession with the importance of diction. His aim was to avoid trite vocabulary, the everyday and usual. He turned to forgotten writers in pursuit of the out-of-the-way and eye-catching word without which grand sentiments could not be fittingly clothed. Here for him was the failure of Cicero: not that his rhetorical technique left anything to be desired, but that he made no cult of unusual vocabulary. The hunt for diction led Fronto into what was properly the grammarian's territory: the combing of texts for rare usages, the examination of correct usage and orthography. It is fitting that Gellius' *Attic nights* show Fronto so often playing the grammarian's game, refuting the professionals at their own craft. Gavius Bassus' essay 'On the meaning of words' was characteristic reading-matter for this circle.[12]

Interest in words is the common factor that links Suetonius to the archaists, whether Probus with his observations on archaic language, Hadrian questioning the correct usage of *obiter* or Fronto, Gellius and their circle. Indeed Suetonius reveals no cult of the archaic in his own style. That is because he is writing technical prose, without stylistic pretensions, which has no need to shirk the trite and everyday. Nevertheless he was well up in the game of combing out-of-the-way and archaic sources, in pursuit of names of various types of clothing or the meaning of *puerperium* for the ancients.

Suetonius' philological interests thus place him in the mainstream of the culture of his day. Much of the writing of the mid second

11. The absence of archaising tendencies from S was stressed by Dalmasso (1905/6) who goes on to cast S as a 'classicist' and a follower of Quintilian; similarly Cizek (1977) 14-17. But how can the unrhetorical S be deemed a follower of Quintilian? Of S's essay on the *de Republica* of Cicero nothing is known except that it was a riposte to the Alexandrian scholar Didymus (Roth p.281, Reifferscheid fr.204). Yet it is clear S admired Cicero: see above ch.3 and Macé (1900) 287f.

12. The philological interests of the Frontonian circle are stressed by Marache 150-1; Leeman 371, 'rhetoric and antiquarian scholarship tend to melt together in their studies' (of Fronto and Gellius). On Gellius' picture of this circle, above ch.2; *Noctes Atticae* 19.10 for an example of Fronto catching out a grammarian at his own game.

century AD was to be marked not by creativity and imagination but rather by learning. In the works that have come down to us from the period, the scholarly and technical bulk large: not only in Fronto and Gellius, but in the jurists, land-surveyors and grammarians, or in Greek in the geography and astrology of Ptolemy and the medicine of Galen. The 'Golden Age' of the Roman Empire encouraged the systematisation of knowledge and a stock-taking of the literature of preceding generations. If Suetonius was more of a scholar than an artist, he was not alone.

BIBLIOGRAPHY

This is not a complete guide to further reading on Suetonius. I have listed only the most important editions and a selection of commentaries (A), and books and articles on Suetonius referred to in the notes by author's name and date of publication (B). I have excluded numerous unpublished doctoral dissertations. For further reading on subjects other than Suetonius and his writings the notes should be consulted.

A. *EDITIONS AND COMMENTARIES*

Quae supersunt omnia: ed. C.L. Roth (Teubner, Leipzig 1858).
Praeter Caesarum libros reliquiae: ed. A. Reifferscheid (Leipzig 1860).
De vita Caesarum: ed. M. Ihm (Teubner, Leipzig, ed. maior 1907, ed. minor 1908).
(Caesars, Grammarians and Rhetors, Poets): trans. J.C. Rolfe, 2 vols. (Loeb Classical Library, 1914).
Vies des Douze Césars:trans H. Ailloud, 3 vols. (Coll. Budé, Paris 1931-2).
De Grammaticis et Rhetoribus: ed. G. Brugnoli (Teubner, Leipzig 1960).
------ :trans. with comm., F. della Corte (Bibl. Loescheriana, Turin, 3rd ed. 1968).
De Poetis: ed. A. Rostagni (Turin 1944, reprinted Arno 1979).
Peri blasphemiōn, Peri paidiōn, extraits byzantins: ed. J. Taillardat (Paris 1967).
Divus Augustus: comm. E.S. Shuckburgh (Cambridge 1896, reprinted Arno 1979).
------ : comm. M.A. Levi (Florence 1951).
------ : comm. J.M. Carter (Bristol Classical Press 1982)
Tiberius: Ch.1-23 comm. M.J. du Four (Philadelphia 1941); ch.24-40, comm. J.R. Rietra (Amsterdam 1928), reprinted as single vol. (Arno 1979).

Nero: comm. B.H. Warmington (Bristol Classical Press 1977).

------ : comm. K.R. Bradley (Coll. Latomus 157, Brussels 1978).

Libri VII-VIII (Galba to Domitian): comm. G.W. Mooney (Dublin 1930, reprinted Arno 1979).

Divus Vespasianus: comm. A.W. Braithwaite (Oxford 1927).

B. BOOKS AND ARTICLES

G. Alföldy (1979), 'Marcius Turbo, Septicius Clarus, Sueton und die Historia Augusta', *Zeitschr. für Pap. u. Epigr.* 36, 233-53.

------ (forthcoming), 'Römisches Staats- und Gesellschafts-denken bei Sueton', *Ancient Society* (forthcoming).

G. D'Anna (1954), *Le Idee Letterarie di Suetonio* (Florence).

P. Bagge (1875), *De elocutione C. Suetonii Tranquilli* (Upsala).

B. Baldwin (1975a), 'Suetonius: birth, disgrace and death', *Acta Classica* 18, 61-70.

------ (1975b), 'Was Suetonius disgraced?' *Echos du Monde Classique* 19, 22-6.

C. Baurain (1976), 'Suétone et l'inscription d'Hippone', *Les Etudes Classiques* 44, 124-44.

G. Bowersock (1969), 'Suetonius and Trajan', in *Hommages à Marcel Renard (Coll. Latomus* 101) 1, 119-25.

K.R. Bradley (1973), 'The composition of Suetonius' *Caesares* again', *Jnl. Indo-Europ. Stud.* 1, 257-63.

------ (1976), 'Imperial virtues in Suetonius' *Caesares*', Jnl. Indo-Europ. Stud. 4, 245-53.

------ (1981), 'The significance of the *spectacula* in Suetonius' *Caesares*', *Rivista storica dell' Antichità* 11, 129-37.

K. Bringmann (1971), 'Zur Tiberiusbiographie Suetons', *Rhein. Mus.* 114, 268-85.

G. Brugnoli (1968), *Studi Suetoniani* (Lecce), reprints of articles published between 1954 and 1964.

C. Brutscher (1958), *Analysen zu Suetons Divus Iulius und der Parallelüberlieferung* (Noctes Romanae 8).

T.F. Carney (1968), 'How Suetonius' lives reflect on Hadrian', *Proc. African Class. Ass.* 11, 7-24.

E. Cizek (1977), *Structures et idéologie dans 'Les Vies des Douze Césars' de Suétone* (Bucharest-Paris).

F. della Corte (1967), *Svetonio, Eques Romanus* (Florence 1958; ed. 2, 1967)

J. Couissin (1953), 'Suétone Physiognomoniste dans les *Vies des XII Césars*', *Rev. Et. Lat.* 31, 234-56.

J.-M. Croisille (1969/70), 'L'art de la composition chez Suétone, d'aprés les vies de Claude et de Néron', *Annali dell' Instituto Italiano per gli studi storici* 2, 73-87.

J.A. Crook (1957), 'Suetonius ab epistulis', *Proc. Camb. Phil. Soc.* n.s. 4, 1956-7, 18-22.

------ (1969), *CR* n.s. 19, 62-3, reviewing della Corte.

E. van't Dack (1963), 'A studiis, a bybliothecis', *Historia* 12, 177-84.

L. Dalmasso (1905/6), 'Un seguace di Quintiliano ...', *Att. Ac. Sc. Torino* 41, 805-25.

A. Dihle (1954) reviews Steidle, *Gött. Gel. Anz.* 208, 45-55.

S. Döpp (1972), 'Zum Aufbau der Tiberiusvita Suetons', *Hermes* 100, 444-60.

H. Drexler (1969), 'Suetons Divus Iulius und die Parallelüberlieferung', *Klio* 51, 223-66.

J. Ektor (1980), 'L'impassibilité et l'objectivité de Suétone', *Les Etudes Classiques* 48, 317-26.

D. Flach (1972), 'Zum Quellenwert der Kaiserbiographien Suetons', *Gymnasium* 79, 273-89.

J.W. Freund (1901), *De Suetonii Tranquilli usu atque genere dicendi* (Diss. Breslau).

G. Funaioli (1932), 'Suetonius', *RE* IV A, 593-641.

------ (1947), 'I Cesari di Suetonio', in *Raccolta di scritti in onore di F. Ramorino* (Milan, 1927), 1-26, reprinted in *Studi di letteratura antica* (1947) 2,2, 147-79.

J. Gascou (1976), 'Suétone et l'ordre équestre', *Rev. Et. Lat.* 54, 257-77.

------ (1978), 'Nouvelles données chronologiques sur la carrière de Suétone', *Latomus* 37, 436-44.

H. Gomoll (1935), 'Suetons bibliotheksgeschichtliche Nachrichten', *Zentralblatt für Bibliothekswesen* 52, 381-8.

H. Gugel (1977), *Studien zur biographischen Technik Suetons* (Wiener Studien Beiheft 7: Vienna).

------ (1970), 'Caesars Tod (Sueton, *Div. Iul.* 81,4-82,3). Aspekte zur Darstellungskunst und zum Caesarbild Suetons', *Gymnasium* 77, 5-22.

R. Hanslik (1954), 'Die Augustusvita Suetons', *Wien. Stud.* 67, 99-144.

F. Leo (1901), *Die griechisch-römische Biographie nach ihrer literarischen Form* (Leipzig).

G. Lewis (forthcoming), 'Suetonius' *Caesares* and their literary antecedents', in H. Temporini (ed.), *Aufstieg u. Niedergang der römischen Welt* II (forthcoming).

G. Luck (1964), 'Ueber Suetons Divus Titus', *Rhein. Mus.* 107, 63-75.

A. Macé (1900), *Essai sur Suétone* (Paris).

E. Malcovati (1977), 'Augusto fonte di Svetonio', in *Festschrift für Rudolf Hanslik* (Wiener Stud. Beiheft 8), 187-95.

E. Marec – H.G. Pflaum (1952), 'Nouvelle inscription sur la carrière de Suétone, l'historien', *Compt. Rend. Ac. Inscr.*, 76-85.

A. Momigliano (1971), *The Development of Greek Biography* (Cambridge, Mass.).

B. Mouchova (1968), *Studie zu Kaiserbiographien Suetons* (Acta Univ. Carolinae; Phil. et. Hist. Monogr. xxii; Prague).

W. Müller (1972), 'Sueton und seine Zitierweise im "Divus Iulius"', *Symb. Osl.* 47, 95-108.

H. Naumann (1974), 'Noch einmal: Suetons Virgil-Vita', *Philologus* 118, 131-44.

------ (1979), 'Lücken und Einfügungen in den Dichter-Viten Suetons', *Wien. Stud.* 92, 151-65.

E. Paratore (1946), *Una Nuova Ricostruzione del 'Del Poetis' di Suetonio* (Rome 1946, 2nd ed. Bari 1950).

------ (1959), 'Claude et Néron chez Suétone', *Rivista di cultura classica e medioevale* 1, 326-41.

P. Ramondetti (1977), 'La terminologia relativa alla procedura del senatum habere in Svetonio', *Atti. Ac. Sc. Torino* 111, 2, 135-68.

T. Reekmans (1977), 'La politique économique et financière des autorités dans les Douze Césars de Suétone', in *Historiografia Antiqua . . .in honorem W. Peremans* (Louvain), 265-314.

P. Sage (1979), 'Quelques aspects de l'expression narrative dans les *XII Césars* de Suétone', *Rev. Belg. Phil.* 57, 18-50.

D. Slusanski (1975), 'Suétone-critique littéraire. Problèmes de vocabulaire', *Actes XII Conf. Int. Et. Class. Eirene (1972)*, 115-19.

W. Steidle (1951), *Sueton und die antike Biographie* (Zetemata 1; Munich 1951; reprinted 1963).

D.R. Stuart (1928), *Epochs of Greek and Roman Biography* (Berkeley).

R. Syme (1980a), 'Guard Prefects of Trajan and Hadrian', *JRS* 70, 64-80.

------ (1980b), 'Biographers of the Caesars', *Museum Helveticum* 37, 104-28.

------ (1981), 'The travels of Suetonius Tranquillus', *Hermes* 109, 105-17.

C.St. Tomulescu (1977), 'Les Douzes Césars et le droit romain', *Bull. Inst. Dir. Rom.* 80, 129-58.

G.B. Townend (1959), 'The date of composition of Suetonius' *Caesares*', *CQ* n.s. 9, 285-93.

------ (1960), 'The sources of the Greek in Suetonius', *Hermes* 88, 98-120.

------ (1961a), 'The Hippo inscription and the career of Suetonius', *Historia* 10, 99-109.

------ (1961b), 'The post *ab epistulis* in the second century', *Historia* 10, 375-81.

------ (1962), 'The trial of Aemilia Lepida in A.D. 20', *Latomus* 21, 484-93.

------ (1967), 'Suetonius and his influence', in *Latin Biography*, ed. T.A. Dorey (London), 79-111.

------ (1972), 'Suetonius and literary biography', abstract in *Proc. Class. Ass.* 69, 27.

P. Venini (1974), 'Sulle Vite Svetoniane di Galba, Otone e Vitellio', *Rend. Inst. Lomb., Cl . Lett. Sc. Mor. St.* 108, 991-1014.

P. Wessner (1917), 'Isidor and Sueton', *Hermes* 52, 201-92.

A.E. Wardman (1967), 'Description of personal appearance in Plutarch and Suetonius: the use of statues as evidence', *CQ* n.s. 17, 414-20.

INDEX

Index

WITHDRAWN FROM HAVERING COLLEGES
SIXTH FORM LIBRARY

Havering Sixth Form College Library

6520647